How to Prepare Now for What's Next is a must-read for all those who wish to remain relevant. Michael points out the speed of change in our world and that now is not the time for leaders to simply tweak our organizations. Now is the time for change. Congratulations Michael on providing us with a useful path to follow.

—**Barry Rassin**, President, Rotary International 2018–19

In business today, you can't design your future by analysing the past. With our world changing so fast, the counsel of a wise and practical futurist such as Michael McQueen is more important than ever.

—**Andy Berry**, Managing Director, Ricoh Australia

Disruption is a concept that is widely cited but often poorly understood. In his latest book, Michael McQueen provides the insight and strategies that leaders have long been seeking. This book is your practical guide to future-proofing your business in an age of disruption

—P⸺ ⸺ ⸺ ⸺ g Officer,
national

This book offers a powerful ro⸺ ⸺ leader should read. Michael provides ⸺ ⸺ ⸺ the future and asks all of the questions you will ⸺ ⸺p you get there.

—**Brendan Sheehan**, Global Council Member,
Association of Chartered Certified Accounts (ACCA)

With Michael's tips for success, this book is a must-read for anyone looking to stay relevant and embrace the future.

—**David Maiolo**, Senior Manager Learning & Development,
Bendigo and Adelaide Bank Limited

In this new book, Michael McQueen de-clutters a very complicated business world with thorough research and real-life case studies. *How to Prepare Now for What's Next* is your ultimate guidebook to retaining relevance.

—**David Mulham**, Chief Field Development Officer,
USANA Health Sciences

Michael has done it again. This book is a true wake up call. Read it now—tomorrow will be too late.

—**Fiona Ross**, Regional Head of Marketing, Travelport

Complacency is failure in the new economy. As a 112-year old organisation, [for us] Michael's unique viewpoint in this book is invaluable if we are to serve our members for another 112 years.

—**Ian Gillespie**, Group CEO, RACQ

In this book, Michael McQueen has clearly identified the unstoppable disruptions that will impact every sector in the coming years. In my industry, healthcare, understanding and proactively addressing the trends he highlights will undeniably result in business success but more importantly in improved patient outcomes.

—**James Britton**, Senior Corporate Development Manager, Multinational healthcare company

How to Prepare Now for What's Next captures Michael McQueen's unique insight into what the future holds. This book is smart, provocative and a great resource for helping any leader prepare for what is next.

—**Jennifer Jones**, 2017 Global Vice President, Rotary International

Michael has an innate ability to simplify the enormous complexity of change and then provide practical advice to business leaders. *How to Prepare Now for What's Next* is a compelling read and an invaluable tool for anyone wanting to stay ahead of the game.

—**Karin Sheppard**, Regional Chief Operating Officer, Intercontinental Hotel Group

Michael's books have changed how I think about the strategic direction of our company. We can't solve our issues with yesterday's thinking. Michael's thought-leadership is refreshing and invaluable.

—**Kevin Guest**, CEO, USANA Health Sciences

Michael does a superb job of simplifying the complex and provides leaders with a structured approach they can follow in order to stay one step ahead of disruption.

—**Mark Merritt**, Associate Director, KPMG

How to Prepare Now for What's Next implores us to accept the inevitability of change and face it by empowering those we lead to help create the future. Michael McQueen will inspire you by shining a light on the path forward for any business or industry.

—**Martin Nelson**, Automotive Industry Executive

Michael McQueen has an uncanny knack of making very complex topics seem simple. This book offers techniques that will help you make good business decisions in the eye of a proverbial perfect storm of disruption.

—**Steven Johnston**, Chief Executive Officer,
ProVision Optometry Group

The future is here—you just need to know where to look. Through his new book Michael brings the future to our doorstep.

—**Mike Baird**, former NSW State Premier

Michael is one of those rare people who make the complex simple. This book has all the ingredients for learning how to thrive in turbulent times.

—**Nick Hakes**, General Manager

HOW TO
PREPARE
NOW

FOR
WHAT'S
NEXT

HOW TO PREPARE NOW FOR WHAT'S NEXT

A GUIDE TO THRIVING IN AN AGE OF DISRUPTION

MICHAEL MCQUEEN

WILEY

First published in 2018 by John Wiley & Sons Australia, Ltd
42 McDougall St, Milton Qld 4064
Office also in Melbourne

Typeset in 11.5/13.5pt ITC Cheltenham Std

© John Wiley & Sons Australia, Ltd 2018

The moral rights of the author have been asserted

 A catalogue record for this book is available from the National Library of Australia

Cover design by Wiley

Cover image © o-che / Getty Images

Author image: © Toby Zerna

Printed in USA by Quad/Graphics

V008099_091118

Disclaimer
The material in this publication is of the nature of general comment only, and does not represent professional advice. It is not intended to provide specific guidance for particular circumstances and it should not be relied on as the basis for any decision to take action or not take action on any matter which it covers. Readers should obtain professional advice where appropriate, before making any such decision. To the maximum extent permitted by law, the author and publisher disclaim all responsibility and liability to any person, arising directly or indirectly from any person taking or not taking action based on the information in this publication.

To my firstborn, Max.

You will inherit the world depicted in this book and I am honoured to help prepare you for the future that awaits.

CONTENTS

ABOUT THE AUTHOR

Michael McQueen understands what it takes to thrive in a rapidly evolving world.

Widely recognised for having his finger on the pulse of business and culture, he has helped some of the world's best-known brands navigate disruption and maintain relevance.

As a leading specialist in social shifts, change management and future trends, Michael features regularly as a commentator on TV and radio and has written five best-selling books.

Michael is a familiar face on the international conference circuit, having shared the stage with the likes of Bill Gates, Dr John C. Maxwell and Apple co-founder Steve Wozniak. He has spoken to hundreds of thousands of people across five continents since 2004 and is known for his high-impact, research-rich and entertaining conference presentations.

Michael was recently named Australia's Keynote Speaker of the Year and was inducted into the Professional Speakers Halls of Fame.

He and his family live in Sydney, Australia.

www.michaelmcqueen.net

INTRODUCTION

As I walked out the doors of my grandmother's nursing home on a sunny autumn day a few months ago, my mind was still processing the four hours I had spent with her that morning.

At the ripe old age of 93, my grandmother isn't showing any hint of slowing down. She's sharp as a tack and disarmingly irreverent. That day I had cleared my schedule to sit down with her and capture elements of her life story and my family heritage. As we sifted through scores of brown leather journals filled with beautiful handwritten script, dusty photo albums and countless loose documents, many of the names and stories I had heard throughout my childhood came to life.

My grandmother reflected on her career as a nurse and welled up when she recounted the day soldiers returned from war, maimed and broken. 'Shells of men' was the way she remembered them.

She recalled how as a young girl she'd watched the Sydney Harbour Bridge take shape over many months and wondered how cars would ever be powerful enough to drive up its steep arches — unaware that the arches were little more than a scaffold for the suspended road plate below.

As I drove home through the very suburbs in which many of the stories I had heard that morning had played out, I tried to imagine how the same city looked, sounded and smelled in my grandmother's early days.

My train of thought was interrupted by a phone call from my publisher, Lucy Raymond. I had left a message on Lucy's voicemail the previous day mentioning I had an idea for a new book.

'I'm excited to hear about this new book,' she said. 'What have you got in mind?'

In a flash, my thoughts were jolted from imagining how the street I was driving down would have looked in the 1930s to pitching the premise for the book you now hold in your hand. As I described my vision for a book that would help leaders and organisations navigate disruptions ranging from artificial intelligence to driverless cars and nanotechnology, the contrast with the morning I'd just spent with my grandmother couldn't have been more stark.

STUNNED BY THE PACE OF PROGRESS

I'm sure you know the feeling. Every now and again most of us catch ourselves reeling at the nature and pace of change around us.

As someone who has spent well over a decade studying trends and forecasting disruption, I still find myself amazed when I reflect on the things I take for granted today — things that would have been utterly inconceivable a few short decades, much less centuries, ago.

To this point, celebrated blogger and TED speaker Tim Urban offered a great little thought experiment in a 2015 blog post where he encouraged readers to imagine teleporting a person from the nineteenth century to the modern day.

As Urban suggests:

> *It's impossible for us to understand what it would be like for him to see shiny capsules racing by on a highway, talk to people who had been on the other side of the ocean earlier in the day, watch sports that were being played 1,000 miles away … This is all before you show him the Internet or explain things like the International Space Station, the Large Hadron Collider, nuclear weapons, or general relativity. This experience for him wouldn't be surprising or shocking or even mind-blowing—those words aren't big enough. He might actually die.*[1]

And so while the modern day is extraordinary enough, much of my time is dedicated to forecasting the trends and changes that would spin our minds were we able to travel even a few decades forward in time.

THE PERILS OF PREDICTION

Now, to be clear, this is not a book about pie-in-the-sky futurism. As stimulating as it can be to gaze into crystal balls, predicting the future can be a pretty risky business. As I recently heard one business strategist suggest, when it comes to predicting the future, humility is a virtue.[2]

Consider how many bold predictions by intelligent people throughout history have proven to be just slightly off the mark:

∞ Ken Olsen, founder and chairman of computer giant DEC, said in 1977, 'There is no reason anyone would want a computer in their home'.[3]

∞ The legendary American businessman and inventor Alex Lewyt predicted in the 1950s that 'Nuclear powered vacuum cleaners will be a reality within 10 years'.[4]

∞ A Boeing engineer boasted 'There will never be a bigger plane built' when Boeing's 10-seater Model 247 was launched in 1933.[5]

∞ Lord Kelvin predicted in 1883 that we would one day discover that x-rays were a hoax all along. (It bears mentioning that Lord Kelvin was no fool. In fact, he was instrumental in formulating the first and second laws of thermodynamics and devised the method for measuring temperature we still use today.)[6]

∞ Steve Jobs predicted the failure of Amazon's Kindle ereader upon its release because, in his words, 'It doesn't matter how good or bad the product is, the fact is that people don't read anymore'.[7]

If nothing else, this list underscores just how hard it can be to predict the future with any degree of certainty. In the words of legendary film producer Samuel Goldwyn, 'Only a fool would make predictions — especially about the future'.[8]

And yet of all the sensational business predictions that have emerged in recent years, one stands out in my mind above the rest. In June 2015, the retiring CEO of Cisco, John Chambers, delivered his final keynote address. He left the audience in stunned silence (and panicked much of the business world) when he said, '40 per cent of businesses in this room, unfortunately, will not exist in a meaningful way in 10 years'. [9]

Now while you could dismiss this prediction as misguided hyperbole, the reality is that Chambers may well be spot on. After all, according to the work of Professor Richard Foster of Yale University, 'the average lifespan of a major listed company has shrunk from 67 years in the 1920s to just 15 years today'.[10]

The coming decades will see many businesses and industries disrupted in ways they cannot imagine today.

I have spent much of the Past decade interacting with and interviewing some of the brightest and most visionary thinkers on the planet and their consensus is that the coming decades will see many businesses and industries disrupted in ways they cannot imagine today — and certainly are unprepared for.

My interest in this started back in 2011. As significant businesses crumbled in rapid succession (from Borders to Kodak, Saab and Nortel, then BlackBerry and Blockbuster), what started out as a blog post for my website turned into a three-year research project examining the dynamics of business demise. Over the course of those three years, I tracked 500 brands, organisations and institutions around the world in an effort to answer two questions:

1. Why do the mighty fall?

2. Why do the enduring prevail?

My goal was to try and discover the habits, culture and mindset that separated enduring brands from their endangered counterparts. Those three years of research culminated in a book called *Winning the Battle for Relevance*.

While that book proved helpful for leaders and organisations trying to stay at the cutting edge, I quickly discovered that the scope of my research had been too limited. After all, it only identified the factors that were driving obsolescence for organisations and brands in the present.

In the years since that book's release, the scope of my research has shifted to what lies ahead and the specific trends and disruptions that are set to shake up the status quo in significant ways.

A UNIQUE TIME IN HISTORY

Having spent much of the past few years absorbed in the future, there is little doubt in my mind that we are standing at the precipice of the most significant change our world has known.

Historian and United States Senator Ben Sasse agrees:

> When people say we're at a unique moment in history, the historian's job is to put things in perspective by pointing out that there is more continuity than discontinuity, that we are not special, that we think our moment is unique because we are narcissists and we're at this moment. But what we are going through now — the past 20 or 30 years, and the next 20 or 30 years — really is historically unique. It is arguably the largest economic disruption in recorded human history. [11]

Political scientist and international relations expert David Rothkopf agrees that we are at a significant and historical moment. That said, in his excellent book *The Great Questions of Tomorrow*, Rothkopf does liken this current point in history to one experienced by our fourteenth-century forebears who had little idea of the sweeping societal changes that the Renaissance was about to usher in:

> As was the case during the fourteenth century, we too are living in what might be described as the day before the Renaissance. The epochal change is coming, a transformational tsunami is on the horizon, and most of our leaders and many of us have our backs to it. [12]

Rothkopf suggests that this lack of awareness of and preparedness for what lies ahead is a function of our very human nature. As humans, we operate with a range of biases and we expect the world to confirm them. As a result, we mishear, misread and misinterpret events around us. We live in a world where 85 per cent of the time today's weather is the same as yesterday's weather; people tend to let the immediate past shape their expectations of the future. [13]

> As humans, we operate with a range of biases and we expect the world to confirm them.

And yet the future is going to be very different from what any of us have known.

We are sailing into uncharted waters. We are at an inflection point where we cannot discern what the future will hold by looking to the past.

And that's the purpose of this book — to get a clear sense of what's next so we can start preparing now.

In part I, we're going to look at what the future holds and how to identify the trends and disruptions that are going to radically redefine the status quo.

In part II, I am going to outline a plan for navigating the turbulent times that lie ahead.

So strap in: things are about to get a bit bumpy. But my commitment is to give you the insights and strategies necessary to thrive in an age of disruption.

PART I

THE FOUR KEY DISRUPTIONS

When Harvard Business School professor Clayton Christensen first introduced the notion of disruptive innovation in his 1997 bestseller *The Innovator's Dilemma*, I wonder if he had any sense of just how profoundly impactful his ideas would become.

And yet while most of the leaders and organisations I work with understand the principles of disruption, many find themselves with little idea of how to predict or pre-empt the very disruptions that are looming large over their businesses and industries. What they often lack is a framework for making sense of the overwhelming barrage of changes they are facing.

After all, it tends not to be linear, incremental or evolutionary; disruption is generally unpredictable, fundamental and revolutionary.

Offering such a framework is my goal in part I of this book. By its very nature disruption is hard to forecast. After all, it tends not to be linear, incremental or evolutionary; disruption is generally unpredictable, fundamental and revolutionary.

So while predicting specific disruptions is difficult, identifying categories or patterns of disruption is far more useful. To this point, I'd suggest that the disruptions that will re-shape the landscape for businesses and organisations in the coming years will fall into one of four broad categories:

1. widescale automation
2. empowered consumers
3. unconventional competition
4. emerging generations.

Part I will feature a chapter dedicated to each of these four disruption categories that will highlight what is driving the change along with a look at how the disruption is set to play out in a range of industries.

In the words of London Business School professor Gary Hamel, 'You can't outrun the future if you don't see it coming.'[1] To Hamel's point, the next four chapters are designed to give you the clearest possible picture of what is coming so you can get a head start.

Quick tip: Before you go any further, I'd highly recommend you flick to appendix A at the back of this book to complete a diagnostic tool called 'The Disruptibility Index'. This revealing exercise will give you an objective measure of just how prone your organisation or business is to disruption at this very moment.

Your disruptibility score may well provide a helpful context for what you'll learn in the coming chapters.

CHAPTER 1

WIDESCALE
AUTOMATION

It's not every day that a stocking manufacturer makes history—especially one with an unremarkable name like Ned.

And yet in the late 1770s, that's exactly what happened. Incensed by the gradual encroachment of new automated knitting machines that threatened to put him out of work, a stocking maker named Ned decided to take matters into his own hands. Smashing a number of these time-saving contraptions to bits in a fit of rage, little did Ned know that he had just sown the seeds of a revolution.

Taking up the cause a few short years later, a group of English weavers and textile artisans banded together in a coordinated assault on the industrial age. Inspired by Ned's act of defiance, this band of weavers and artisans was soon destroying a few hundred automated looms each month.

As you can imagine, the wealthy factory owners who owned the looms weren't thrilled. Using their political sway in the British Parliament, these industrialists arranged for almost 15 000 soldiers to descend on the loom smashers to put an end to the destruction. They even managed to have a law passed making the breaking of weaving frames a crime punishable by death—a fairly extreme reaction even by early eighteenth century standards. Dozens of the 'revolutionaries' were executed or exiled to penal colonies such as Australia.

Things simmered down in the years that followed, the revolution crushed.[2]

You may not have heard of Ned but you likely know his surname and the movement he inspired. Ned Ludd and his band of self-described 'Luddites' have been widely ridiculed in the history books as backward, small-minded and anti-progress. Even to this day the term 'Luddite' is used to describe an individual who stubbornly and naively tries to hold back the march of technological advancement.

It's important to note that progress was not the chief complaint of the Luddites. Instead, it was the power imbalance and erosion of dignity that automation technology led to that caused most frustration. In fact, Luddites were primarily concerned with negotiating the employment conditions that we take for granted today—you could almost call Luddites visionaries! The Luddites were not opposed to the idea of using machines to increase efficiency and productivity—they simply believed that some of the additional profits these efficiencies led to should go back to ensuring the welfare of workers in the form of pensions, minimum wages and safe working conditions.

Regardless of whether you agree with the Luddites' behaviour or beliefs, it is the context of this uprising and its parallels with the modern age that offer an important lesson as we begin considering the automation-driven disruptions that lie ahead.

The late 1700s were, after all, a time of significant upheaval in the English textile business. War with France had resulted in trade barriers that had a huge commercial impact on British manufacturers. Added to this, fashions had rapidly changed and men no longer wore leggings—opting for trousers instead. All of this culminated in a time of enormous cost pressure for wealthy textile manufacturers. In this perfect storm of upheaval, steam-powered looms came onto the scene offering sizeable productivity and efficiency gains for mill owners. It was the perfect recipe for a clash.[3]

THE ATTRACTION OF AUTOMATION

Looking at the context we find ourselves in currently, the parallels are striking. Facing mounting pressure to decrease costs and increase productivity, businesses today are again looking to widescale automation as the answer. What's significant about this first of the four forms of disruption we explore in part I is that automation is both a *result* of change and a *driver* of it. In other words, many of the shifts we've seen in recent years have left businesses with little choice but to automate. However, this in turn is going to kick off a wave of disruption that will re-shape entire business sectors and potentially leave untold millions out of work.

> **Automation is both a *result* of change and a *driver* of it.**

This era we are about to enter is one that the World Economic Forum's founder, Klaus Schwab, has labelled the 'Fourth Industrial Revolution'.

While many of us refer to the 'Industrial Revolution' as if it were a single period of technological and social upheaval, Schwab suggests that there have actually been four distinct industrial revolutions that have brought us to the point where we find ourselves today:

∞ *First Industrial Revolution (1760–1840).* This first phase of industrialisation saw society move from muscle power to machine power. It was this transition that gave rise to the Luddite movement as mechanical production became increasingly mainstream. Railroads were constructed as the invention of the steam engine transformed productivity forever.

∞ *Second Industrial Revolution (late 1800s – early 1900s).* This second phase of industrialisation saw the introduction of electricity and the development of the production line, which made mass production possible.

∞ *Third Industrial Revolution (late 1960 – early 2000s).* Sometimes referred to as the digital or computer revolution, this age of information technology catalysed development of mainframes, personal computing and the Internet. Knowledge became ubiquitous, the tyranny of distance all but disappeared and digital business platforms transformed the basis of commerce.

∞ *Fourth Industrial Revolution (early 2000s onward).* Building on the digital revolution, this fourth phase of industrialisation has seen mobile Internet, the proliferation of smaller and more powerful sensors, nanotechnology and learning algorithms bring the physical and digital worlds together.

What Schwab refers to as 'the Fourth Industrial Revolution', MIT professors Erik Brynjolfsson and Andrew McAfee refer to as 'the Second Machine Age' and others have labelled 'Industry 4.0'.[4]

Regardless of which label you use, any thoughtful analysis of the current state of play in business and society makes it clear that the years to come will be a time of rapid and fundamental change.

Throughout this chapter, we're going to look at what the coming age of widescale automation is going to mean to a range of different industries and how it will disrupt the status quo in some surprising and extraordinary ways.

To get us underway, let's briefly look at the two significant enablers of this age of widescale automation, as they offer a number of clues as to how this whole trend is going to play out.

Enabler 1: Ubiquitous data

Data today is more plentiful than ever.

It's widely accepted that 90 per cent of the world's data has been created in the past two years[5] and Google's servers alone handle 24 petabytes (equal to 24 million gigabytes) each and every day.[6]

While a lot of this data is generated in monitoring the mechanical world of turbines, tyre pressure and thermostats, a somewhat creepy amount of it is actually about us as individuals. Consider this: private companies today collect and sell as many as 75 000 individual data points about the average individual consumer.[7]

The raft of web-enabled devices and sensors churning out this data is often referred to as a trend called 'the Internet of Things' and it is a trend that's only just getting started. It is estimated that by 2020 there will be 50 billion connected devices in use and more than a trillion sensors monitoring every conceivable facet of our lives.[8] By 2025, forecasts are that a full 10 per cent of the population will be wearing clothing or reading glasses that are connected to the Internet.[9]

Owing to its scope and volume, this 'big data', as it is often referred to, is transforming the nature of business. Reflecting on this, former GE chairman and CEO Jeff Immelt suggests that every company today is in the software and analytics business—whether they want to be or not.[10]

IT giant Cisco estimates that the move toward a connected world will increase corporate profits by a massive 21 per cent by the mid 2020s and create $14.4 trillion in value.[11] As a case-in-point, they highlight Canada's oil sector, which is set to enjoy 11 per cent operational cost savings thanks to data-driven insights—savings that equate to more than $100 billion per year.[12]

Keeping with the oil theme, my friend and fellow futurist Chris Riddell goes as far as to suggest that data will in fact 'be the oil of twenty-first century—wealth and power will belong to those who can find it, mine it and refine it'.

And he is spot on.

Retailers were one of the first industry groups to recognise the benefits of monitoring the purchasing data of customers in order to identify trends. In the words of former Woolworths CEO Grant O'Brien, 'Data is the new eyes of the retailer. Without it the shopper is invisible'.

In the agricultural world, data is transforming efficiency and profitability too. Farmers in New Zealand are using technology to take hundreds of measurements per second across a large area—data that allows farmers to distribute dairy cows more effectively for feeding. It also alerts farmers to areas of low production that may need additional fertiliser. This precision-agriculture technology has resulted in a significant increase in farm output.[13]

How does this all enable the Fourth Industrial Revolution and the era of widescale automation, you ask? Well, the very insights necessary to automate the processes and professions we examine in this chapter are all data-driven. Data is the fuel that will drive the automation machine.

As we will shortly see, the data itself is not what is powerful; rather, it's what the data enables that counts.

Enabler 2: Artificial intelligence

For many of us, the very mention of artificial intelligence (AI) conjures up futuristic notions of Skynet and the malevolent robots that rose up to destroy humankind in the *Terminator* film series.

In reality, however, artificial intelligence is already here and it's not out to kill us—well, not yet, anyway. Our computers are smarter than most of us realise and they're getting smarter all the time.

I had an eerie moment of this realisation recently when searching my iPhone camera roll for some photos of a trip to the Cotswolds in the UK a few years ago. I opened up the search bar and started typing the word C-o-t-s-w but only got up to the third letter when an album of images popped up featuring me and my heavily-pregnant wife assembling a cot for our soon-to-be-born son, Max.

What made the hairs stand up on the back of my neck was the fact that I had never given these photos a caption or category that could have indicated the content of the image. My phone had somehow 'inspected' the image and identified that it indeed featured a cot.

I quickly discovered that my phone was far from unique or special in its ability. In the weeks that followed I noticed that Facebook had begun recognising the faces of friends in the photos I was about to post without me having to manually tag them. The AI-driven technology that underpins this somewhat unnerving development has achieved an astonishing degree of accuracy in recent years. For instance, the error rate of image recognising software fell from more than 30 per cent in 2010 to roughly 4 per cent in 2016—a figure that is especially amazing when you consider that the album used in the accuracy tests included several million photographs of common, obscure or downright weird images.[14] Facebook's own face recognition software can correctly identify the faces of individuals in images 97.25 per cent of the time—a degree of accuracy only marginally lower than our 97.53 per cent strike rate as humans.[15]

The capability we call 'artificial intelligence' today is actually older than most of us would assume. Researchers first started experimenting with computers that thought for themselves back in the late 1940s. They called it 'deep learning'.[16]

By the late 1950s, industry pioneers Herbert Simon, Marvin Minsky, Claude Shannon and John McCarthy developed a computer program called a 'general problem solver', which was designed to solve any logic problem. It was in fact one of these pioneers, John McCarthy, who first coined the term 'artificial intelligence'.[17]

From the very outset, predictions about the promise and potential of AI have proven to be ambitious. In 1957 Herbert Simon boldly predicted that computers would beat humans at chess within 10 years. In reality this feat took four times as long to accomplish, but it did eventually happen when, on 11 May 1997, an IBM computer called Deep Blue beat the world chess champion Garry Kasparov.[18]

THE AI SPECTRUM

When we talk about artificial intelligence (or learning algorithms, deep learning or machine learning, as it is sometimes labelled), it's important to clarify that it exists in various forms across a wide spectrum.

For the purposes of our discussions here, we're going to discuss AI in terms of three broad categories[19]:

1. *Artificial Narrow Intelligence (ANI).* A long way from the sort of rudimentary AI that beat chess players in the late 1990s, ANI is 'narrow' only because it is specialised to the function for which it has been developed. Just because ANI has a limited scope does not mean it's of limited potency or significance. As we will shortly see, much of the technology running our smartphones, online purchases and social media apps is in fact ANI.

2. *Artificial General Intelligence (AGI).* This second level of AI is where things get even more interesting. AGI is generally referred to as 'human-level AI', because it describes the capacity of a computer that is as smart as a human across the board — a point often referred to as 'Singularity'. This is the stage where computers possess the ability to plan, reason, problem-solve and comprehend abstract and complex ideas. Once we have conquered AGI, computers will possess the power to learn from experiences and develop intelligent conclusions as fast as, or perhaps even faster than, the human brain.

3. *Artificial Super Intelligence (ASI).* Now this is the scary Skynet stuff. ASI is the point at which computers possess an intellectual capacity far greater than that of human beings. Furthermore, they would possess the capacity for social skills and general knowledge that would increase exponentially over time. It is this level of artificial intelligence that worries many of today's leading thinkers, including Elon Musk, Stephen Hawking and Frank Wilczek.

As you can probably gather, right now we are on the verge of moving beyond the first level of AI, where computers aid and assist us as willing servants, to the point where they will equal our mental capacity and perhaps one day even surpass it.

Achieving AGI will be an extraordinarily complex challenge. It will require computers that are significantly more powerful and nuanced than those we currently possess. However, there is little doubt we will overcome these challenges. And soon.

Just how long it will take to create AGI is a source of much debate. Some, such as Google's director of engineering and pre-eminent AI expert Ray Kurzweil, believe computers will reach AGI by 2029 (followed by ASI in 2045). In case you are unfamiliar with Kurzweil's name and reputation, he is definitely someone worth listening to. In addition to being a celebrated inventor, engineer and entrepreneur, Kurzweil has been awarded 20 honorary doctorates as well as the American National Medal of Technology. He has also been inducted into the US Patent Office's Hall of Fame and *Inc.* magazine named him the 'rightful heir' to Thomas Edison.[20] So when Kurzweil makes a prediction about the future of technology, it is worth paying close attention to.

Despite this, many believe that Kurzweil's forecast and timeline are ambitious at best. When hundreds of the world's brightest scientific minds were surveyed recently, the average estimate given was that we would pass the AGI threshold by 2040.

Regardless of the timeline, one thing every expert agrees on is this: it is only a matter of time before humans will be outwitted by technology. Reflecting on the significance of this, David Rothkopf points out: 'There has never been a moment when our species did not possess the most powerful intellectual capacity on the planet'. Rothkopf suggests this distinction is unlikely to survive the twenty-second century.[21]

AI in everyday life

While the ethics and practicality of AGI are still up for debate, consider the myriad ways you are already benefiting from and using ANI, whether you are aware of it or not:

∞ Virtual assistants, such as Siri or Google Assistant, can not only recognise what you say in natural language but even ascertain context and intent based on your tone of voice and request history.[22]

∞ Voice recognition technology already enables you to speak a sentence in one language and have it translated to the listener's language in real time.

∞ Recommendation algorithms on Pandora or Amazon make intelligent suggestions of products, books or music you may like.

∞ The map software on your phone makes route suggestions based on your previous travel patterns and current traffic conditions.

From a commercial and business perspective, the current capabilities of ANI are extraordinary.

PayPal are using ANI to prevent money laundering while cybersecurity company Deep Instinct are using it to detect malware. JPMorgan Chase introduced a system for reviewing commercial loan contracts, which means work that once took loan officers 360 000 hours is now completed in a few seconds.[23]

One Brazilian online retailer implemented an ANI system to predict the likelihood of customers clicking on certain advertisements, allowing them to make ad placements more effective, resulting in $125 million in additional revenue.[24]

Of all the commercial applications of ANI, Google's recent mapping of the exact location of every business, household and street number in France stands out as especially remarkable. Traditionally a job this enormous would have required hundreds of GPS-enabled humans to manually go suburb to suburb and would have likely taken well over a year. Using ANI, Google was able to program its image-recognition software to trawl through the millions of images in its street view database to identify street numbers. The entire process took less than 60 minutes.[25]

THE IMPACT OF AUTOMATION

When you consider the efficiency, accuracy and productivity gains that automation offers, it's clear that embracing this technology is irresistible for businesses. The twin enablers of ubiquitous data and AI mean we are on the precipice of a level of automation the eighteenth-century Luddites could scarcely have imagined.

In fact, it's hard even for us in the present day to conceive the impact that automation will have over the coming years. As Amara's Law tells us, while we humans can often overestimate the impact of technology in the short term, we tend to wildly underestimate its impact in the long term.

In the coming pages, we're going to explore how this move towards widescale automation is going to significantly disrupt a range of industries and sectors including:

∞ transportation

∞ retail

∞ personal and professional services

∞ logistics and distribution

∞ medicine

∞ communication.

Transportation

While autonomous cars have received a fair amount of media attention in recent years, it may surprise you to learn that innovating the driver out of the driver's seat has been something automakers have been working on for a really long time.

While we humans can often overestimate the impact of technology in the short term, we tend to wildly underestimate its impact in the long term.

Back in 1939 at the World's Fair in New York, General Motors unveiled the concept of radio-guided cars and less than 20 years later they released a test model called the Firebird, which was designed to travel along tracks wired with electrical cables (much the same technology used by cable cars in San Francisco).[26]

As you can well imagine, these thought bubbles and slightly off-kilter inventions never got traction. However, the notion of self-driving cars is well and truly back on the agenda in a big way because the technology is finally good enough. As processing power has improved, data-generating sensors have become more powerful and less expensive, AI has become functional, and automated cars have become a distinct possibility.

Within a few short years, Google has assembled a functioning autonomous prototype and by the end of 2016 had clocked up a staggering 2 million hours of successful driverless operation on public roads. And Google are far from the only ones who've been tinkering with driverless car technology in recent years. Tesla, Volvo, Mercedes, Volkswagen, Audi, Ford, Baidu, Apple and even Intel have been busily working away at autonomous car technology.

How far are driverless cars from being a reality?

And now we stand at a point of critical mass. With automakers across the board all working to create a future where drivers are no longer necessary, just how far away is the reality of a driverless world?

In characteristically ambitious fashion, Tesla founder Elon Musk suggests we will see true autonomous driving available to the public by 2020.[27] *Quartz* magazine's Zack Kanter is equally optimistic, predicting that autonomous cars will be commonplace by 2025 and have a near monopoly by 2030.[28]

One of the more thorough examinations of how the self-driving age will unfold has been conducted by Tony Seba and James Arbib of the think tank RethinkX. According to Seba and Arbib, autonomous vehicles will be an overnight sensation with disruptive ramifications that will rival those brought by the printing press. They predict that by 2027, 90 per cent of passenger miles in the US each year will be travelled in autonomous vehicles and that many of those vehicles will not be owned by the 'driver'. Instead, this 90 per cent of travel will be done in driverless Uber-style vehicles, which will make up 60 per cent of the vehicles on the road.[29] (Similar forecasts from the Boston Consulting Group predict that Seba and Arbib's predictions are likely to be spot on.[30])

So the bottom line is this: a driverless world is far closer than most of us realise. In fact, it will only be user reluctance or regulator anxiety that prevents driverless cars from hitting our roads even sooner.

Naturally there are those who question the pace and impact of autonomous driving technology. For instance, in November 2016 the head of the National Highway Traffic Safety Administration, Mark Rosekind, suggested that truly autonomous cars are actually a long way off and that for the next 20 to 30 years we'll see a mixed fleet on public roads with different levels of automation.

Then there are those who suggest that driverless vehicles will never be able to truly replicate the nuances of human judgement on the road. They wonder if driverless cars will ever really be able to understand the intent of a police officer yelling through a bullhorn or process nonverbal cues from other drivers.[31]

However, even if the predicted timelines regarding driverless cars are out by 5 to 15 years, my own son and certainly his children will likely never get a driver's licence, much less ever own a car.

From a disruption standpoint, this likely reality is what's keeping the auto industry awake at night—or at least it should be.

The disruption of a driverless age

Within 25 to 30 years, owning a car could be like owning a horse today—something you do if it's a passion or hobby, but not as your primary mode of transportation.[32] Barclays Capital analyst Brian Johnson has said US vehicle sales will likely decline by 40 per cent by 2040.[33]

Within 25 to 30 years, owning a car could be like owning a horse today.

Senior analyst with Navigant Research, Sam Abuelsamid, suggests that the greatest opportunity for automakers may well be to establish their own ride-sharing services to rival existing leaders such as Uber and Lyft.[34] McKinsey predicted in 2016 that if automakers get it right, on-demand mobility and other new digitally driven services could create up to $US1.5 trillion in new revenue for the automotive industry by 2030.[35]

Everyday life in an autonomous era

Beyond the commercial changes, *The Wall Street Journal*'s Christopher Mims offers a compelling insight into what the actual experience of commuting to work may well look like in the post-driver age:

> *Imagine a world in which hardly anyone owns a car. Instead, most people subscribe to a service for self-driving cars. The service is great. You whip out your circa-2025 smartwatch, which has all but replaced your phone, bark a command and a self-driving car appears from a fleet circulating nearby.*[36]

Sound fantastical? Maybe so. Yet very possible and even probable.

But what about the period of time between now and when you cease to own a car? As the vehicle you own becomes increasingly autonomous in the coming years, what impact will that have on your transport experience?

First, the way you travel will change. Highways will be filled to the brim with cars travelling about a metre apart while going between 100 and 110 kilometres per hour. This will significantly increase the capacity and efficiency of roads.[37]

Once you arrive at your destination, you're unlikely to pay to park your driverless car. After all, your vehicle may drop you at the desired destination and then head off to a designated wait area or perhaps even drive home only to return and pick you up when you need it. Even if you do need to pay for parking, your car might look after the process for you once you've been dropped off. Brand-new technology developed by TechCrunch Disrupt NY hackathon team Val.ai allows self-driving cars to bid for parking spots that are soon to be vacated by other cars. If the fuel cost of driving around before the parked car's next pick-up is less than the money that can be made from the sale of the car park, it can accept the bid. The parked car will then leave as the winning vehicle arrives.[38]

I suspect you're beginning to see just how significant and unprecedented the disruption posed by autonomous cars will be. The autonomous age will likely see the end of taxi services entirely. A Columbia University study suggested that with a fleet of just 9000 autonomous cars, ride-sharing services such as Uber 'could replace every taxi cab in New York City and that passengers would wait an average of 36 seconds for a ride that costs about $0.50 per mile'.[39] As you would imagine, ride-sharing companies are champing at the bit for driverless car services to become a possibility. Former Uber CEO Travis Kalanick pointed to the enormous cost savings of removing drivers from the ride-sharing equation.[40]

Looking further afield, consider how significant an impact driverless cars will have on the $198 billion automotive insurance market, the $98 billion automotive finance market and a range of other industries ranging from rental car companies to panel beaters.[41]

The auto insurance industry specifically is set for a massive shakeup as driverless cars become mainstream. After all, if you do happen to be unlucky enough to have an accident in an infinitely safer driverless vehicle, who will actually be at fault? By extension, what would the purpose of car insurance be? KPMG estimate that as much as 80 per cent of auto insurer's revenues could evaporate in coming decades.[42]

'Change is coming and we need to get ahead of it,' said Allstate Chief Executive Tom Wilson in a recent interview. 'It isn't going to happen tomorrow but it is going to happen soon.'[43]

Chris Urmson, one of the engineers who led Google's driverless car project, suggests that current US law makes it clear that the car's manufacturer would be responsible in the event of an accident.[44] This was reinforced recently when Volvo went on record to announce they would accept responsibility for accidents caused by their autonomous vehicles.[45] Beyond legalities, there are moral and ethical implications of driverless vehicles too, so much so that a panel of experts in Germany met in June 2017 to produce the world's first ethical guidelines for self-driving cars. The number one guideline was that the protection of human life, above the destruction of property or other creatures, would always be the top priority.[46]

The benefits of autonomous cars

While there is little doubt that autonomous vehicles will prove to be an existential disruptive threat to a large range of industries, they also offer a number of significant positives. Beyond seeing an estimated 90 per cent decrease in road fatalities,[47] driverless technology will save millions of hours in lost productivity from time wasted driving in traffic. Repeated studies have examined the link between commute time and a poor quality of life. One in particular found that people who commute for longer than 40 minutes each day are unhappier, more stressed and generally experience more worry than those who have only a 10-minute commute.[48]

As our commute times decrease or can be re-purposed into meaningful and productive time, the quality of life benefits could be enormous. This trend will also allow people to live further away from their workplaces and we may well see a significant surge in real estate values in areas once deemed too far from the epicentres of commerce.

The end of truck drivers

While the world has been obsessed with the emerging technology of driverless cars, many people have failed to recognise that automating our personal vehicles is only part of the story.

Looking to a much larger format vehicle, trucks too are well down the road to becoming driverless in some significant and disruptive ways. In the remote Pilbara mining region of Western Australia, driverless trucks have been hauling 240 tonnes of dirt 24 hours a day without drivers for a number of years now. And this is a sign of things to come.[49]

The director of engineering and safety policy for the American Trucking Association, Ted Scott, admits that ubiquitous, autonomous trucks are 'close to inevitable'.[50]

Uber has acquired self-driving truck technology 'Otto', which, among other features, allows any truck with an automatic transmission to be retrofitted with true self-driving capabilities.

While it currently only works on the highway, within a few short years technology like Otto will transform the entire point-to-point logistics business.[51]

Retail

Imagine a world where you enter a retail store and are instantly identified by your mobile phone. Your preferences, credit card details and buying history are immediately recognised along with your identity and, from that moment on, the entire in-store experience is customised to your needs and desires.

You will select products either by scanning a code on your smartphone or by placing items in a physical shopping cart the old-school way.

When you are finished shopping, there are no cash registers, no lining up to pay for your goods: RFID tags in the packaging of every product means your shopping tally is calculated as you walk past sensors near the exit and the amount owing is immediately charged to your default credit card.

Sound fanciful or futuristic? Well this is almost precisely the automated retail experience shoppers are already enjoying in Amazon's brick-and-mortar retail stores.

However, Amazon are not the only ones transforming physical retailing. Square have developed and released technology that will identify you upon entry to a store. Their Pay By Name system works by sensing when a known mobile phone is in the defined area, identifying the potential buyer, and showing their face on the register so that the person behind the counter can complete the transaction by doing no more than tapping the buyer's picture.[52]

While each of these current technologies relies on customers' smartphones as the primary interface for retail automation, we are not far off removing the need for phones in the process. Before long, biometric technology will recognise our voices, fingerprints or retinas as we walk into a store and kickstart the automation process. Chinese payment giant Alipay even unveiled technology called 'Smile to Pay' in September 2017, which allows customers to verify their identity and 'pay' for a meal via facial recognition.[53]

Who benefits from retail automation?

The primary beneficiaries of retail automation will initially be the retail owners and operators themselves. In addition to reducing staff costs, an increasingly automated retail experience will generate data that will give store owners powerful insights into consumer behaviour, all while increasing the degree of personalisation and targeting that can be done (think reactive talking billboards similar to the ones featured in the movie *Minority Report*).[54]

While the big losers from retail automation will undoubtedly be the workers whose jobs will increasingly disappear, shoppers themselves may also lose out. The process of discovery and creativity in retail purchasing is often a result of choosing products we may not normally choose. It's the thrill of finding something out of the box, unique and unusual that even our spouse may never have guessed we'd like. So in a world where technology makes a lot of assumptions about us based on historical purchasing data, how much of the thrill, emotion and joy of shopping will disappear? Perhaps we'll see a counter-trend of bespoke, low-tech, high-touch retailers and artisans emerge in much the same way farmer's markets have been a reaction to the large-scale grocery businesses. (More on this theme in chapter 10.)

We'll see a counter-trend of bespoke, low-tech, high-touch retailers and artisans emerge.

The CEO of the Carl's Jr. restaurant chain, Andy Puzder, suggests that despite our desire for traditional human engagement, the drive for convenience will win out in the coming years—especially for younger generations.

Puzder is currently working on a 100 per cent–automated restaurant model that would lead to a hyper-convenient customer experience all while reducing wage costs. He suggests that it is younger generations who will drive demand for this degree of automation: 'Millennials like *not* seeing people,' he says.

> *I've been inside restaurants where we've installed ordering kiosks… and I've actually seen young people waiting in line to use the kiosk where there's a person standing behind the counter, waiting on nobody.*[55]

While a lot of the automation we will see in the retail sector is purportedly designed to enhance the customer experience, some of it is downright creepy. Take Walmart's recent patent filing to employ AI technology to detect whether customers are unhappy or frustrated. The company suggests it will result in better customer service, but the infringement on privacy is hard to ignore![56]

Personal and professional services

In much the same way that humans will quickly disappear from retail service in the coming years, many personal and professional service businesses will likely experience significant automation.

Take the financial planning and advice business, for instance. Traditionally a high-trust business, financial advice has been rocked by a series of scandals in recent years, leaving many clients asking whether human advisers and the fees they command are actually a necessary part of the wealth management process.

While advisers who are expert financial strategists with extraordinary people skills will remain in high demand for many years to come, those advisers who are stuck in transaction mode will likely find their clients gravitating toward automated 'robo advisers'.

These automated investment advice algorithms incorporate a client's goals and risk profile in order to make intelligent wealth management recommendations at a fraction of the cost of a traditional adviser or funds manager.[57]

Carolyn Colley, chief executive of software firm Decimal, says the range of automated advice platforms is likely to grow significantly in the coming years and that by mid 2017 they were already managing $19 billion of investments in the United States.[58]

In the related field of accounting, similar moves towards automation have been underway for some time now. Automated bank feeds and cloud-based accounting software have all but removed the need for bookkeepers—and accountants themselves could be next in the firing line.

The accounting profession, not one known for its flamboyant characters, actually has a long history of embracing new technology that allowed practitioners to work more quickly, simply and accurately. They eagerly adopted adding machines in the nineteenth century, and calculators and computers in the twentieth century.[59]

However, while these previous technological advancements enhanced the work of accountants, we're entering an era where automation technology has the potential to threaten the relevance of accountants entirely.

For instance, KPMG recently announced a goal of having 30 per cent of client audits completed by robots within a few short years. That's the bread-and-butter work of a lot of accountants instantly disappearing.

Like financial advisers, smart accountants will recognise automation technology for the opportunity that it is and adjust their value proposition accordingly. The days of simply managing the compliance, financial administration and lodgement requirements of clients will soon be long gone. As one of the more visionary accountants I have worked with once said: accountants need to shift from seeing themselves as the score keeper at the end of the game (or financial year) to being the coach on the sidelines offering advice and support throughout the game.

I love this metaphor and he is so right. Automation in accounting will free up practitioners to become trusted and valuable business advisers and coaches instead of bean counters. In contrast, those accountants who fail to make this shift will likely see themselves out of a job more quickly than they realise.

Automating personal services

Automation will have a similarly significant impact to personal services. Consider recent developments in automation that are seeing human-like robots acting as:

- ∞ *waiters.* Robotics giant Motoman have developed automated waiters that are currently serving tables in restaurants around China, Japan and South Korea.[60]

- ∞ *secretaries.* A robotic secretary is already a reality at the Jones Lang LaSalle headquarters in Sydney. 'JiLL', as she is known, is a 57-centimetre-tall humanoid whose job description is to 'handle a range of front-of-house tasks, including check-in for meetings, providing directions, contacting hosts and reporting building maintenance issues.' JiLL also has 'in-built facial recognition software to enable her to respond differently to team members as opposed to external visitors'.[61]

- ∞ *hairdressers.* Panasonic recently created a 24-fingered hairwashing robot that's already operating in Japanese hair salons.[62]

- ∞ *aged-care workers.* The Japanese are also at the forefront of automating the aged-care sector. This is partly due to the demographic realities facing Japan: an ageing population and a severe worker shortage. In response, Japanese auto giant Toyota has built a nursing aide named 'Robina'. Weighing 60 kilograms and standing at 1.2 metres tall, Robina communicates in a broadly human manner using words and gestures, and has a brother named 'Humanoid' who is a general home assistant for the elderly, performing tasks such as washing dishes.[63]

Despite advancements in the automation of personal and professional services, I do believe there are some things that only humans will be able to do for a long while yet. For instance, you may be able to automate *care-giving* but you can't automate *caring*. The virtues of compassion and empathy are uniquely human.

That said, the pace of automation in the service sector will increase dramatically in the years to come. Those who resist the trend or ignore it will likely find themselves disrupted in the blink of an eye. However, those who can embrace automation and see it as an enabler for the uniquely human traits that personal and professional services can offer will flourish.

> **You may be able to automate *care-giving* but you can't automate *caring*.**

Logistics and distribution

Recently I was doing some strategic planning work with the team who head up distribution for one of the world's largest FMCG (Fast Moving Consumer Goods) companies. As our discussions turned to the theme of automation, each of the attendees pointed to the fact that increased use of AI and robotics would be an enormous boon for their industry—allowing them to achieve greater efficiency, productivity and transparency in the order-fulfilment process.

Acknowledging the benefits, I then asked if they foresaw any ways in which automation could pose a disruptive threat to their business model.

'Well someone's got to get the boxes from point A to point B so we're hardly going to disappear entirely,' one of the attendees declared.

Then I shared the details of a patent application made by Amazon just two weeks earlier and the room went very quiet, very quickly.

This patent application was for what Amazon referred to as an 'Airborne Fulfillment Center'.

These massive flying warehouse 'blimps' would hover above metropolitan areas at an altitude of 45 000 feet (13 700 metres). When a customer makes an order via their smartphone, a drone would promptly deliver the ordered item to the customer in minutes.[64]

As I described Amazon's plan, what my clients understood very clearly was that automation of this kind had the potential to disrupt them enormously—even cutting them out of the product distribution process altogether. Walmart are certainly taking the threat of this disruption seriously, having lodged their own patent application for airborne fulfilment centres in late August 2017.[65]

While plans such as these may seem unrealistic, it's worth bearing in mind that Amazon in particular have been steadily disrupting the world of distribution for well over a decade now and don't show any signs of slowing.

In 2012, they acquired a warehouse robotic system named 'Kiva' for a cool $775 million and steadily began rolling out the Kiva robots in their warehouses—quickly making scores of human order-fulfilment workers redundant. In recent years, other companies such as Toys R Us,

Gap, Walgreens and Staples have followed suit, purchasing Kiva robots of their own. It is widely estimated that Amazon's warehouse robots have allowed companies to cut order fulfilment costs by as much as 40 per cent.[66]

While Kiva robots do much of the heavy lifting in warehouses, Boston-based company Rethink Robotics has been steadily working on technology designed to do the finer pack and dispatch work traditionally requiring human dexterity. Rethink's humanoid robot 'Baxter' has been a significant breakthrough in this area.

With a price tag of less than the average warehouse worker's annual wage, the beauty of Baxter is that it can be 'trained' by simply moving its arms through the required motions in order to model what you want it to do. Baxter can perform a remarkable variety of tasks, including the transfer of parts on conveyer belts, tending machines used in metal fabrication and packing products into shipping boxes. This third skill is one that Baxter especially excels in. A toy company in Pennsylvania named K'NEX found that Baxter was so good at packing its products tightly into shipping boxes that 20 to 40 per cent fewer boxes were required than when humans did the packing.[67] On top of the skill advantage, one of Baxter's key selling points is the fact that 'he' works 24 hours a day, 365 days per year for the equivalent of about $4 per hour.[68]

There's a robot at the front door

Robots are beginning to change the game at the delivery end of the distribution channel too. The US state of Virginia recently passed a law allowing delivery robots to operate on footpaths and street crossings. Under the new law, robots will not be able to exceed 10 miles (16 kilometres) per hour or weigh more than 50 pounds (23 kilograms) but they will be allowed to operate autonomously. Companies such as Marble, Dispatch, Postmates and DoorDash are leading the way in making delivery-to-the-door robots a reality.[69]

Returning to the example of Amazon's airship warehouses, it's clear that much of the future automation in the delivery and logistics field will depend on drone technology. With their first commercial drone delivery in December 2016, Amazon are again at the cutting edge of employing disruptive technology.[70]

The World Economic Forum's Klaus Schwab suggests that as drones become more adept at sensing and responding to their environment, they will do more and more work across a wide range of industries.[71]

Naturally, a proliferation of drones will pose practical challenges when it comes to airspace use, but these problems will be far from insurmountable.

Medicine

Of all the sectors that automation is set to transform in the coming years, medicine is perhaps the most exciting. While we will see many of the challenging or negative impacts of automation, as with the other industries we've looked at, in the case of the medical sector the disruption may mean the difference between life and death for patients (in a good way!).

For instance, Google has recently developed a contact lens that contains a tiny glucose detector and wireless chip. These lenses can continuously monitor glucose levels in real time, making the maintenance and treatment of diabetes significantly less invasive and painful than current alternatives.[72]

In a similar vein, Proteus Biomedical and Novartis have recently developed smart pills that monitor how the body is interacting with medications and transmit that data to your phone in real time.[73]

New AI-powered diagnostic tools are revolutionising the detection of skin and cervical cancers in some exciting ways too. While examining Pap smear results can be time-consuming and costly, new automated imaging systems can scan samples rapidly and detect more than a hundred visual signs of cell abnormality. The computer then ranks the tests based on the likelihood of disease and, if risk factors are deemed high, passes the tests on to human pathologists to investigate further. This technology is achieving significantly more accurate results than human pathologists alone and roughly doubles the speed of processing tests.[74]

On the treatment side, doctors have recently begun treating certain cancers with tiny robots that are temporarily inserted into the human body to release radiation.[75]

Nanotechnology, the branch of technology that deals with the manipulation of individual atoms and molecules, is also having a significant impact on product design and functionality, with an estimated three to four nanotech products hitting the market every week. In the field of medicine, 'Smart Dust', an array of microscopic computers that can organise themselves inside the human body, can perform a wide range of functions. The applications of Smart Dust are almost unfathomable. Imagine swarms of these nano-devices, called 'motes', attacking early cancer or bringing pain relief to a wound. In the coming years, Smart Dust will enable doctors to essentially get inside your body without traditional surgical procedures at all.[76]

> In the coming years, Smart Dust will enable doctors to essentially get inside your body without traditional surgical procedures at all.

The disruptive impact of medical automation

Despite all the medical possibilities that AI and nanotechnology present, there are a number of ways in which widescale automation will significantly disrupt the medical profession.

For instance, the primary role of medical doctors and their expertise is coming into question with the advent of IBM's Watson supercomputer. Using AI, Watson is able to give accurate medical diagnoses without human help by drawing on its encyclopaedic brain.[77]

A new player in the space, Alibaba Health, also recently unveiled an AI service for disease diagnosis called 'Doctor You'. As an example of the power of this revolutionary technology, Doctor You can be used for medical image diagnosis of CT scans to identify early indicators of cancer.

According to vice president of Alibaba Health Ke Yan, 'Within the coming decade, A.I. will be capable of taking more than half of the workload from doctors in China'.[78]

In surgical wards, automation is proving to be a game changer too. A full 40 per cent of robots currently sold worldwide are designed for surgical purposes. Every year the number of robotic surgeries is increasing by 30 per cent and at the time of writing more than one million Americans have undergone robotic surgery.[79]

The da Vinci robot is proving to be an enduring success story in automated surgery. When I was working with a key player in the medical device sector recently, they told me that as many as 80 per cent of prostate surgeries today are done using some form of intervention by robotic technology such as the da Vinci.

While some in the medical fraternity caution against a reliance on robots in the operating room, the reality is that many surgical robots are able to perform procedures with greater proficiency than humans. In New Zealand a team of surgeons recently trialled the use of a robot to carry out a procedure to remove a throat tumour. This technology resulted in a far more accurate procedure that was less invasive and therefore led to faster recovery times for patients.[80]

It's pretty clear that medical progress is on the verge of significant change in the coming years due to AI-powered automation and robotics. Whether in a traditional operating theatre or at the most microscopic scale, these innovations will forever change the paradigm and profit models of traditional medicine. Some businesses, products and professionals will fall prey to the disruptive impact of these changes but we the patients will undoubtedly be the big winners.

Communication

To round out our look at the key industries that will be disrupted in the coming years by widescale automation, it's only fitting we turn our attention to the notion of how we communicate.

While communication has evolved rapidly in recent decades with the advent of the telephone, fax machines, the Internet, email and social media, the years to come will likely see communication become automated in some very significant ways.

First, we are going to find ourselves communicating fluidly with robots in ways that may have seemed unimaginable just a few short years ago. Amazon's Alexa-enabled Echo, along with Google Home and, most recently, Apple's HomePod, are set to transform the way we interact with and rely upon technology in our day-to-day lives.[81]

Amazon's Alexa is gaining knowledge at a rapid rate, making it ever more useful, reliable and easy to interact with. As of June 2017, the voice assistant had gained more than 14 000 'skills'.[82]

The chatbot revolution

While speaking to machines in our homes and asking them to play music, confirm the current date or read out the news headlines is pretty cutting-edge stuff, the reality is that you and I have been communicating with and relying on robots conversationally for a while now without even knowing it.

I recently presented at a conference where the speaker following me began his address by mirroring his computer monitor with the big screen, logging in to a chat portal and starting an interaction with a call-centre customer service assistant named Kate. After answering a series of Kate's chatty questions about the speaker's age, health status and geographic location, Kate came up with a range of insurance product options that would be a good fit for him. The speaker selected one of the quotes and then progressed to the policy application process.

Watching this in real time, I was impressed with how seamless the quote process was. I was floored to discover that Kate didn't actually exist—she was a computer-generated service assistant otherwise known as a 'chatbot'.

If you've interacted with any large company online or even over the phone in recent months, there is every chance you were actually speaking with a chatbot like Kate rather than a real person.

By 2020, technology research leader Gartner estimates that AI-powered chatbots will be responsible for a full 85 per cent of customer service interactions.[83] It's easy to see why companies are rushing to implement this automated customer service technology—after all, it costs a fraction of what human service assistants do. It is also far more efficient.

According to Juniper Research, healthcare and banking providers using chatbots are seeing average service interactions being cut by just more than four minutes per enquiry—equating to average cost savings in the range of $0.50 to $0.70 per interaction. The research's author, Lauren Foye, suggests, 'As Artificial Intelligence advances, reducing reliance on human representatives undoubtedly spells job losses'.[84]

Never get lost in translation again

Beyond chatbots and AI-powered home assistants, it is the advances in automating language translation that have perhaps captured my attention most in the research for this book.

Having grown up in Australia, where learning a second language is uncommon, I have always found myself at a loss when travelling overseas and interacting with people in foreign languages.

So when I read about a new product called Translate One2One, I got very excited.[85] Powered by IBM's Watson AI technology, Translate One2One is a translation earpiece that works in almost real time and doesn't rely on bluetooth or wi-fi connections like older generation solutions. It currently supports eight languages, and the possibilities of this technology are enormous for the world of commerce. It also stands to transform the travel experience for linguistically challenged tourists like me.

Fans of *The Hitchhiker's Guide to the Galaxy* will recognise the likeness of this technology to the Babel fish, which was a creature that, once inserted into the ear, allowed a person to understand speech in any language.[86] Science fiction is indeed becoming a reality.

Professional translators will of course point out that no device can allow for the range of nuances, inflections, slang and dialect variances in language and perhaps they are right—for now. But the technology is getting better all the time. Accuracy of human language recognition technology such as that used in Microsoft's Cortana, Apple's Siri, Google Now and Amazon's Alexa is in the range of 96 to 98 per cent.[87]

While language recognition and translation technology is not yet perfect and may never be, all I can say is that I wouldn't want to be a language translator in the coming years. That said, anyone involved in online customer service, call centre operation or insurance quote assistance is looking vulnerable too!

Automation is going to change the way we communicate in some profound, disrupting and enduring ways in the very near future.

∞

In appendix B at the back of this book I take a detailed look at some of the societal implications of widescale automation. With predictions of up to 47 per cent of current occupations at high risk of being automated or made redundant by artificial intelligence, this first form of disruption is one that has ramifications not just for industries and businesses but also for individuals, families and the very fabric of our society.

So feel free to flick to the back of the book to get a better sense of the occupations that are safest, those that are not, and the skills required to navigate the disruptions ahead as an individual.

As we draw this chapter to a close, however, I'm sure you are left with little doubt that automation is going to change the status quo for all of us in the years to come.

In the same way that the Luddites resisted the destruction of their livelihoods by industrialisation, we will likely see scores of individuals and industries rail against the very changes we have explored in this chapter. Automation will either be an opportunity or a threat depending on whether you embrace it or not. In the words of the technologist Tim O'Reilly, 'We must not fall into the trap of trying to protect the past from the future'.[88]

Questions for reflection

∞ How will the increasing availability and prevalence of data change decision making for you in the coming years?

∞ In what way will AI be a threat or an opportunity for your role, organisation or industry?

∞ What do you suspect the moral and ethical implications of widescale automation could be in your context?

∞ What is the unique value you or your organisation add that cannot be readily automated?

∞ How could you better engage and communicate with customers by using automation technology?

CHAPTER 2

EMPOWERED
CONSUMERS

Since the dawn of time, the deck has always been stacked against the individual.

Power belonged to organisations—be they religious institutions, government bureaucracies or corporate behemoths. While we have tried to harness our collective clout from time to time and pinned our hopes on brave revolutionaries who railed against authority, at the end of the day, the individual has always lacked power.

Until now.

Recent years have seen the balance of power shift rapidly away from organisations. The individual today has access to information, options and a platform for making their voice heard that previous generations could have only dreamed of.

Organisations and institutions are not the only ones losing power though—professions are too.

REAL CHALLENGES FOR REAL ESTATE

To see how profoundly consumer empowerment is already disrupting our world, look no further than the real estate industry.

In years past, real estate agents enjoyed a position of power over both the buyer and the seller. The agent's office had the once-critical window displays in which to feature a property. Agents had preferential pricing agreements with print advertising in newspapers and magazines. They had relationships with photographers and copywriters who knew how to profile properties in the most favourable light. And most of all, agents had access to databases of previous local sales and proprietary software for sharing your property with other agents through multiple listing services. Add their all-powerful rolodex of potential warm buyers, their local knowledge and their understanding of regulatory requirements and real estate agents were a truly indispensable part of the property transaction. In fact, not that many years ago it would have been inconceivable to sell or buy a property without an agent. This reality was reflected in the generous fees they could command.

Having worked extensively with many real estate agents and agency groups, I have seen firsthand how significantly things are changing—and it's only just begun.

From a seller's side, online listings websites have made an agent's window displays, multiple listing services and print advertising largely irrelevant. The comparable sales figures and historical records required to create property valuations are also now easily accessible to everyone.

Added to this, the paths to market that involve little or no agent intervention are growing by the day. In Australia, services such as buyMyplace.com.au allow owners to list their properties for a fee of just $650.[1] Reflecting on the 22 per cent per quarter increase in new listings on buyMyplace.com.au, the company's chief executive, Paul Heath, suggests the growth is a function of people's growing frustration with the traditional ways of selling real estate. He points to data that shows that the average seller can save $20000 on a median-value home transaction by using a direct-to-market sales service and avoiding agent's commissions.[2]

Around the world, the same trend is gathering momentum. In the United States, around 20 per cent of homes are sold without an agent and in Canada it's as high as 30 per cent.[3]

Even those sellers who still opt to use a traditional real estate agent are enjoying a newfound power through accessing and writing reviews on individual agents. Websites such as ratemyagent.com.au and openagent.com.au have become the TripAdvisor of real estate. Sellers now have the ability to research and compare individual real estate agents based on reviews of past sellers before deciding who to list their property through.

On the buyer side of the property equation, the individual is enjoying unprecedented power too.

Searching for properties is now done on data-rich apps rather than by browsing the window displays of local agents. Instead of wasting time inspecting properties that look good on paper but don't match your needs, online virtual tours help buyers make informed decisions as to which properties should make the shortlist without stepping out the door.

Even once buyers have found a property of interest and turn up to inspect it, it is not uncommon for them to arrive at an open for inspection knowing more than the agent about the property's features, historical comparable sales and local amenities such as schools and public transport. This is putting buyers in an ever-stronger position to negotiate and means agents are more accountable for underquoting or other bad behaviour than ever before.[4]

For those buyers who still opt to search for properties by scoping out a neighbourhood in person, apps such as Snaploader are changing that experience too. Sometimes described as Shazam for real estate, with Snaploader you can photograph or 'snap' a house for sale and it will use advanced visual recognition technology to immediately retrieve photos, viewing and auction times, the status of the listing and a 3D image of its internal structure. Interested parties can also be updated after an offer or an auction.[5]

And this is just the beginning. In the years to come, new technologies and players will continue to offer consumers information and options that will increase the power they have in the property transaction process. For real estate agents, the key to remaining relevant will lie in the unique experience they can offer clients—an experience not easily replicated by technology. Agents who provide trusted advice, a remarkable customer experience and local knowledge stand to do very well while those who remain in transaction mode will disappear entirely.

THE EMPOWERED AUDIENCE

In my own industry I have had to come to terms with an increasingly empowered marketplace. In the world of writing and professional speaking, typically the greatest source of value is intellectual property. The traditional paradigm is that the content, ideas and insights a person creates must be guarded and protected at all costs. For years, common decency and general awareness of copyright restrictions have stopped readers or audience members from photocopying and disseminating my work or setting up a video camera at the back of the room to record a live presentation.

But this has changed. Today, every audience member turns up to a live presentation with a video camera in their pocket and they are not hesitant to use it. Curiously, while it would have seemed odd or presumptuous to set up a tripod at the back of a room to record a presentation in the pre-smartphones days, propping up your phone from the comfort of your seat and doing the same thing now seems entirely reasonable and permissible.

A few years ago I began noticing audience members doing this and then would subsequently discover their unauthorised footage on YouTube and Facebook. I'm embarrassed to admit that my initial response was one of indignation. I even 'called out' a few audience members during a presentation, asking them to stop recording. It was always an awkward experience but, worst of all, it did little to dissuade others.

Then the next trend was to take photos of every PowerPoint slide. At some stage a few years ago, audience members seemed to all decide that writing notes was old-school and that photographing slides was now the done thing. Again, at first I found this off-putting because audience members would take photos of my proprietary content and then immediately share them on social media.

In speaking with my colleagues on the conference circuit, I quickly learned that this sort of behaviour was happening across the board and I realised I needed to make a choice. Clearly trying to control or change the behaviour of audiences with web-enabled smartphones was futile, so the only thing I could control and change was my own paradigm.

Rather than perceiving audience members' recordings as an infringement of my intellectual property, I chose to see it as marketing. Every person who shared a video or an image of my content was helping me leverage my ideas and brand!

THE THREE SOURCES OF CONSUMER POWER

Regardless of the industry you are in, I bet you are grappling with similar challenges and frustrations to the ones I have just described. The truth is that consumers and the marketplace at large will grow increasingly powerful in the years to come as a result of three things:

i. information

ii. options

iii. a voice.

i. Information

If there is one piece of technology that has enabled the empowerment enjoyed by consumers today, it would have to be the smartphone.

The average consumer today is merely a few taps or swipes away from more information than entire nations possessed a few decades ago. Conventional wisdom tells us that knowledge is power, and perhaps nothing has increased our knowledge more than our web-enabled smartphones.

We need look no further than the world of retail to see how smartphones have tipped the power balance in favour of the consumer. Consider the fact that 81 per cent of consumers today will have researched a product online before entering the store.[6] The consumer will likely know more about the product's features and price comparability than the store assistant they are speaking to. This uncomfortable new normal is one businesses must adjust to.

Even in the online shopping world, new levels of access to information are transforming the power dynamic. A recently released feature of Microsoft's digital assistant, Cortana, will advise customers of the best price and availability of similar products across dozens of major retailers when they are looking at a product online. At a moment's notice, you can check if shopping through a competitor's website will offer you a better deal.[7]

Not to be outdone, Google are also leveraging the power of artificial intelligence to give consumers access to real-time information that will inform their purchasing decisions. Among other things, Google Lens will allow consumers to point their smartphone camera at any business or product and instantly have reviews, ratings and price comparisons pop up on their screen.[8]

When I spoke at a global electronics manufacturer recently, a number of audience members shared that consumers' awareness of a lack of pricing uniformity across markets had become a significant challenge in recent times. Like most multinationals, my client had product pricing that varied based on the country or region. Any number of factors such as import tariffs, local tax regulation and currency fluctuations influenced these price variations.

In the past, price inconsistencies hardly mattered. After all, a customer in Spain was unlikely or unable to compare the price of a product they were purchasing with the price being paid by a customer in New Zealand. Today, however, pricing transparency means consumers can and do compare—in ways that can do immeasurable damage to a company's reputation and perceived trustworthiness.

Considering how important access to information is to consumer empowerment, there is every chance the coming years will see Internet connectivity designated as a key human right. The UN Special Rapporteur for Freedom of Opinion and Expression has gone as far as to suggest that disconnecting people from the Internet constitutes a human rights violation and Estonia has even passed the world's first law enshrining this right.[9]

The genie is well and truly out of the bottle. Consumers know more than ever before and there is little that companies and professionals can do to change it.

ii. Options

In their book *How Companies Win*, authors Rick Kash and David Calhoun suggest that the twentieth-century model for business success centred on protecting, controlling and defending distribution channels at all costs. They point to companies such as AT&T, Ford and IBM, who succeeded by doing just this.[10] In the years to come, however, a protectionist approach simply won't work. The days of controlling the market by restricting options are over.

In the same way that direct-to-market platforms are changing the game for real estate agents, the age of 'disintermediation' means that consumers have the option to deal directly with service providers by circumventing the established channels of old.

Take travel agents for instance. Almost half of the respondents indicated that when researching a trip online, they prefer purchasing travel services such as accommodation, flights or tours directly from the supplier rather than through a travel agent.[11]

The age of empowered consumers means product and service providers can no longer simply be gatekeepers standing between suppliers and end users. On the contrary, middlemen must be adding real value (and not merely adding 'clip the ticket' costs) in the distribution process if they hope to remain indispensable rather than become irrelevant.

The retail sector is also grappling with a consumer base that has more options than ever. With tech giants such as Amazon massively changing the retail landscape in recent years, with initiatives such as the Prime Wardrobe service that allows shoppers to truly 'try before they buy', online retail is becoming a genuine option for consumers.

iii. A voice

In early November 2014, Tony and Jan Jenkinson checked out of the Broadway Hotel in the seaside resort town of Blackpool on England's north-west coast. Presumably, their experience at the Broadway was less than amazing: they promptly posted a review on TripAdvisor describing the hotel as 'rotten' and 'stinking'. And that was the end of the story — or so the Jenkinsons thought.

To their surprise, a few days later they discovered a £100 charge on their credit card from the Broadway Hotel. When they rang to query the unexpected transaction, the hotel manager promptly informed them that it was company policy to charge £100 for negative reviews. When they asked the hotel manager if he was joking, he informed them that he certainly was not.[12] When the Jenkinsons took their story to the media, things quickly escalated. In the face of widespread outrage, the Broadway Hotel eventually bowed to public pressure, offering to refund the £100 fee and scrap the policy.

Apart from breaching local contract fairness regulations, the Broadway Hotel's behaviour revealed a mindset dangerously out of step with the modern age—the belief that businesses can control their brand. While this may have been the case in years past, consumers today have a voice that has never been louder, more persuasive and harder to ignore.

Sadly, many businesses have a similar mindset to the Broadway Hotel, even if their practices and policies are less outrageous.

The global soapbox

There was a time when a consumer's voice only travelled so far. If you had a bad experience with a company or brand, you might have told your family and friends, who might in turn have shared it with theirs.

Online review sites and social media have thoroughly turned the tables.

But that's where it would have stopped. If you were really incensed, you might have written a letter to the editor of a local newspaper, organised a boycott or even contacted the government department concerned with consumer protection. But at the end of the day, the power of a consumer's voice was dwarfed by the clout and reach of a company's marketing budget.

And yet today, online review sites and social media have thoroughly turned the tables. Ninety per cent of consumers trust peer reviews while only 14 per cent trust advertisements.[13] In order words, what you say about yourself and your products matters less than it ever has before. In contrast, what your customers say about you speaks volumes.

In addition to confronting the challenges of increasingly informed patients, doctors and medical professionals are also dealing with an increasingly loud consumer voice.

Doctor rating websites now allow patients to rate their doctors on price, bedside manner and service levels. Former head of Australia's competition regulator Graeme Samuel says this represents a 'new paradigm' for both consumers and healthcare providers. 'Providers used to say to me, "Health is different, because consumers don't understand … ",' Samuel says:

> Of course medical providers don't like it. But I can't think of a single business that likes to have its success or the quality of what they're doing exposed, unless they're the best quality and they're proud of it.[14]

∞

Regardless of which of these three sources of empowerment stands to disrupt your business or industry most in the coming years, the bottom line is that consumers have a power that cannot be ignored. Taking customers for granted and restricting options or information will never work like it once did. Further still, a good reputation may take years to build but only minutes to lose, so you must be on your best behaviour at all times and constantly keep the consumer's needs and desires front and centre.

In truth, shouldn't that have been what businesses were doing all along?

3D PRINTING AND THE RISE OF THE PROSUMER

While consumers empowered by information, options and a voice will continue to disrupt businesses and industries in the years to come, there is one form of empowerment that is scarcely on the radar today but will have a greater disruptive impact than most of us realise. I'd go as far as to suggest it will be the most profound form of disintermediation since the beginning of the Industrial Revolution.

That disruption? 3D printing.

Unlike recent forms of disintermediation, which have forced middlemen such as retailers, wholesalers, distributors and brokers to clarify the value they add, 3D printing disintermediates the *entire* supply chain—including the manufacturer. The moment the consumer becomes the producer (a hybrid known as a 'prosumer'), the game changes for countless businesses and industries.

3D printing is actually not a new technology. Hideo Kodama of Japan's Nagoya Municipal Industrial Research Institute invented the first working 3D printer as far back as 1982.[15] Since then, 3D printing technology has remained at the fringes of commerce—mainly used for prototypes, architecture, construction, aerospace or the military.

The years to come will likely see 3D printing become mainstream in some powerfully disruptive ways. In their book *Abundance: The Future is Better Than You Think*, Peter Diamandis and Steven Kotler name 3D printing as one of the world's most exciting new technologies—referring to it as the 'democratisation of distribution'.[16]

I suspect Diamandis and Kotler may be spot on.

A few years ago I was doing some consulting work with the executive team of a large electrical hardware manufacturer. During our discussions about potential disruptions to their business, I asked how seriously they were taking the threat of 3D printing. The general consensus was that it wasn't something that needed to be on their radar, so I shared a hypothetical scenario that is not far from becoming a reality.

I asked them to imagine a scene where someone accidentally cracks the wall-mounted power-point casing while vacuuming. In the present day, to fix the broken unit you'd have to either head down to your local hardware store to buy a replacement case (likely manufactured by the company I was working with) or order one online. The executive team around the table nodded their heads.

I then shared an alternative future scenario where, upon breaking the power-point casing, you'd log on to a website such as thingiverse.com and purchase for less than a dollar the exact design file for the power point cover you'd broken. You'd then proceed to 3D print your own replacement cover without leaving your home (or purchasing any product produced by my client company or their competitors). This scenario would be a case-in-point of where a consumer becomes the producer.

Sound far-fetched?

This scenario could become a reality sooner than you think.

The current market leader in small-scale residential 3D printers, MakerBot, are going beyond creating low-priced and easy-to-use 3D printers—they are helping create the very ecosystem of downloadable designs that will make personal printer ownership viable and attractive.[17]

The numbers give some indication of how quickly 3D printing is moving towards the mainstream. In 2016 more than 278000 home desktop 3D printers were sold worldwide, and by 2020 it is forecast that the global revenue of the 3D printing industry is expected to top $21 billion. Driving this march towards the mainstream, Siemens predicts that 3D printing will become 50 per cent cheaper and up to 400 per cent faster by 2020.[18]

Printing a new pair of shoes

To see how 3D printing could change the game and tip the scales of power toward consumers, consider recent advancements in the printing of consumer goods such as shoes.

In the past few years, all the major shoe manufacturers, including Nike, Adidas and New Balance, have taken significant steps toward 3D printing.

To date, many of these advancements have centred on the creation of printed insoles and orthotics designed to prevent or eliminate foot pain. However, printing insoles is just the beginning. Soon we'll be printing the whole shoe.

Nike COO Eric Sprunk recently weighed in on the possibility of 3D printed shoes. Speaking at the 2015 GeekWire Summit, Sprunk discussed how making Nike's Flyknit Lunar shoes involved simply sending a computer file to a machine.

> *Do I envision a future where we might still own the file from an IP perspective… and you can either manufacture that in your home or we will do it for you at our store? Oh yeah, that's not that far away.*[19]

In a similar vein, New Balance CEO Robert DeMartini reported in mid 2016 that his company was working on a design for 3D-printed running shoes, predicting a similar future to Nike. 'It's really just the beginning,' DeMartini said.[20]

Will 3D printing live up to the hype?

Like any new transformative technology, there is no shortage of sceptics who question whether there will ever be a day when the majority of residential households own a 3D printer.

Gartner have gone as far as to create a Hype Cycle which suggests that within a few years we will have passed what they refer to as the 'peak of Inflated Expectations' and that 3D printing will eventually find its natural level as a niche prototyping technology.[21]

Others, such as Martin Ford in his book *Rise of the Robots*, suggest that the low economies of scale, slow speed of the machines and questionable value of customisation will mean that 3D printers are unlikely to become ubiquitous any time soon.[22] At best, Martin predicts that 3D printing will merely alter the supply chain, seeing manufacturing move closer to the consumer.

What does go without saying is that consumer 3D printing has not yet lived up to the hype surrounding it in the past. The price of the hardware, the availability of printing designs and the limitations of printable materials have all prevented 3D printing from breaking into the mainstream.

In the words of Hod Lipson in his book *Fabricated*, what 3D printing needs is a 'killer app' — the one capability that will cause it to become an irresistibly attractive option for everyday households.

According to Lipson, this killer app may well come in an unexpected form: food.

Printing tonight's dinner

While food printers are already creating designer cookies, pastries and chocolates, the significant shift will occur when restaurants and households can use these printers to create entire meals using 3D printing technology.[23]

One company is already making inroads towards this reality. Spanish company Natural Machines predicts its Foodini 3D food printer will become as common as home microwaves within the decade.

Moving from the kitchen to the bathroom, the consumer benefits and applications of 3D printing are far reaching. For instance, the US Food and Drug Administration recently approved the first 3D-printed drug with a view to make a wide range of pharmaceuticals printable in the years to come.[24]

The US Food and Drug Administration recently approved the first 3D-printed drug.

The rise of the prosumer is something no business or industry can afford to ignore. 3D printers are set to change the game for all manufacturers, distributors and retailers in the years to come.

∞

I hope you are beginning to get a clear sense of the disruptive impact of consumers, who have more power than ever.

Whether by having more information, greater options or an increasingly loud voice, the consumers of tomorrow will hold many if not all of the cards. Organisations and industries will need to quickly adjust to this new reality if they haven't done so already.

The age of empowered consumers means that 'good enough' no longer is. Businesses, professions and industries must be on their A game at all times lest customers exercise their newfound power and make a quick move for the door—writing an online review about you as they walk through it.

> The age of empowered consumers means that 'good enough' no longer is.

Beyond the information, options and voice that consumers enjoy, the rise of prosumerism through 3D printing represents one of the most significant economic shifts we have seen in centuries. In an age where consumers have the power to produce their own customised goods, every player in the manufacturing supply chain will need to radically rethink their value proposition.

Questions for reflection

- ∞ How are you seeing the increasing power of consumers playing out in your context?

- ∞ In what ways is greater access to information tipping the power scale in favour of consumers in your context?

- ∞ What new options and paths to market are consumers enjoying and how will these grow in the years to come?

- ∞ What impact is an increasingly loud consumer voice having on you or your organisation/industry? What is the best response to this?

- ∞ How do you see the rise of 'prosumerism' through technologies such as 3D printing changing the game for you?

CHAPTER 3

UNCONVENTIONAL
COMPETITION

Preparing to speak at a conference in Singapore recently, I was doing some research and discovered that much of what I had been told in history class about the country's fall to the Japanese during World War II was not in fact true at all.

I'd always been told that the British were essentially caught off guard by the Japanese invasion—that they were ill equipped and failed to recognise the threat until it was too late. In reality, the British were anything but unprepared *militarily*. The challenge was that they were unprepared *mentally*.

The established paradigm in Singapore during World War II was that any significant threat of invasion would come from the sea. As a result, a British naval base was built in Sembawang, and Singapore's coastline was heavily fortified with massive guns designed to fend off naval attacks. This preparedness contributed to an arrogant mindset that the island nation was virtually impossible to conquer—it was even referred to by military experts at the time as being a 'Gibraltar of the East' and a 'fortress' that was 'impregnable'.[1]

As the Japanese made their way progressively down the Malay Peninsula during the early months of 1942, the officer in charge of defending Singapore, Lieutenant General Arthur E. Percival, was operating under the strong assumption that the Japanese would attack near the Sembawang naval base, and so he placed his strongest forces there.[2]

It was inconceivable to British military planners that the island could be attacked in any way other than what they had assumed. It was certainly unimaginable that the Japanese forces would traverse the jungles and mangrove swamps of the Malay Peninsula in order to mount an invasion from Singapore's north-west.

But that's exactly what they did.[3]

On 8 February 1942, Japanese forces used collapsible boats to cross the Johor Strait into Singapore and overran the startled and unprepared British forces with extraordinary speed and ruthlessness. Continuing to adopt unconventional military tactics, the Japanese used bicycles as an extremely swift and effective means of transport.[4]

To this day, the fall of Singapore is considered one of the greatest military disasters in the history of the British army.

LESSONS FROM HISTORY

When we consider business strategy in the face of disruption, I suspect there is much to learn from the annals of history—especially the arena of armed combat. In fact, I'd suggest that the very missteps and mistakes that contributed to the fall of Singapore ought to serve as a warning to every business leader today.

The reality is that the British *were* prepared. They were ready. They'd done all they could do based on the assumptions they held and the information they had. What they weren't prepared for was an unconventional adversary coming at them from an unexpected direction and in an inconceivable manner.

And it's the same in business. When I'm working with clients, my strong encouragement is to stay alert to unconventional competitive threats because these are often dismissed or go undetected until it's almost too late.

The challenge with this third form of disruption is that it's the hardest one for business leaders to prepare for or pre-empt. History is full of examples of leaders underestimating, dismissing or ignoring the threat posed by unconventional competitors.

Take this assertion from Blockbuster's CEO, Jim Keyes, in 2008: 'Neither RedBox nor Netflix are even on the radar screen in terms of competition'.[5] This, just a few years after Netflix's founder, Reed Hastings, had offered to sell his company to Blockbuster for a mere $50 million. Blockbuster declined.

Nokia's Chief Strategy Officer, Anssi Vanjoki, dismissed the threat Apple posed to his company's dominance in mobile phones: 'With the Mac, Apple attracted a lot of attention at first, but they have remained a niche manufacturer. That will be their role in mobile phones as well'.[6]

Then there's former Microsoft CEO Steve Ballmer who confidently proclaimed in 2007, 'There is no chance iPhone will get any significant market share'. (This from the same man who dismissed Google in its early days: 'Google's not a real company. It's a house of cards'.[7])

While it's easy and even a bit unfair to use the benefit of hindsight to scoff at such assertions, if nothing else these predictions show just how dangerous underestimating the threat of unconventional competition can be—whether this is through naivety, closed-mindedness or sheer arrogance.

According the Klaus Schwab of the World Economic Forum, business leaders would be wise to 'consider their biggest threat to be competitors that are not yet regarded as such'. In other words, Schwab challenges leaders to regularly ask themselves: who are the outliers, the new entrants or the players in parallel industries who may not be on your radar yet as competition but could become so in the blink of an eye? Further still, he warns business leaders not to fall into the trap of assuming unconventional threats will only come in the form of fledgling tech startups: 'Digitization enables large incumbents to cross industry boundaries by leveraging their customer base, infrastructure or technology. Size can be a competitive advantage if smartly leveraged,' he suggests.[8]

Consider Google's foray into the job search business in June 2017, allowing job hunters to search for jobs across virtually all of the major online job boards such as LinkedIn, Monster, WayUp, DirectEmployers, CareerBuilder and Facebook.[9] This at a time when recruitment agencies are facing a multitude of other unconventional competitors moving into their space, including dating site eHarmony. With extensive experience in using algorithms to help match potential mates, it was only ever a short step for eHarmony to help potential employees find their perfect employment match too![10]

As I reflect on recent years of working with clients across a wide range of industries, there have been a number of striking examples of how disruptive unconventional competition can be. Here are just a few:

∞ Uber has evolved from being solely a ride-sharing service to a full-fledged logistics firm delivering packages, food and groceries.[11] This is already having a significant impact on freight, logistics and delivery industries and will continue to do so.

∞ The auto-refracting technology Opternative allows users to do full eye examinations at home, using the camera on their smartphone or computer. Once a diagnosis is complete, the customer is provided with their prescription and they can then purchase glasses online from any number of suppliers. The completed glasses are delivered to the customer's home — removing the need to enter a physical optometrist's office at all.

∞ The meat and livestock industry is bracing for the arrival of lab-grown meats. Driven by ethical and environmental considerations, lab-grown meat has existed for a number of years but is now becoming economically viable.[12] The decision in August 2017 by Bill Gates and Richard Branson to invest in Memphis Meats — a company that develops meat from stem cells — is indicative of how much attention and interest the technology is attracting.

∞ As a final example, look at how Dollar Shave Club upended the men's shaving market in recent years. From the moment the brand launched, its edgy, irreverent and unconventional YouTube marketing was hard to ignore. Taking on global behemoth Gillette, Dollar Shave Club took inspiration from Netflix's original mail-order business model and it worked. Dollar Shave Club quickly grew to be a $60 million per year business with no salespeople, no distributors, no retailers and no TV commercials.[13] Its growth shattered conventional wisdom and challenged established industry norms to the point where Gillette's market share dropped from 70 per cent in 2010 to just 54 per cent by 2016.[14]

Beyond these specific examples of disruption, in the pages ahead we're going to explore some of the key unconventional competitive threats that will affect a range of industries:

∞ media and entertainment

∞ automotive

- ∞ energy
- ∞ travel and tourism
- ∞ banking and finance.

MEDIA AND ENTERTAINMENT

Jim Keyes' dismissal of the threat Netflix posed to Blockbuster's business is far from an isolated case in the world of media and entertainment. When asked in a 2010 interview what he thought of Netflix, Time Warner CEO Jeff Bewkes scoffed: 'It's a little bit like, is the Albanian army going to take over the world? I don't think so'.[15]

In a similar vein, NBCUniversal's president of research and media development, Alan Wurtzel, underplayed the threat of streaming services in 2016: 'The notion that [companies like Netflix] are replacing broadcast TV may not be quite accurate. I think we need a little bit of perspective'.[16]

Rather tellingly, by the middle of 2017 NBCUniversal's parent company, Comcast, announced a record-breaking loss of 45 000 residential customers in one quarter,[17] Fox 21 Television Studios head Bert Salke was labelling Netflix as 'public enemy No. 1', and another network executive likened Netflix's onslaught to that of Genghis Khan.[18]

There is little doubt that Netflix has significantly changed the game for entertainment providers. According to Nielsen, among people aged two to 34, prime-time viewing dropped by 34 per cent between 2012 and 2017.[19] Over the same period, eight million US households have abandoned traditional pay TV.[20] But Netflix are not the only unconventional competitive threat to have recently disrupted the media and entertainment status quo.

Consider the fact that at the time of writing, 1.5 billion viewers visit YouTube every single month—20 per cent of the world's population. Even more significantly, the average viewer spends more than an hour per day watching YouTube on mobile devices alone.[21] When all this is added up, the total number of hours viewers spend on YouTube each day totals more than one billion and YouTube is now the largest TV network in the world.[22]

Indicative of how profoundly the media landscape has changed, toy giant Hasbro recently launched a new product range via YouTube rather than television. Says Hasbro's SVP of global digital marketing, Victor Lee:

> *It was time to get with the times. Today people watch what they want, whenever they want. So as brands, we have to be consistently present—and let people binge-watch and engage further if they'd like.*[23]

YouTube was an unconventional competitive threat that the incumbents couldn't or wouldn't accept a few short years ago. In 2006, the executive of a large media company dismissed it entirely: 'If you add up every video ever watched on YouTube, it is less than the viewership of even low-rated television shows on obscure cable networks. We don't have to worry about this garbage.'[24]

In fairness, this executive could have been forgiven for holding this view. After all, in the mid 2000s YouTube was indeed little more than a fledgling service mostly populated by pirated videos.[25]

And yet that is the very problem with unconventional competitive threats — it may be tempting to ignore, dismiss or ridicule them when they first appear. But by the time they become a clear and present danger, it can often be too late.

AUTOMOTIVE

As discussed in chapter 1, the move towards driverless cars is seeing a range of non-traditional players enter the auto sector, from Apple to Google to Samsung.

Many automakers are struggling to adjust to this new competitive landscape. In early 2016 Porsche's CEO Oliver Blume dismissed the entry of tech giants such as Apple, saying, 'An iPhone belongs in your pocket, not on the road'.[26]

However, it is another new entrant that most underscores how significantly the highly mature auto market has been disrupted through unconventional competition. In a milestone that was as significant as it was symbolic, in April 2017 Tesla overtook General Motors to become the most valuable automaker in the United States — this from a company that had only released its first model nine years earlier.[27]

While some detractors suggest that Tesla's market cap is overhyped and overvalued, the disruptive impact of this one company can't be overstated.

Right from the outset, Tesla's business model disrupted and unsettled the entire automotive sector. Rather than following a traditional dealer distribution channel, Tesla sold directly to the market in its early days. And unlike other electric vehicle (EV) manufacturers that relied upon established service stations or users' own homes for powering a vehicle, Tesla began constructing their own network of innovative charging points around the country.[28]

However, more than its business model, it is Tesla's philosophy and technology that have most blindsided its rivals. While other automakers had dabbled in making electric vehicles over the years, it wasn't until Tesla that these vehicles became sexy, fast and a genuine alternative to traditional internal combustion engines.

ENERGY

In an energy market that has long been dominated by coal-fired power stations and lucrative poles-and-wires distribution networks, the entrance of alternative power sources represents a significant disruption.

It is predicted that wind and solar will make up 34 per cent of all power generated by 2040—in contrast with 5 per cent in 2017.[29] Over the same time period, the cost of offshore wind farms will decrease by a staggering 71 per cent and the cost of solar generation will slide by 66 per cent.[30] The impact on the coal-generation power business is already being felt, with 369 gigawatts of projects scheduled at the time of writing set to be cancelled in the short term.[31]

> **The entrance of alternative power sources represents a significant disruption.**

While large-scale alternative energy projects are having a significant disruptive impact on the energy sector, it is what's occurring at a smaller scale, in the home, that is most significant. Although the impact of residential solar power generation and storage was dismissed by many utilities companies at first, there is a growing awareness of how significant the threat posed by this trend really is. In a recent report from the Edison Electric Institute, a warning was issued to power providers the world over: 'One can imagine a day when battery storage technology or micro turbines could allow customers to be electric grid independent,' the report said, likening the speed of the coming transition to the one from landlines to mobile phones in the mid 2000s.[32]

There's little doubt that this prediction is rapidly coming true. Increasingly cheap solar panels and increasingly powerful batteries are seeing regulated power monopolies in competition with their very own customers.

According to Ravi Manghani of GTM Research, utilities aren't doomed but they will need to undergo a radical transformation. Manghani suggests that utilities will need to become facilitators and minders of an increasingly distributed grid, rather than the centralised power producers they are today.[33]

Again, it will likely be the great unconventional disruptor Elon Musk and his company Solar City that will enable this change to occur. Solar City's revolutionary solar panel roof tiles unveiled in October 2016 could well prove to be a game changer. Musk's goal is ambitious if nothing else:

> The goal is … to make solar roofs that look better than a normal roof, generate electricity, last longer, have better insulation and an installed cost that is less than a normal roof plus the cost of electricity.[34]

In estimating a timeline for the wide-scale adoption of these solar roof tiles, Musk is uncharacteristically conservative. He suggests that the time horizon will be close to 50 years for full adoption but that within 15 years the tiles will become commonplace.[35]

While utilities may dismiss even this timeline as unrealistic, it's good to remember that Elon Musk's Tesla became the world's most valuable automaker in nine years—so there's no reason to doubt he could disrupt the energy business more broadly in double that time.

TRAVEL AND TOURISM

Perhaps one of the most potent examples of unconventional competition is what's become known as the 'sharing economy'.

I remember the day that the significance of this trend really became clear to me. My wife and I were looking to upgrade our outdoor furniture and so we decided to place an ad for our old set on eBay. Within a day, we had secured a buyer for our used furniture at a price even higher than we'd hoped for. When the buyer arrived to pick up her purchase, she was driving a van she'd hired for the hour from a car-sharing service called GoGet. The buyer informed me that she didn't own a car so she just rented one when she needed it.

As she was measuring up the furniture before loading it into the van, she told me it was the perfect size for the deck outside the lower level of her two-storey home—which she rents out almost every week of the year on Airbnb.

As I watched this woman pull out of my driveway that Saturday afternoon, it struck me how significant the new economy is—it's an entire exchange of goods that could not and would not have occurred in the years before the sharing economy.

According to forecasts from PricewaterhouseCoopers, one of the biggest sectors to be affected by the sharing economy is travel and tourism.[36]

The fact that Airbnb is worth twice as much as hotel giant Hyatt and has more than four million listings[37] in 34 000 cities around the world underscores how profoundly disruptive this one unconventional competitor has become.[38]

> **Airbnb is worth twice as much as hotel giant Hyatt.**

In Australia, Airbnb has gone from being an accommodation provider at the fringes of the industry to being thoroughly mainstream. Their partnership with Qantas, allowing customers to earn frequent flyer points when booking through Airbnb, was a symbolic move that rattled the travel industry. A partnership with travel giant Flight Centre, focusing on the highly lucrative corporate travel market, has left traditional hotel providers in no doubt—what started as a cute idea by two young guys in San Francisco has become a serious threat.[39]

However, it's not just the hotel chains that ought to be nervous about the unconventional threat of Airbnb. The company's recent initiative called Airbnb Trips is positioning them as a full-scale travel agency that will cater for every element of the travel experience—not just the accommodation.[40] Airbnb are also looking to break into the flight-booking market in an effort to take on giants such as Priceline and Expedia.[41]

Looking further afield, fellow Silicon Valley giants Facebook and Google are steadily disrupting the travel industry in some unconventional ways. In the case of Facebook, the social media giant's City Guides tool is proving to be a significant disruptor of the travel guide market and even the dominance of TripAdvisor. City Guides allows Facebook users to see any of the friends in their network who have visited a destination and discover where they went and what they liked, such as hotels, restaurants and attractions.[42]

In the case of Google, it is the company's Google Flights that is causing the biggest waves. With Google Flights, users can get access to powerful information ranging from price alerts to intelligent route suggestions.[43]

Beyond the technology disruptors, working with the executive team of a large hotel chain recently gave me an insight into how many unconventional competitive threats exist even outside the tech world. For instance, the head of events told me about the challenge posed by the many serviced office towers that were being built at a rapid pace within a few blocks of her CBD hotel. 'All the office towers have their own on-site catering facilities and meeting spaces,' she said. 'We're losing a lot of conference bookings to them and it's increasingly hard to compete.'

BANKING AND FINANCE

'Silicon Valley is coming.' This ominous warning to shareholders from JPMorgan Chase CEO Jamie Dimon gives some indication of how seriously banks are beginning to take the threat of unconventional competition. 'There are hundreds of start-ups with a lot of brains and money working on various alternatives to traditional banking,' he continued.[44]

My colleague and banking trends expert Brett King agrees. King suggests that the banking industry will experience more disruption in the next 10 years than in the previous 300 years—and much of it from unconventional sources. 'This will hurt,' he says.[45]

The sources of unconventional competition in the financial services technology—or 'fintech'—sector abound. Just to name a few: Square (merchant payments); Nutmeg (wealth management); Symphony (online peer-to-peer lending) and TransferWise (international payments).

Reflecting on the pace and scale of unconventional fintech competition, former head of Barclays Bank Antony Jenkins predicts that employment in financial services and in branches could drop by as much as 50 per cent before 2025. Jenkins also points to research from McKinsey suggesting that profits from credit cards, car loans and lending for retail may be wiped out by two-thirds over the same time period.[46]

While banks are rapidly gearing up and developing technology to counter the Silicon Valley threat (a third of Goldman Sachs' employees are now engineers), Jenkins questions whether huge banking institutions will be courageous enough to move at the pace required to get ahead of the curve.[47]

While there is little doubt that banking services will become increasingly important in the future, banks in the traditional sense may not be. As former Wells Fargo CEO Richard Kovacevich admits: 'Banking is essential, banks are not'.[48]

When money no longer exists

Although banks and financial institutions themselves are facing a swarm of unconventional competition, the bigger story in financial services is a significant change to the very notion of currency.

Currency has historically been tied to national sovereignty, with notes and coins bearing the face or insignia of the sovereign. They were also intrinsically linked to the physical world—consider how the very names of currencies such as the peso, shekel and British pound are all derived from terms relating to weight.[49]

However, the emergence of virtual currencies and the blockchain technology that underpins them represents the most significant change to financial services in decades and possibly centuries.

Known as 'distributed ledger technology', a blockchain is essentially a secure protocol

> The emergence of virtual currencies represents the most significant change to financial services in decades and possibly centuries.

where a network of computers collectively verify a transaction before it can be recorded and approved. The most common and well-known virtual 'cryptocurrency' using blockchain is Bitcoin, although at the time of writing there are more than 900 virtual currencies being traded.[50]

In reality, blockchain could be a great opportunity for banks and financial institutions to improve customer service and efficiency. As evidence of this, in September 2016 Barclays carried out the world's first trade transaction using blockchain — cutting down the time it took to process the transaction from seven to 10 days to roughly four hours.[51]

However, it could well be that blockchain becomes a significant disruption by threatening the very revenue banks and financial institutions earn from facilitating transactions. Bypassing intermediaries in the financial system was, after all, the clear goal of Bitcoin's creator, Satoshi Nakamoto.[52] It is predicted that blockchain will reduce settlement and transaction costs by up to $20 billion (revenue that is currently being gobbled up by traditional banking institutions).[53]

Mobile phones and a cashless world

The move towards a cashless world represents another significant disruption to the financial sector — especially as a number of non-traditional providers such as telcos enter the industry.

We are seeing the clearest indication of how profound this change can be in poorer parts of the world, where traditional banking services are scarce.

Take for instance fintech startup Abra, which is quickly gaining popularity in places where people live too far from bank branches or don't have the documentation required to open accounts. While they may not have bank accounts, these consumers all have smartphones and Abra allows them to deposit income, withdraw funds and send money using only an app on their phone.[54]

Abra is tapping into a trend identified by the Bill and Melinda Gates Foundation in their 2014 annual review. According to this report, it is predicted that two billion people in unbanked and under-banked communities will be storing money and making payments using mobile devices by 2030.[55]

Perhaps the most famous and wide-reaching example of non-bank banking services being conducted via smartphones is M-Pesa. Like Abra, M-Pesa allows users to send and receive money through their smartphone without a traditional bank account.

Launched in Kenya and Tanzania by a telco named Safaricom in 2007, M-Pesa has quickly grown in popularity around Africa, Asia and Eastern Europe. Within five years of its launch, M-Pesa boasted 19 million accounts in Kenya (equivalent to nearly two-thirds of the country's adult population) and 25 per cent of Kenya's GNP flows through the network at the time of writing.[56]

Technology giants such as Facebook, PayPal, Snapchat, Google, WeChat and Alibaba are also getting into the game.

In the case of Google, while Google Wallet has been integrated into Gmail since 2013, its extension to the mobile app in 2017 marked a significant step forward. Now Gmail users can send or request money with just a tap. It's a similar story with Snapchat's Snapcash and Facebook's Messenger app cash transfer function.[57] All of these apps cut out banks from transactions that would typically take place through them.

Unlike with M-Pesa, each of these technology-driven currency transfer solutions still require users to have a stored bank account or credit card—but for how much longer, who knows?

Macquarie's banking analysts say up to $27 billion is under threat from so-called digital disruptors in the banks' key payments businesses. Longer term, however, the same analysts suggest it is the business of lending money that will face the stiffest competition from unconventional sources in the coming years.[58]

The changing landscape of lending

The current wave of peer-to-peer lending providers such as Lending Club and Prosper are just the first glimpses of what will become a $150 billion business by 2025, according to PricewaterhouseCoopers.[59]

Recent moves by Square give some indication of how this unconventional and non-bank lending market will evolve. Square moved well beyond their traditional focus on facilitating transactions with the June 2017 launch of Square Capital.

With Square Capital, merchants using the Square system can apply for an instant loan of up to $10 000 with the click of a button — and then pay it back at a low interest rate as a percentage of the transactions being put through their merchant account.[60]

This move makes sense for Square. Not only does it diversify their business away from a heavy reliance on narrow-margin transactions, but it also leverages one of Square's unique assets: their deep, data-driven knowledge of a merchant customer's day-to-day operations. This significantly reduces the risk of extending finance. Square's founder hinted in June 2017 that the next step would be to broaden Square Capital's reach to consumers as well.[61]

In the words of one industry insider, 'Square is creeping further from Silicon Valley and closer to Wall Street'.[62] In September 2017 it was revealed that the company is seeking to establish a fully fledged bank called Square Financial Services. In doing this, they join a raft of other recent unconventional entrants to the banking sector, including Social Finance and Varo Money.[63] As barriers to entry are lowered and technology levels the playing field, unconventional competition will continue to affect the financial services sector — and it's only going to increase in the coming years.

RESPONDING TO UNCONVENTIONAL COMPETITION

Having looked at the various ways that unconventional competition will change the game for businesses and industries in the coming years, the key question then is how to respond to it.

The general manager of a big hotel recently shared how he'd had to ask himself this very question a few years ago. Increasing numbers of hotel guests had begun using smartphone apps to order food from outside the hotel. Mindful of the impact on hotel revenue from lost room service orders (plus the 'look' of pizza delivery guys trudging through the lobby), initially the hotel tried to ban food delivery people from entering the premises.

Ignoring, dismissing or discounting unconventional competitors is never the answer.

As you can imagine, this got complicated. Food delivery people aren't always easy to identify, so stopping them is tough. Some guests even tried to circumvent the rule by meeting delivery workers in the back alley outside the hotel.

Eventually the hotel realised their ban was untenable and they began allowing food delivery to guests.

This example, and a myriad others, leaves me with little doubt that ignoring, dismissing or discounting unconventional competitors is never the answer.

In the same way, fighting unconventional competitors or trying to leverage your power and size to lobby regulators to protect the status quo will only work for so long. It's like trying to hold back the tide; the pressure will grow to a point where you can contain it no longer. Added to this, nimble and creative startups have a knack for getting around the tools of established power—just see what Uber and Airbnb have done over recent years to circumvent various regulators' attempts to block them.[64]

∞

Despite the disruptive threat posed by unconventional competition, it's important to maintain a degree of perspective and discernment. After all, not every unconventional competitor is a disruption—some are little more than a distraction. However, the key is to remain alert. Businesses and leaders must be constantly scanning the horizon while also looking over their shoulder. And when unconventional competition emerges from the periphery, keep a close eye on it. Engage with, learn from and be sharpened by it.

> **Not every unconventional competitor is a disruption — some are little more than a distraction.**

In the case of the hotel general manager who had initially resisted food deliveries, he eventually realised the best response was to begin packaging their room-service food to look like the meals people were ordering on their smartphones. So rather than serving pizzas on white china plates with silver lids, they began delivering pizzas to in-house guests in high-quality rustic pizza boxes—and it worked.

Even better than mimicking the tactics of unconventional competitors, it pays well to tackle them head-on. This is precisely the approach of

AccorHotels' global CEO Sebastien Bazin, who is spearheading a major push by the hotel brand into the private rental accommodation market by investing in platforms such as Travel Keys, Onefinestay and digital concierge business John Paul:

> *I am trying to adapt. I am saying what [Airbnb] do is nice and it's growing, so why not tap into their territory.*

In a revealing insight into the mentality that is driving Bazin's approach at Accor, he says:

> *Twenty-four hours a day I have my eyes open and I am listening ... to find ... what can we do to create top line growth.*[65]

It is this posture of openness and alertness that is most important for any organisation or leader today. While it is tempting to dismiss the threat posed by unconventional competitors, you do so at your own peril.

Questions for reflection

∞ What long-held assumptions about the competitive landscape could leave you vulnerable to unconventional threats in the coming years?

∞ Who are some of the emerging unconventional competitors that may prove to be game changers for you or your organisation/industry?

∞ Considering the challenges posed by alternate forms of energy production, new car technology, digital media providers and a cashless society, how could some of these unconventional threats affect you?

∞ How have you responded to unconventional competition in the past—have you fallen into the trap of dismissing, denying, ridiculing or ignoring it? What can you learn from this experience?

∞ How can you foster the sense of alertness necessary to identify unconventional threats when they emerge?

CHAPTER 4

EMERGING
GENERATIONS

Your laundry habits reveal more about your generation than you realise!

While the generation gap is often described in terms of our tastes in music, our social attitudes, or our openness to technology, apparently whether or not you use fabric softener is a powerful indication of the era you were raised in.

This has certainly been the lesson Procter & Gamble (P&G) have learned the hard way in recent times.

The consumer-products giant, which enjoys 50 per cent of the $1.3 billion US market for liquid fabric softener, has come to the realisation that no-one born after 1980 uses the product. Shailesh Jejurikar, P&G's head of global fabric care, admitted recently that most Millennials don't even know what the product is for.

Part of the reason is that they've grown up in an era where it hasn't been necessary. In the 1960s, when fabric softener was popularised, it solved the common problem of clothes emerging from washing machines scratchy and rough. However, washing machines and clothing fabrics have evolved to the point where this is no longer the issue it once was.

In addition, younger and more eco-conscious consumers are more actively trying to limit the number of chemicals they use in their homes and some popular athletic gear even comes with instructions to avoid using softener because it will damage the fabric.

As a result, sales in the US liquid softener industry fell 15 per cent between 2007 and 2015 while sales of P&G's market-leading Downy brand slumped 26 per cent, according to Euromonitor.

For laundry giants such as P&G, engaging the younger generation is vital because consumers form their laundry habits in the first few years after they move out of home. This is the window of time when companies have the ability to influence purchasing decisions and consumption habits customers will often keep for life. As a result, P&G have recently re-badged Downy as a 'fabric conditioner' in the hope consumers will draw the parallel with the conditioner they use each time they wash their hair. They've also added 'scent boosters' which promise to help your clothes smell clean for longer. Early indications are that the strategy is working, with US softener sales jumping 5 per cent in 2016.[1]

P&G, along with beauty giants Estée Lauder and Coty, are facing generational disruption on another front — the anti-ageing business.

Recent years have shown that Millennials are less willing to invest in expensive skin creams than older generations were in their twenties and thirties. Rather than purchasing products that offer hope in a jar and long-term results, younger consumers are opting for makeup or masks that offer more immediate outcomes.

As an indication of how significantly this trend is already re-shaping the beauty business's bottom line, sales of skin-care brands Estée Lauder and Clinique fell 2.5 per cent in the first quarter of 2016, while makeup sales rose 7.3 per cent, driven by growth in MAC, Smashbox and Tom Ford.

It is a similar story over at P&G, with the company's iconic Olay skin-care brand sagging despite a concerted effort to revitalise it.[2]

WHICH DEMOGRAPHICS NOW DOMINATE

While industries and brands have always needed to stay relevant to the next generation of consumers, it will matter even more in the coming years. Younger generations can either represent a breathtakingly large opportunity — or one of the most significant disruptions any brand or industry is likely to face.

Generational changes and their impact on businesses and organisations have fascinated me for a number of years now. In fact, this topic is where my trends research began back in 2004. Over the course of three years, I travelled the globe interviewing and speaking with more than 80 000 young people in order to get an idea of what was driving and defining the next generation (Millennials and younger). My first book, *The 'New' Rules of Engagement*, was essentially an exploration of the key findings of this research.

While changes in generational attitudes and behaviours are already having a significant impact on organisations and brands (as evidenced in their shift away from fabric softener and face creams), we haven't seen anything yet. As we look to the next 10 to 15 years, engaging the next generation is going to be vital if you hope to thrive and maintain relvance.

In this chapter I am going to explore what is making Millennials tick, what they'll be looking for in the coming years, and how they are going to disrupt a range of industry sectors. The reason we're going to focus on Millennials (roughly, those born in the 1980s and 1990s) rather than Gen X (born in the mid 1960s to late 1970s) or their younger cousins, Gen Z (born 2000s to mid 2010s), is because the size and impact

The Millennial cohort are the largest generation in history.

of the Millennials is hard to ignore. Added to this, they are going to be entering their peak consumption years in the coming decade.

According to celebrated economist Harry S. Dent, an individual's peak spending years are between the ages of 46 and 50. So, if you consider that the vast bulk of the enormous Baby Boom generation passed through this window between the mid 1990s and mid 2000s, it is no surprise that our economy prospered during those years.[3] The Millennials will begin entering this same peak spending phase in the mid 2020s.

When you consider the demographic size of the Millennial cohort, it's easy to see why they are such a game-changing group. They are the largest generation in history, making up one in three persons on the globe — 86 per cent of whom live in emerging markets.[4]

Drilling down to specific geographic regions, the numbers are no less staggering:

∞ In North America, they are 79 million strong—which makes Millennials marginally larger than even the Baby Boomers.[5]

∞ In the Asia–Pacific region, Millennials makes up more than 30 per cent of the population—in China alone there are 200 million people between the ages of 22 and 34. In India, more than half of the country's population is under the age of 35.[6]

∞ In parts of the Middle East and North Africa, the influence of the youth demographic is even more pronounced, with 65 per cent of the region's population under the age of 30.[7]

According to recent consumer research, by 2020 Millennials will wield an extraordinary $1.4 trillion spending power in the United States alone,[8] and account for 30 per cent of retail sales.[9]

So with Millennials representing such a huge opportunity, what makes them tick and how can brands and organisations engage rather than estrange this emerging generation?

THE MILLENNIAL MINDSET

Here are some high-level insights that begin to paint a picture of the key mindsets and expectations of Millennial consumers. As a cohort, they tend to be:

∞ *digitally tethered.* On average, Millennials own 7.7 connected devices and use 3.3 each day.[10]

∞ *online-obsessed.* The 18-to-34 age group make 54 per cent of their purchases online.[11] When asked about how they will make their next online purchase, 32 per cent of Millennials said they planned to do it on a laptop or desktop computer, 25 per cent said a smartphone and 24 per cent said a tablet. Only 11 per cent would shop in a physical retail store.[12]

∞ *experience-driven.* Seventy-eight per cent of Millennials would rather choose to spend money on a desirable experience than a physical item.

∞ *socially minded*. Ninety-two per cent of Millennials believe that business success should be measured by more than just profit.[13]

∞ *passionate about openness*. Millennials say it's okay to publicly share about mental illness (70 per cent), coming out (70 per cent), going to rehab (55 per cent) and having a miscarriage (50 per cent).[14]

∞ *post-modern*. Having grown up in an era where truth is relative and open to personal interpretation, 32 per cent of Millennials believe there is no such thing as 'the truth'.[15]

∞ *attention-seeking*. Seventy per cent of Millennials admit to choosing activities, products and experiences that will give them something to post about on social media.[16]

∞ *empowered*. Sixty-one per cent of Millennials honestly believe they can change the world or at least have an influence on it.[17]

∞ *selectively loyal*. Seventy per cent of Millennials say they come back to brands they connect with, relate to and love.[18]

∞ *peer-influenced*. Forty-eight per cent of Millennials report that social media and word-of-mouth referrals from peers influenced their product purchases far more than traditional advertising.[19]

Despite the possibilities and opportunities that Millennials represent, many brands and organisations are ill-equipped to ride the demographic wave that is building on the horizon. This young cohort is buying different things, in different ways and for different reasons than older generations. Attracting, engaging and communicating with them is a different game.

Millennials buy different things, in different ways for different reasons than older generations.

For instance, consider the challenge of communicating with various generations. Recent research indicates that the channel you use to get a message through can make all the difference. While 63 per cent of Baby Boomers prefer companies to contact them by phone, only 12.3 per cent of Millennials report the same. On the other hand, 48 per cent of Millennials want companies to connect with them using social media or online chat tools—compared with only 32 per cent of Gen Xers and 9 per cent of Baby Boomers.[20]

To continue the approach used in previous chapters, in the coming pages we're going to explore how generational disruption is going to play out in the following industries:

∞ retail

∞ automotive

∞ banking and finance

∞ travel

∞ sport.

RETAIL

When Michael Ford of Australian appliance chain The Good Guys suggested that retailers needed to brace for a Millennial 'tsunami', he wasn't mincing words. As Ford argues, 'Retail has been a pretty sleepy old industry for the last 150 years,'[21] and now is the time to embrace new technology or get left behind.

Ford is spot on. In the Amazon age where the online retail experience is seamless, personalised and cheap, brick-and-mortar stores have their work cut out for them in showing relevance to the next generation.

But it's not just Amazon that have transformed the expectations of Millennials when it comes to retailing. Online-first brands such as Warby Parker (glasses), Casper (mattresses) and Joybird (furniture) have built enormously successful retail businesses by targeting Millennials with strong return policies, authentic reviews and social media validation that can alleviate a shopper's buying concerns at the checkout screen.[22]

If retailers are going to engage the next generation of consumers, competing on price or range is not going to be enough.

None of this is to say that traditional retailing is going to disappear anytime soon. Rather, if retailers are going to engage the next generation of consumers, competing on price or range is not going to be enough. The in-store experience needs to be just that—an experience. Stores need to recapture the multi-sensory, rich and enjoyable experience of shopping. This is going to mean adopting new store formats and shifting the retail culture to being radically customer-centric.

American retail giant Target is beginning to wake up to this reality, having recently experienced a significant decline in sales and a corresponding 13 per cent drop in their share price. Recognising that younger shoppers are increasingly buying their essentials online, Target are in the process of abandoning their traditional big-box store format and opting instead for smaller stores that occupy the same locations and vibe of neighbourhood grocery stores. COO John Mulligan admitted that they are 'rethinking everything' in order to attract Millennials. This even includes transforming the purpose of their stores to become pickup locations for the very items that Millennials are ordering online. If you can't beat 'em, join 'em I guess.[23]

Beyond new store formats, personalisation is also vital for Millennial shoppers. Accenture recently conducted an online survey of young consumers across eight countries in an effort to understand what motivates this cohort.[24]

The main conclusion was this: Millennials demand a shopping experience that is personalised and customised to their wants and needs. As one survey responder put it, 'There is [something] about the product and its cost, but there's also a big part about being treated like a valued customer'.

In other words, while price comparability and product quality matter, what Millennials want more than anything else is a sense that they are known and valued by a store. However, this level of personalisation doesn't just begin when they walk into the store. Ninety-five per cent of Millennials in Accenture's study said they wanted brands to actively court them, and the most persuasive tactic is by offering targeted coupons.

While this degree of personalisation can be time-consuming and costly, the payoff if you get it right with Millennials will be huge. Remember that by 2020 they'll be spending one in three retail dollars spent. The question is who they will be spending those dollars with. The answer is up to retailers and how they prepare for this approaching tsunami.

AUTOMOTIVE

While automakers are scrambling to prepare for the mid 2030s, when self-driving cars could make vehicle ownership a thing of the past, in the meantime it is demographic disruption that is causing automakers no end of anxiety.

Put simply, younger generations are buying fewer cars and are choosing not to get driver's licences in record numbers. According to research conducted by the University of Michigan, the percentage of 20- to 24-year-olds with driver's licences dropped to 81 per cent in 2010—down from 92 per cent for the same age group in 1983.[25] This is far from a US-only trend. In the words of a 2014 Public Research Interest Group study, 'All over the developed world, Millennials are turning their back on the car'.[26]

There are a myriad reasons for this decline. High fuel prices; the economic downturn of 2007–08 that forced young people onto public transport; young people choosing to live in inner-city suburbs; the rise of car-sharing services such as Zipcar; and ride-sharing services such as Uber, to name a few contributing factors. Even technology has a role to play—recent Australian research found that Millennials were deriving independence and social connection from online interactions, rather than through owning a car as previous generations did when coming of age.[27]

Automakers have certainly tried to lure young car buyers back, with limited success. Toyota created the Scion brand for Millennials, Ford released the Fiesta and GM partnered with Disney and MTV to help train dealers with tactics for attracting young buyers.[28]

Iconic motorcycle brand Harley-Davidson are also grappling with demographic disruption. Having lost 4 per cent of motorcycle market share in the space of two years, Harley-Davidson is desperately keen to reach out to new, non-traditional buyers—especially Millennials.

The challenge for Harley-Davidson is that its brand is so closely tied to ageing Baby Boomer men. It's an old-school, masculine brand that has worked for years, but it isn't appealing to younger buyers the way it did their fathers.

One Tennessee-based Harley-Davidson dealer, Scott Maddux, has taken steps to address this generational disconnect. Maddux has begun organising concerts in his store featuring younger country stars. He also donates bikes and parts to local high schools so students can learn by customising them. 'It's all about exposing young people to our brand,' he says.[29]

In addition, Maddux has looked to hire more young staff members, upon the realisation that in the past his employees looked a bit like 'Santa Claus in leathers'.

While this doesn't mean that young staff are necessarily the key to attracting young customers, it gives an indication of the need to overhaul everything about a brand if you are going to stay relevant to the next generation. What has worked in the past may not work in the future — in fact, it is unlikely to.

BANKING AND FINANCE

Of all the demographic cohorts banks are struggling to engage, Millennials would have to be at the top of the list.

A recent widescale survey revealed that 71 per cent of Millennials would rather visit the dentist than their local bank branch. Even more tellingly, 73 per cent said they would rather handle their financial services needs through Google, Amazon, Apple, PayPal or Square than a traditional bank. To add insult to injury, American respondents to the survey voted all four leading US banks among their least-loved brands.[30] Ouch.

There are a number of reasons for Millennials' active dislike of traditional banks. The bureaucratic approach, the recent litany of scandals revealing banks' unscrupulous practices and banks' often woefully inadequate mobile technology are chief among their complaints.

This last factor is significant when you consider 72 per cent of Millennials prefer to do banking primarily on mobile devices—compared with 50 per cent for Generation Xers and just 19 per cent for Baby Boomers. If the mobile experience is clunky, Millennials will be heading straight for the door.[31]

Another important factor in Millennials' disaffection with traditional banks is the perceived lack of anything remarkable or impressive on offer. Well over half of Millennials don't believe their bank offers anything unique—a dire situation that we look at strategies for addressing in chapter 10.

All of this adds up to a significant customer retention challenge for banks looking to engage young consumers. A recent study showed almost one in five Millennials had switched their primary banking provider within the previous 12 months (compared with 10 per cent of Gen Xers and just 3 per cent of Baby Boomers).[32] In truth, you could dismiss this as a function of the fact that people become more entrenched as they get older and their financial affairs become more complicated. But even so, Millennials are on the hunt for value, trust and a great customer experience from banks and they'll readily switch if they perceive these things are on offer elsewhere. This can either be a massive threat or a terrific positive.

One of the key areas of opportunity with younger consumers is in the sheer number who haven't yet built up a significant credit history and therefore can find gaining approvals difficult. Add to this the growing number of young people whose incomes don't fit traditional moulds (many of them are freelancers or earn their income from the sharing economy as Uber drivers, and so on.). Banks that can develop business models to engage this enormous group of non-traditional young customers (15 million in the United States alone) while appropriately managing risk will stand to win big in the years to come.[33]

Some emerging banking and finance players have recognised the opportunity that high-tech Millennials pose and have crafted their business models specifically to engage this group.

Examples such as commission-free share trading platform Robinhood and robo advisers Wealthfront and Betterment have all made an active play for the Millennial consumer. The online money management platform LearnVest has set out with the express goal of making managing your finances as easy as streaming music or ordering a product on Amazon—activities that have set the base expectation of seamless service for Millennials.

Traditional banks and financial institutions would do well to learn quickly from the example of fintech startups such as the ones mentioned. After all, a recent international study by Australian telecommunications giant Telstra found that 67 per cent of Millennials prefer to receive advice on financial products and services via a digital platform—without a printed product disclosure statement in sight. The two key reasons for this preference for digital advice? A desire for faster response times and the perception of greater independence. Tellingly, more than 50 per cent of high-net-worth Millennials saw digital financial advice as more independent than that given by human financial advisers—a scathing reflection of the perceived trustworthiness of financial advisers and the institutions they represent.[34]

TRAVEL

In the travel and tourism sector, Millennials are shaking things up in equally fundamental ways.

With younger generations having driven many of the key travel disruptors, such as Airbnb, over the past decade, their influence is likely to continue in the coming decade.

It's important to remember that many travellers born after 1990 have never used a traditional travel agent. With TripAdvisor and a myriad online platforms such as Expedia and Orbitz at Millennials' disposal, travel agents have their work cut out for them to communicate their value proposition to the next generation.

Many travellers born after 1990 have never used a traditional travel agent.

Mind you, the travel planning process for Millennials is changing in ways that are far more fundamental than just the platform they use to do the booking. On average, Millennials will check more than 10 sources before booking travel. In addition to review sites such as TripAdvisor or Yelp, social media is playing an increasingly important role and new technologies such as Google Lens will transform in-the-moment travel decisions about tours, restaurants and even accommodation.

Although the travel industry has always prided itself on being high-touch and service-driven, early indications are that Millennials may prefer *less* human interaction than previous generations. Hotel brands such as Aloft and Yotel are pioneering a quality automated check-in experience using self-service kiosks. For Millennials, this low-touch and high-convenience solution doesn't equate to a low service level. In fact, 36 per cent of Millennials prefer human-free automated kiosk check-ins compared to 19 per cent of the older generations.[35]

As business travellers, Millennials are quickly changing the game too. Whereas hotel rooms were traditionally designed with desks for older-generation travellers who typically catch up on work in their rooms, Millennials want to work in so-called 'third spaces', such as lobbies and restaurants. Recent research found that almost 40 per cent of Millennials prefer to work in the lobby area of a hotel (compared to 17 per cent of older generations). Chains such as Marriott's Courtyard have specifically designed their lobbies with this in mind, featuring pod seating to encourage group work in a relaxed but professional environment.[36]

SPORT

The sporting arena is also coming to terms with the shifting preferences of Millennials in some significant ways.

Consider golf. Between 2009 and 2013, golfing participation rates among people aged 18 to 34 fell roughly 13 per cent, while participation rates for this demographic in other active sports, such as running, rose 29 per cent. Reflecting on why this might be the case, Matt Powell of SportsOneSource points to the fact that 'Golf is slow, takes a long time to play and is expensive. As a sport it doesn't reflect the kind of values Millennials like such as diversity and inclusion'.[37]

This dropoff is beginning to take a toll. In July 2014, 46-year-old Florida chain Edwin Watts Golf Shops filed for bankruptcy, blaming a decline in the sport's popularity. Just days later, international chain Dick's Sporting Goods laid off more than 400 golf professionals as it reduced store space for golf in favour of women's and youth apparel. The bigbox retailer is also rethinking its specialty retailer Golf Galaxy, which was acquired in 2007 for $226 million.[38]

Golf, like many other tradition-bound games, will likely be forced to adapt the cultural expectations and format of the game to engage the next generation.

Other sports have had significant success in doing just this over recent years. Cricket's gradual move away from five-day test matches to the higher-octane and faster-paced Twenty20 and Big Bash formats has proven a huge winner. While traditionalists decried the flashier, louder and more sensational formats, they have proven to be a winner with live crowds and broadcast audiences alike.

In the tennis world, new formats are also being experimented with in order to capture and keep the attention of fickle younger generations. The Australian Open's 2017 inclusion of the Fast4 series showed enormous promise and will likely see tennis transformed in much the same way cricket has in recent years.

ENGAGING MILLENNIAL CONSUMERS

There are many good books dedicated to helping brands and businesses effectively engage Millennials as a consumer cohort, and it's not my intention to focus on the theme in detail here.

However, it's important to note that Millennials have grown up in the age of advertising and are highly attuned to the tips and techniques that marketers use. So you can't necessarily use the same playbook that worked with older generations.

> **Make your marketing messages short, sharp and highly shareable.**

In a brilliant article on Inc.com, journalist and digital consultant John Boitnott offers five of the common mistakes and pitfalls that can cause Millennial marketing efforts to backfire spectacularly:

1. *It looks like an ad.* Boitnott suggests that the less a content marketing piece looks like an ad, the better. Focus on being interesting, arresting, high-value and even controversial but be mindful of having big logos and blatant calls to action front and centre. Millennials will switch off quickly if this is the case.

2. *It's unoriginal.* Millennials tend to be fun-loving, irreverent and even a bit quirky—make your marketing the same if you want to connect with them. The more unique, compelling and entertaining, the better.

3. *It's boring.* This is especially the case if you are marketing using digital media. Instagram, Vine and Snapchat have conditioned Millennials to become accustomed to media-rich soundbites and if your marketing video is too long, visually bland or static, for instance, you'll lose their attention or not gain it in the first place. Make your marketing messages short, sharp and highly shareable.

4. *It's irrelevant.* Millennials have become used to personalised and bespoke communication. The more you can segment and target your marketing to this group, the more effective it will be.

5. *It's deceptive.* Millennials are sceptical about the claims of marketers. If it appears to be too good to be true or too convenient to reflect reality (any '99.9 per cent' claims, for instance), they'll dismiss your messages outright. Be upfront, honest and even self-deprecating. Carlsberg's 'Probably The Best Beer In The World' campaign was a good example of a brand not pretending to be anything more than it was. Statistics or more concrete claims about their pre-eminence would never have worked as well as their tongue-in-cheek suggestion.[39]

MARKET THROUGH THEM, NOT TO THEM

Having helped countless brands craft marketing strategies to engage Millennials, the most important principle I can offer you here is this: market *through* Millennials, not *to* them.

Use the established networks of trust that Millennials rely upon to get your messages out to the market. Social media is an absolute gift for marketers if you use it well. To this point, 34 per cent of Millennials report using social media as their primary source of information when making a purchase.[40]

From a brand awareness perspective, social media is equally powerful. The jackpot is when your marketing messages become so entertaining, shocking or random that Millennials begin sharing them to the point of virality.

While viral marketing is the holy grail, the good news is that social media can be tremendously powerful even if you don't make the big time.

I remember doing some work in the hospitality sector and speaking to a bar owner who had used social media very strategically to attract the attention of young patrons. Having taken over a run-down establishment that had almost zero brand recognition, the new owner hired staff to wander around the bar on a busy Friday night encouraging people to 'like' the bar's Facebook page — even offering free drinks to do so.

These staff would then take photos of the patrons who had liked the page—tagging them in the images.

Within weeks, the strategy began to work magnificently. One day the owner was looking at his Facebook page's administrator panel and did some numbers. He realised that one photo of two tagged patrons would be typically liked by 24 of their friends. Because of the network multiplier effect, within two hours this photo and the bar's branding would be seen in the newsfeed of more than 3700 people who were in the related networks of those liking the image. It's hard to put a value on the impact of this, and the only cost had been a few drinks to entice patrons to like the page.

MILLENNIALS AS A DISRUPTIVE WORKFORCE

Before we finish this look at the disruptive impact of emerging generations, it would be remiss of me to not address the effect that Millennials are having in the workplace as well as the marketplace. Engaging the next generation is in fact a key strategy for actioning many of the strategies we explore in part II.

Beyond their innate technology skills, this young generation offer a range of characteristics that are indispensable in an age of disruption. They are innovative, entrepreneurial and adaptable by nature. On top of all this, they are entering businesses and industries with fresh eyes, a different worldview and a bold confidence to challenge the status quo.

All the benefits aside, Millennial employees will be impossible to ignore in the years to come from a sheer numbers perspective. By 2025 they are set to make up more than half of the working population in Australia and 75 per cent of the labour force in the United States.[41] If you are not engaging the talented, innovative and entrepreneurial members of this massive cohort, your competition likely will.

Millennials in the workplace

Deloitte have conducted arguably the most detailed research examining how disruptive the attitudes and expectations of a Millennial workforce will be in the coming years. Having surveyed 7800 Millennials from 29 countries, they found that the paradigm of this young group of employees could best be described as:

∞ *purpose-driven.* Seventy-seven per cent of this group report their company's purpose was part of the reason they chose to work there.[42]

∞ *transient.* During any given year, one in four Millennials will leave their current employer and role to join a new organisation or do something different. That figure increases to 44 per cent when the time frame is extended to two years.[43] When you consider that it costs an average of $24 000 to replace each Millennial employee who churns through an organisation, it's clear that there is a financial imperative to engaging and retaining this group.[44]

∞ *ambitious.* Sixty-three per cent of Millennials surveyed say their 'leadership skills are not being fully developed'. In some markets, such as Brazil and the South-east Asian nations of Malaysia, Singapore and Thailand, the figure exceeds 70 per cent.[45]

∞ *socially minded.* Eighty-seven per cent of Millennials believe that the success of a business should be measured in terms of more than just its financial performance and well over half of them would choose not to work for an organisation whose values don't match their own.[46]

∞ *flexibility-focused.* Eighty-eight per cent of Millennials expressed a strong desire to have some control over start and finish times and 75 per cent would like to have greater scope to work from home or other locations where they feel most productive. In contrast, only 43 per cent of organisations allow the sort of work-location flexibility Millennials are looking for. Reflecting on how a lack of trust tends to drive a lack of employee empowerment, Adam Henderson of consultancy firm Millennial Mindset asks, 'If you can't trust your employees to work flexibly, why hire them in the first place?' It's a great question.[47]

As I reflect on my interactions with businesses and leaders across a range of industries, there's often a clear mismatch between the employee values of Millennials and the culture of many organisations.

In the accounting profession, for instance, the traditional culture and systems of larger firms is turning off Millennials en masse. Michael

Macolino, co-founder of accounting technology firm Accodex, points to the fact that many young accountants in large firms feel trapped in number-crunching mode working within a 'this is how we've always done it' culture and bound by outdated technology.[48] To this last point, my colleague Chris Riddell shared with me that he'd recently heard one Millennial worker jokingly describe work as 'the period during the day where I have to use old technology'.

Peter Docherty of CPA Australia agrees with Macolino's assessment. CPA Australia's data shows the average age of accountants leaving large firms to go out on their own has dropped from mid forties back in 2000 to early to mid thirties in 2017. Some of this is a function of the entrepreneurial spirit of Millennials, while much more of it has to do with the fact that this young group is rejecting the status quo in large, bureaucratic firms.

> There's often a clear mismatch between the employee values of Millennials and the culture of many organisations.

According to Docherty,

A lot of [Millennials] have heard horror stories or had horror stories about expectations of working hours. They are looking at the potential to be pigeon-holed into one area of specialisation and want to provide more broad-based advisory services to clients.

He goes on to argue that Millennial accounting graduates want a lot more out of their career now, demanding more client engagement and more control over their destiny.[49]

It's a similar story in the financial services sector. For years, investment houses and big banks worked on the formula that young workers had to grind out years of marathon workweeks and menial tasks in order to earn the right to climb the ranks and enjoy the perks of leadership. However, Millennials are simply not willing to play this game the way previous generations were.

According to analysis conducted by LinkedIn for *The Wall Street Journal*, young associates in 2015 were leaving positions at a dozen investment banks after an average of 17 months—compared with an average tenure of 30 months back in 1995.[50]

Co-head of Goldman Sachs' investment banking division John Waldron says Goldman and fellow banks JPMorgan Chase and Citigroup are waking up to this reality and looking to change: 'We're focused on trying to understand what's important to the folks we hire right out of school'. Among other things, the banks are looking to revamp their rules, add sweeteners for young employees and tweak their traditional delayed-gratification model to better suit the expectations of the Millennial generation.[51]

∞

While the trends and changes in emerging generations we have discussed in these pages can be confronting, there is some good news. Unlike the previous three forms of disruption we have examined, generational disruption is perhaps the most linear and incremental. Although the fickle tastes and preferences of Millennials can change quickly, the all-pervasive impact of this group is one that can be anticipated and prepared for with greater accuracy than, say, the impact of AI or unconventional competition.

As Peter Drucker observed, one of the great things about demographic shifts is that, while they can be difficult to predict, they do have long lead times.[52]

Questions for reflection

∞ How have you seen generational attitudes and expectations change in your context over recent years?

∞ Considering the demographic and economic clout of Millennials, how important will this group be to your organisation or industry in the coming decades?

∞ Which elements of the mindset of Millennial consumers represent an exciting opportunity for you — and which represent a threat?

∞ How can you more effectively engage Millennials by marketing through them, not to them?

∞ If Millennials will soon make up a sizeable portion of the workforce, what are the implications of this and how can you better engage this young cohort?

9 KEYS TO THRIVING IN AN AGE OF DISRUPTION

Having spent part I identifying the key disruptions you are likely to face in the coming years, we're now going to change tack.

Despite the turbulent times and uncharted waters we are all heading into, there are solid and proven principles that can act as your lodestar. While the pace of disruption is greater than ever, the reality is that scores of businesses and industries have successfully navigated periods of immense change and upheaval over the years and their experience can offer us insights and inspiration.

Consider the list of brands and organisations that have prevailed despite enormous disruption. From Coca-Cola to Corning, Dupont to Disney, Bosch to BASF and Chanel to Cadbury, the very principles that have seen these brands thrive in the face of turbulence are timeless and we can learn much from them.

One of my mentors years ago was fond of saying that failure leaves clues — and he was right. There is a lot we can learn from the mistakes and missteps of others who've gone before us. However, I have come to learn that success leaves a lot of clues too.

Part II is dedicated to identifying these clues.

CHAPTER 5

DIG THE WELL
BEFORE YOU GET
THIRSTY

I was recently catching up with an old client and she admitted that the previous few weeks had been an incredibly stressful time. When I asked what was going on, she shared that she'd spent day and night racing to and from the vet clinic to care for her seriously unwell pet rabbit.

While I was naturally sympathetic, I didn't really grasp the significance of her situation until she explained, 'The hardest thing is that by the time you have any idea that a rabbit is sick, it's often too late to do anything about it'. She said it was still touch-and-go for her 'furry baby'.

Researching it further after our conversation, I learned that unlike other domestic pets, rabbits will go to great lengths to conceal any hint of illness—a behaviour that works to their advantage in the wild where an obviously sick animal will become an easy target. This means that often rabbits will be within a few hours of death before there is any hint that anything is wrong and then it can be too late for medical intervention.

WITH BUSINESSES AS IT IS WITH BUNNIES

As I reflected on this dynamic, I was struck by the parallels between the behaviour of rabbits and the behaviour of organisations and businesses. Many businesses act much the same way when things start to get a bit wobbly. When external threats or internal dysfunction begin to affect the health and viability of a business, there is often a redoubling of efforts to conceal any hint of concern or crisis. In an effort to appear fine, business leaders will even ramp up the rhetoric of excitement for the future and satisfaction with the present. Everything seems rosy until, one day, the cracks begin to appear. Then all of a sudden these cracks become gaping chasms and before you know it, everything is falling apart.

This all-too-common process reminds me of Hemingway's quote about how a man goes broke: 'Gradually and then suddenly.'[1]

When it comes to the effect of disruption on a business, it is much the same. The impacts of change aren't felt or communicated gradually over time. In fact, sometimes business leaders aren't even consciously hiding the impact of disruption—they may not even be aware it's happening, as the change can be imperceptible or inconceivable.

The challenge for any business or organisation hoping to thrive in an age of disruption is to respond quickly and decisively when change hits. Winston Churchill knew to never let a good crisis go to waste and many of us were taught as children that necessity is the mother of invention. And so smart leaders will always leverage the urgency and hunger created by crisis and respond swiftly.

However even smarter leaders will pre-empt disruption and change before the crisis hits and they are left with no other option. They will change before they are forced or, as our chapter title suggests, dig the well before they get thirsty.

The key benefit of adapting before disruption hits is that it keeps you in strategic mode.

If you wait until a crisis unfolds, you will be operating from a position of survival, not strategy. The drive for survival may be exhilarating but it is far from conducive to making measured and wise decisions.

> **If you wait until a crisis unfolds, you will be operating from a position of survival, not strategy.**

Better still, it is always best to innovate and reinvent yourself when times are good because that is when you have resources, time and perspective on your side. However, it requires visionary leadership and courage to embrace change and embark on reinvention when there is nothing wrong—after all, why rock the boat if everything seems fine?

This is what Scott D. Anthony calls 'the Innovator's Paradox': 'when times are good, you have the *ability* to do things differently but not much *urgency* or *desire*'. However, 'when times are bad, you urgently need to do things differently, but it's punishingly hard'. When a crisis hits, momentum has slowed, cash flow has often dried up and your options seem limited. Any new-growth efforts look too small to address today's problems, and so the focus becomes on pursuing the 'one big dramatic thing' that will turn the tide. However, big, dramatic cure-all efforts rarely work and can even speed up decline. Often the efforts that companies take to plug growth gaps actually result in larger, not smaller, gaps—something often referred to as the 'growth gap death spiral'.[2]

THREE WAYS TO DIG THE WELL BEFORE YOU GET THIRSTY

If you are going to successfully dig the well before you get thirsty and change before you are forced to, here are three key guiding principles for doing so:

i. watch the tides

ii. cannibalise your own business

iii. identify your sources of unfair advantage.

i. Watch the tides

One of the biggest challenges in pre-empting change is to discern the difference between waves and tides.

Waves are the short-term trends, aberrations and fads that come and go. They tend not to leave a mark and, while they are dramatic and even exciting, can easily be strategic distractions.

Tides, on the other hand, are the broad-based, slower moving and all-pervasive changes that can alter the entire landscape. They are not dramatic and are therefore easy to miss—and that's why so many people do. Leaders and organisations ignore the shifting tides at their peril.

In order to thrive in turbulent times, you must get good at identifying the difference between distractions and disruptions—between waves and tides. Jump at every wave and you'll soon lose the leadership credibility required when you sense the tide is finally turning.

Business theorists will often refer to these 'tides' as discontinuities. In an organisational context, 'discontinuities' are defined as unpredictable and unforeseen changes that confound existing assumptions or expectations. Sometimes labelled 'Black Swans', these are the 'unknown unknowns' that Donald Rumsfeld referred to all those years ago.

The fact that discontinuities are unpredictable by their very nature means they represent a huge opportunity for the alert, the prepared and the adaptable. After all, as Harvard Business School professor Clayton Christensen points out, 'By the time the writing is on the wall, everyone can read it'.[3]

Celebrated entrepreneur and investor Marc Andreessen was able to pioneer the idea of a web browser because he recognised the potential of the Internet early on. In order to stay one step ahead of change, Andreessen suggests that the key is to 'Pay attention to things that are taking off, even if they're only taking off at a small scale'.[4]

Identifying the tides of discontinuity in their earliest stage is where the greatest opportunity lies. Those who fail to notice or choose to ignore these discontinuities early on will be rudely shocked by those who do.[5]

Gary Hamel puts it best: 'Individuals who get startled by the future weren't paying attention'.[6] In other words, digging the well before you get thirsty will require you to stay alert.

Examples abound of business leaders choosing to ignore discontinuities and paying a heavy price. In an April 2017 interview, Barclays CEO Jes Staley said, 'I don't think that small fintech companies are going to challenge us. Every day, 30% of Britain's GDP goes through Barclays payment systems ... so I am not concerned that new technologies will harm [us]'.[7]

This paradigm stands in stark contrast with that of Staley's predecessor, Antony Jenkins, who warned that banks are actually facing their own 'Kodak moment' owing to the threat of new technologies. In June 2017, Jenkins predicted that banks would be forced to close up to half of their branches before 2027 and that the path to decline could well mirror that of collapsed video giant Blockbuster. According to Jenkins, this fate is entirely avoidable if banks are willing to acknowledge the change that is upon them and start adapting. 'Banks have to act now. What they really need to do is think about innovation, but also transformation, doing something radically different,' Jenkins says.[8]

Judging by the prevailing complacency and arrogance in many of the world's banks, I suspect Antony Jenkins's warning may well fall on deaf ears.

Encyclopedia Britannica: a surprising success story

In contrast, consider how Encyclopedia Britannica were well prepared for the digital tide that rendered their iconic printed volumes irrelevant.

As far back as the mid 1990s, Britannica started making moves to limit its dependence on print book sales as they could see technology would one day have an impact on their business. It's worth noting that compact discs were only just becoming mainstream and the Internet was still in its very infancy at the point Britannica began gearing up for the future.

In the ensuing years, the company slowly but surely transformed itself from a book printer into an online information provider to the point where, by 2011, 85 per cent of Britannica's revenue was coming from sales of online subscriptions, instructional programs and electronic books. In the very year Britannica announced it would be ceasing printed editions, the company boasted half a million household subscribers to its full-access online database, while more than 100 million people have access to the online Encyclopedia Britannica in schools, libraries and colleges. In the words of the company's president, Jorge Cauz, Britannica had become 'a fully digital company'.[9]

Although it is valuable to identify discontinuities early on, this is not to say that you should immediately take action and overhaul your business. A useful strategy to prepare for the future is to do scenario planning. Develop a range of contingency plans where you rehearse alternate futures based on embryonic trends you have identified. That way, when it becomes clear that the tide is indeed turning and disruption is on the way, you won't be blindsided by it because you've already planned the response and developed a strategy.[10]

As media mogul Rupert Murdoch once said, 'The essential ingredient to business success is the ability to consistently see round the corner'.[11] Ironic, perhaps, coming from a man who ideologically clings to his newspaper business—and yet a wise insight no less.

ii. Cannibalise your own business

One of Steve Jobs' most famous and enduring quotes is also one of my very favourites: 'If you're not willing to cannibalize your own business, someone else will do it for you'.

More than just a pithy platitude, this ethos is one that Jobs truly lived by. Consider how Apple essentially put its own iPod out of business. The popularity of the iPod, once the 'must have' technology device for music lovers everywhere, was largely eroded by the iPhone's release in 2007. Once consumers could listen to their music on their phones, there was no need for a separate device. This, however, had been a deliberate cannibalisation on the part of Apple. In 2005, Steve Jobs warned Apple's board that the ubiquity of mobile phones would render the iPod obsolete almost overnight. Apple's solution, rather than waiting for a competitor to beat them to it, was to invent the 'iPod killer' themselves.

In the same way, Netflix cannibalised its own highly profitable DVD-by-mail business to make room for a more strategic online option. Reflecting on the boldness of this move, Reed Hastings, CEO and co-founder of Netflix, pointed to the genuine difficulties of anticipating change and deciding which future path is the best one to pursue.[12] After all, shifting from mail-order DVDs to content streaming seems like a 'no brainer' in hindsight, but was far from a sure bet at the time Netflix made the leap. Reinventing before disruption hits is by no means an easy feat, and the fact that we often only hear of the success stories in retrospect disguises how difficult cannibalisation can be.

Australian online job search site Seek has recently embarked on a bold cannibalisation initiative. However, rather than attacking their own business model, Seek have set up a contest encouraging others to do it for them. Their new accelerator program will offer grants of $50 000 to a dozen workplace-related startups who demonstrate the skills and smarts to disrupt Seek's existing business. Seek chief executive and co-founder Andrew Bassat said this is just part of the company's commitment to disrupting themselves rather than waiting for others to do so.[13]

A new road for Ricoh

I came across another inspiring example of cannibalisation recently when doing some work with the leadership team at print giant Ricoh. From their beginnings in the 1930s as a photographics company, Ricoh have consistently reinvented themselves as technology has evolved.

In the 1980s and 1990s, Ricoh enjoyed a significant slice of the lucrative print and photocopier market worldwide. Recent years, however, have not been kind to the print industry. The rise of digital rather than printed content has significantly eroded the consumer demand and as such the printing industry worldwide has been searching for new sources of value and relevance.

In the case of Ricoh, I was fascinated to hear about the company's reinvention journey to becoming a leader in workflow management, web-based collaboration technologies and document digitisation.

This third aspect of their new business is perhaps the most visionary one. Think of it for a moment: a company that made its money out of printed documents is now actively helping clients take all their printed materials and digitise them in an effort to make offices truly paper free.

Ricoh Australia's national director shared with me the example of one client organisation that used the company's document digitising technology to get rid of seven truckloads of paper. Genuinely, seven trucks full of old documents that could be dispensed with, freeing up entire office floors that had been jam-packed with filing cabinets for years.

More than just helping their clients move away from paper, Ricoh is practising what they preach. When seven regional Ricoh offices consolidated into one capital city hub a few years ago, they digitised one million of their own pieces of paper.

Probably the most striking component of this cannibalisation is that Ricoh is now encouraging clients to use the very print machines they purchased in years past to do the scanning of these documents in order to digitise them.

Daimler disrupts itself

In the automotive industry, the level of disruption discussed in chapter 1 is going to leave many automakers with little option but to adapt. In an age of driverless car-sharing services, the existing business model of automakers will come under significant threat.

One automaker that has been preparing for and anticipating this disruption for a number of years now is Daimler.

While continuing to develop and manufacture vehicles the traditional way, Daimler AG has been busy exploring ways to cannibalise its traditional business to prepare for the future.

Recognising the opportunity and the threat posed by the sharing economy, years ago Daimler AG developed the wildly successful car-sharing service Car2Go. Today they are at the forefront of driverless technology and have also acquired technology companies including mytaxi and RideScout in order to have a foothold in the trend toward mobility-as-service.[14]

Overhauling higher education

The higher education sector is also doing a pretty extraordinary job of cannibalising their own business model in an effort to ward off disruption.

In large part, the college or university experience has remained largely unchanged for more than a century. Students pick a degree or major, choose a university or college, get the books, go to the lectures, write and submit the papers, sit the exams, get graded, graduate and then work hard to pay off the debt. For years, a university or college degree has been widely considered the right track to a good job. But with a high percentage of graduates failing to find high-calibre work and education costs continuing to rise, students are beginning to ask: Is a degree really valuable?

Richard Miller, president of Olin College of Engineering in Massachusetts, argues that knowledge has become a commodity that's increasingly cheap and easy to acquire. He goes on to question whether charging people a lot of money for education in the age of Internet video is a realistic long-term financial model.[15]

In light of this pending disruption, colleges and universities are beginning to transform their product offering and value proposition.

In the years to come, we will likely see lecture halls disappear and the role of lecturers change entirely. Although the bulk of foundational learning will be done online in massive open online classes (MOOCs), that doesn't mean physical campuses and teachers will become entirely irrelevant. Instead, the value proposition and purpose of colleges and universities will be in their capacity to expose students to new people and new ideas while creating a network of valuable connections.

In the future, online learning will be supplemented by hands-on physical educational experiences where students get the chance to test, apply and expand the knowledge they have acquired online.

Michelle Weise, a senior research fellow at the Clayton Christensen Institute, acknowledges that these changes

> *are wreaking havoc on the way we are used to thinking about higher education. We don't need a person to stand at the front of a room full of hundreds of students and lecture. Now, because information is everywhere, it has to be about a special learning experience.*[16]

Vice-chancellor of the University of Adelaide Warren Bebbington agrees with Weise's assessment. 'Lectures are obsolete,' he admits. 'My view is they're gone; they're never coming back.'[17]

The University of Adelaide in South Australia is at the forefront of tertiary institutions' efforts to cannibalise existing business models. The university has long been offering free online courses in conjunction with Harvard's and MIT's edX programs. However, that was just the beginning.

In 2016, the University of Adelaide began phasing out traditional lectures and replacing them with online learning integrated with small-group work. Having visited the university and seen their technology in action, I can say it is a truly extraordinary example of disruptive innovation.[18]

At Melbourne's Deakin University, a similar paradigm shift is occurring. According to Deakin University's deputy vice-chancellor, Beverley Oliver, universities need to become more like Netflix and allow students to 'binge watch' their courses online in their own time.

Pointing to the example of other industries, Oliver suggests that higher education could learn from the music and entertainment businesses where technology is used to offer customers many different options to suit the way they choose to consume the product.

Deakin's Start Any Time initiative is a significant step toward this reality. The program allows students to commence an online course whenever it suits them.[19]

Digging the well before you get thirsty is not for the faint-hearted.

Naturally, there are many tertiary institutions that will dismiss the moves of colleges and universities such as MIT, Adelaide and Deakin as reckless or even gimmicky. There's no doubt that the innovation strategies of these educational institutions are pretty daring—they are in effect turning their back on centuries of tradition and countless millions of dollars in safe and predictable revenue. However, this is what digging the well before you get thirsty looks like. It's not for the faint-hearted or the fair-weather sailors. It's gutsy work, but vitally important in turbulent times.

iii. Identify your sources of unfair advantage

The third and final key to pre-empting disruption is to identify the skills and capabilities that give you a competitive advantage and a point of leverage.

Since its early days as a glassmaker in the 1850s, Corning has consistently demonstrated an amazing ability to leverage its unique skills and capabilities to navigate disruption.

At the turn of the last century Corning's primary focus was on the manufacture of light bulbs, with half of their revenue coming from this product line. Known for their high-quality and robust glassware, Corning realised that the impending influx of new competitors would see the light bulb market in a race to the bottom on price. And so the company leveraged their reputation for quality by shifting their focus to the manufacture of high-quality cookware and kitchenware.

If you still think of Corning as the makers of the baking dish in your kitchen cupboard, what you may not know is that today the vast bulk of Corning's most lucrative products would never be found in your kitchen and in fact were likely not even invented a decade ago.

Today, Corning specialises in manufacturing cathode-ray tubes, fibre optics for high-definition TVs, and laser technology that enables mobile phones to be fitted with micro projectors.[20] They produce the ultra-durable 'Gorilla Glass' used in iPhones and iPads, and even high-tech translucent diagnostics boards being used in surgical wards around the world today.

I learned about one of Corning's lesser-known products recently when doing some work with the global medical device giant Medtronic. The Medtronic team were telling me that they produce a video camera capsule that is swallowed and then takes high-definition footage as it moves through your digestive system — removing the need for invasive endoscopies. Amazingly, the lenses in these capsules are made by none other than Corning.[21]

Corning are a phenomenal example of a very old company with a very agile mindset. Before successive waves of change and disruption have hit, Corning have been on the front foot, reinventing themselves and leveraging their skills, brand recognition and reputation to stay one step ahead.

National Cash Register (NCR) is another good example of an established business that flirted with irrelevance but managed to recover by leveraging the skills and competencies at their disposal.

Back in the 1970s, NCR were caught off guard when electronic cash registers made the company's traditional product range obsolete almost overnight. Far from digging the well before they felt parched, NCR were almost dying of thirst before they realised the need to pick up a shovel.

Recognising the need to act quickly, NCR identified that their strong brand recognition and established distribution network were two very powerful competitive advantages they would need to exploit if they were to avoid annihilation. They quickly got to work developing a range of electronic registers and successfully set out to re-position themselves as market innovators.[22] In more recent years, NCR have gone on to pioneer self-service checkout technology, thus solidifying the company's market leadership position.

WHAT DO YOU *KNOW*? WHAT DO YOU *OWN*? WHAT CAN YOU *DO*?

When looking to innovate, a good starting place is to identify what you *know*, what you *own* and what you can *do* that gives you an unfair edge. It is these strategic assets and core competencies that you could otherwise take for granted that may point to the path of enduring success and relevance. I have seen this in my local context recently in the scores of retailers who have recognised that their physical position in high-traffic areas makes them ideal pick-up and drop-off points for customers' online purchases or returns. Rather than seeing online shopping as the enemy, these retail stores become a part of the value chain and can enjoy the flow-on effects of customers visiting their stores and making discretionary purchases.

> When looking to innovate, a good starting place is to identify what you *know*, what you *own* and what you can *do* that gives you an unfair edge.

Beyond being a defensive tactic in the face of disruption, sources of unfair advantage can also be a powerful proactive strategy. Consider how Disney have leveraged their reputational assets and skills to develop their children's English language training programs in China. Owing to the familiarity and popularity of Disney's characters with Chinese children, specially trained and licensed instructors teach English to students using these very characters. Testament to how visionary this strategy was, Disney English has become the largest player in China's $2 billion English-teaching industry.[23]

∞

John F. Kennedy said in 1963 that 'To even stand still we have to move very fast'. Those words are perhaps truer today than ever before.

Smart leaders and visionary leaders know that preparing for, pre-empting and embracing disruption is the only way to ensure you don't become a victim of it.

While it can be tempting to dismiss, ignore or fight the tides of change, resistance is futile, foolish and could well prove fatal.

Questions for reflection

∞ How strong is the sense of urgency to transform and reinvent your organisation? Who would be resistant to such a change initiative?

∞ What are some of the emerging trends and discontinuities you would be wise to monitor in the coming years?

∞ What elements of your business or organisation are still working but may be nearing their use-by date?

∞ How could you look to cannibalise your own business and what would this look like?

∞ What do you *know*, *own* or *do* that could give you an unfair competitive advantage in the future?

CHAPTER 6

FAIL FAST,
FREQUENTLY AND FRUGALLY

Six hours' train ride south of Stockholm, in the Swedish town of Helsingborg, you will find one of the more interesting museums you're ever likely to come across. What is most remarkable about this museum is what it celebrates. Inside you will find no exhibits commemorating triumphs of human ingenuity of creativity—rather, you will encounter exhibit after exhibit celebrating, of all things, failure. That's right: an entire museum dedicated to many of the greatest stuff-ups, misfires and train wrecks of human history.

Since it opened its doors on 15 June 2017, the Museum of Failure has given visitors the opportunity to encounter a litany of flops, ranging from Harley-Davidson's ill-fated perfume to the breathtakingly misogynistic Bic pen 'For Her', the Apple Newton and, of course, Google Glass.

Far from ridiculing these embarrassing blunders, the Museum of Failure's director, Samuel West, wants to celebrate them. A former clinical psychologist with a doctorate in innovation, West knows too well the vital role that failure plays in coming up with new ideas. And yet, the stigma attached to failure prevents many organisations and individuals from embracing it. 'We glorify success so much, but at the expense of demonizing failure. And it's from failure that we learn,' says West.[1]

I couldn't agree more.

We live in a culture that is obsessed with success. As someone who spends a lot of his time in the conference world, I can hardly think of a single corporate event where a leader took to the stage and celebrated a mistake or failure. Sometimes we skirt the theme by talking about 'learning experiences' but, in reality, modern business culture loves to showcase the success, the triumph and the victory (while scarcely acknowledging the failures that were part of the success journey).

I am under no illusions: the mantra of 'failing fast' is somewhat tired and even cliché in many business circles of late. And yet, while we intellectually know that failing fast is critical, we're simply not doing it. This is especially the case in large publicly listed companies, where the scrutiny of shareholders and real-time feedback provided by stock prices can drive us to play a dangerously safe game.

The problem is, in the disruptive age we're entering, playing it safe won't cut it. In the words of celebrated physicist Frank Wilczek, 'If you're not making mistakes, you're not working on hard enough problems. And that's a mistake'.[2] You may keep your job this year or keep your shareholders happy this quarter, but you may well be doing so at the long-term cost of your relevance and viability.

In the disruptive age we're entering, playing it safe won't cut it.

In preparing to run a workshop with middle managers of a large bank recently, I asked the client what they'd like me to focus on in my presentation. When I shared the broad overview of the content I had in mind, including a module on the importance of failure, the department leader suggested I might want to leave it out. 'We've heard that a lot in recent years,' he said.

Acknowledging his concerns, I simply replied, 'I did wonder if that might be the case. But are your people doing it? Are they taking risks and openly embracing failure in the innovation process?' His telling silence and sheepish look made it clear that the leadership verbiage wasn't lining up with the grassroots corporate culture. Aspiration and philosophy weren't translating into behaviour.

NO LICENCE FOR RECKLESSNESS

Now, none of this is to say that companies should encourage reckless failure as an end in itself. That would be downright foolish. Further still, people who repeat the same mistake over and over again without learning from it need to be held to account—stupidity or ineptitude are not a recipe for innovation, or anything constructive for that matter.

In contrast, genuine, well-meaning, measured and sensible risks or experiments that result in failure must be applauded and encouraged. It is an appetite for this type of risk that will be critical if you are to thrive in an age of disruption.

Former president of IBM Thomas Watson Jr is widely known for recognising the importance of risk-taking and intelligent failure. One of his better known personal mottos was, 'If you want to increase your success rate, double your failure rate'.

> **An appetite for this type of risk will be critical if you are to thrive in an age of disruption.**

More than simply a pithy credo, this philosophy was one that Watson had inherited from his father, IBM's founder, Thomas Watson Sr.

I love the story Andy Stanley shares in his fantastic book, *Next Generation Leader*, about a staff member's interaction with the elder Thomas Watson. As the account goes, a young IBM employee had made a decision to try something that many of his colleagues warned might not work. However, he was convinced that he knew best and went along with his plans.

Unfortunately, it turned out that his colleagues' judgement had been right and the decision ended up costing the company $10 million. Needless to say, the young man was immediately called to the office of Tom Watson Sr.

Upon entering Mr Watson's office, the nervous young man looked down and said, 'Well I suppose you want my resignation'.

'You can't be serious!' Mr Watson exclaimed. 'We just spent 10 million dollars educating you! You're not going anywhere!'

You can easily see how a response like this set a healthy culture of experimentation and empowerment within IBM that saw the company become the global innovation giant it did.

Sadly, this risk-promoting culture gradually diminished over time and when Lou Gerstner took over as CEO at IBM in 1993 he encountered a very different philosophy — one marked by safe thinking, complacency and denial.

In the years just prior to Gerstner's arrival, things had been dire at IBM. Tellingly, however, the company surveyed 1200 of its top managers and found that four in 10 did not accept the need for change[3] — despite the fact that the company was posting losses that had totalled $16 billion between 1991 and 1993.[4]

The world of computing was quickly shifting focus to laptop technology but IBM was dragging its heels and risked missing the boat entirely. They were 'stuck' in every sense of the word and Gerstner realised he needed to shift the culture — and quickly.

He learned that employees would often approach their superiors and say things like 'You know, I've been thinking...' but they'd typically be shut down before they could even share their idea. So Gerstner addressed the entire workforce and gave them a mandate to stick their neck out, be daring and come up with new ideas. 'If you have a good idea,' he said, 'take it to your manager. If he won't listen, then bring it to me'.

And he meant it. Rumours began circulating of blue-collar workers being flown to New York aboard the company jet to share their innovations with the CEO. This sent a powerful message to the organisation that began shaping culture and reviving the spirit of ingenuity that had once permeated IBM. As Gerstner himself reflected, his job was to teach the elephant to dance again.[5]

Destigmatising failure at Ford

A similar culture of denial confronted Alan Mulally when he stepped into the leadership role of Ford in 2006. Being the first person outside the Ford family to take the helm of the company, Mulally's very appointment sent a message that change was on the agenda.

That year, the automaker had made a huge loss of $12.7 billion and Mulally recognised that Ford's internal culture was largely to blame.

In an effort to address this, Mulally began by establishing a weekly routine of gathering each of his direct reports on Thursdays at 7 am for what would be called 'The Business Plan Review' meeting. For the first of these gatherings, Mulally asked each of his executive team to prepare colour-coded reports: green reports if all was going well in their division, yellow if there were some problems that needed addressing and red if something was significantly wrong.

Considering the company had just posted a multibillion-dollar loss, the fact that each executive entered the first meeting proudly carrying a green folder spoke volumes. While you could put this down to these executives wanting to impress their new boss, it pointed to a more dangerous culture within the company. Namely, that failure was shunned, mistakes ignored or blame shifted.

Addressing the issue head on, Mulally said things needed to change. He gave tacit and explicit permission for executives to be honest in the assessment of their division's performance. Gradually, the colour of the reports began to change. As the leadership culture began to shift, the organisational culture followed.[6]

FAILING SLOWLY IS PAINFUL

Beyond acknowledging and even encouraging failure, it is the speed with which failure is experienced and learned from that can make all the difference. As one colleague of mine put it recently, the reason failing fast makes so much sense is that it's far less painful than failing slowly. And she's right. Identifying a failed experiment or misguided strategy early on and quickly responding can make all the difference.

> **The reason failing fast makes so much sense is that it's far less painful than failing slowly.**

More than simply limiting collateral damage, failing fast maintains momentum and agility. Persist with a failing initiative too long and you'll be bogged down before you know it. Further still, the longer you persist with something that clearly isn't working, the greater the sunk cost risk: 'We've come this far and invested so much, we should at least see it through'. Once our egos and identity get wrapped up in the efforts, walking away or admitting failure gets all the more difficult.

So the key message is this: fail quickly, fail often and don't get too attached to your experiments or ideas. At the risk of sounding cliché, remember that a failure is not a person but an event.

The trick in all this, of course, is to recognise the early warning signs of genuine failure. After all, sometimes it's hard to discern whether you've encountered a setback that warrants persistence and a redoubling of effort, or whether you've arrived at a dead end. Sadly, there is no hard and fast rule I can offer here except to say that trusted advisers and wise colleagues can prove invaluable. Seek the input of seasoned innovators who have run the risk-and-failure gauntlet many times themselves. Their objectivity and perspective will be the best guide in discerning the difference between failing experiments and frustrated efforts.

MAGNITUDE MATTERS

Beyond developing an appetite for fast and frequent failure, the third element in this strategy for navigating disruption relates to the magnitude of the risks you ought to take.

In keeping with the alliteration, any business or leader would do well to not just fail fast and frequently but also *frugally*.

Put simply, when taking innovation risks, don't bet the farm. While taking big risks can be exhilarating and appear bold or visionary, a more measured approach is far wiser.

Good venture capitalists (VCs) know this. By their very nature, VCs are risk-takers—but they're not big risk-takers. They know full well that not everything will work and, by taking risks that are small in magnitude, they can stomach failure and even embrace it.

In their wonderfully practical book *Great by Choice*, Jim Collins and Morten Hansen pick up on this theme and offer a great metaphor for frugal risk-taking—likening it to a gun battle at sea in a bygone era. Only a foolish soldier, they say, would open fire with his one and only cannonball, thereby taking the risk of missing his target and possibly giving the enemy an advantage. Wily tacticians, on the other hand, knew to use a smaller amount of gun power firing bullets to calibrate their weapons so they could then use their one cannonball and achieve a direct hit.[7]

In the same way, smart risk-taking in today's disruptive age will generally involve small innovations, low-cost experimentation and short feedback loops. Once you've experienced a few failures and have zeroed in on the surefire winning strategy, then go in all guns blazing. Until that point, frugal risk-taking is the most sensible and sustainable approach.

> **Smart risk-taking will generally involve small innovations, low-cost experimentation and short feedback loops.**

A helpful rule of thumb for experimentation is that out of 1000 crazy ideas, 100 will merit a small-scale experiment and, of those, only 10 will be worth investing serious money and resources into. Of that 10, realistically only one or two will have the power to transform a business or spawn a new one.[8]

Google's culture of experimentation has been a key element of the company's breakout success. Google co-founder Eric Schmidt describes his company's ethos: 'Our goal is to have more at bats per unit of time and money than anyone else'. Google have always looked to experiment more than the competition and learn cheaply through simulations, role-playing scenarios, cheap mock-ups and by welcoming customer feedback on early stage ideas.[9]

THREE WAYS TO BUILD A RISK-TAKING CULTURE

Returning to my conversation with the banking client who suggested I steer clear of talking about failure because they'd 'heard it all before', as we explored the reason the corporate verbiage wasn't translating into behaviour change, it was clear that culture was a key factor.

And this is where we're going to focus for the remainder of this chapter. You can espouse the value and virtues of failure and the critical role it plays in innovation until you're blue in the face, but until there is a culture that fosters risk-taking, people simply won't do it. They'll colour inside the lines, they'll play it safe, and when things do go wrong they'll hide the bodies or simply shift the blame.

If an organisation is going to truly remove the stigma of failure and foster an appetite for risk-taking, they must do three things:

i. incentivise boldness

ii. build high trust and empowerment

iii. give access to capital and resources.

i. Incentivise boldness

One of the primary reasons people avoid taking risks and failing is that there is little incentive to do so. On the contrary, many organisations tend to actively disincentivise risk. There is no point urging risk-taking but then punishing failure, explicitly or implicitly.

Reflecting on the need for banks to adapt to the disruptions posed by technology, the former CEO of Barclays bank, Antony Jenkins (who featured in the previous chapter), suggests that an appetite for boldness must start at the top:

> Boards will need to accept that we live in a discontinuous world. They should ask executives to take significant but calculated risks by working on projects that no one else is

working on... doing the same thing a little better is now the riskiest thing you can do.[10]

Traditional reward and incentive programs focus on improvement, growth and linear advancement. Employees are encouraged to do what they did last quarter or last year but slightly more profitably, frequently or efficiently. Incentives are tied to the degree to which these improvements are realised.

Structuring incentives this way certainly seems intuitive and even sensible, all things being equal. But that's just the problem. All things are far from equal. Businesses and leaders are going to have to do things in dramatically new and different ways in order to stay at the cutting edge.

Picking up on this, prolific *Harvard Business Review* contributor Scott D. Anthony suggests that leaders would do well to move from rewarding innovation outcomes to rewarding innovation behaviours.[11]

At an informal level, this can be as simple as framing performance review discussions around experimentation. Imagine how the tone and culture of a performance review would change if employees were asked questions such as 'What daring risks have you taken over the past month?' or 'What have you tried that has failed recently—and what did you learn?' While only the especially brave businesses may go on to tie bonus payments to levels of daring or risky behaviour, even affirming this behaviour in discussions and highlighting that it is expected and welcome can be a powerful incentive.

For any readers who are parents, I'd encourage you to apply this approach when fostering a spirit of boldness and openness to failure in your own kids. The payoff in their adult lives may well be huge.

Consider Spanx founder Sara Blakely, who grew up with a keen awareness of the power of failure. Her father would often ask, 'What have you failed at this week?' Learning early on that the one thing worse than failing was to not try, Blakely developed the perseverance necessary to build the billion-dollar empire she has.[12]

Getting creative to re-shape culture

Sometimes it takes a bit of creativity to incentivise and encourage boldness in an organisation. When Jim Donald came to the helm of Extended Stay America in 2012, the former CEO of Starbucks recognised the need to inject a daring spirit into his new organisation. With the national hotel chain having only recently emerged from bankruptcy, the prevailing culture was one of survival. Employees were so focused on not losing their jobs or making mistakes that might cost the company money, there was zero appetite for innovation or inventiveness.

In order to address this fear-driven paralysis, Donald gave everyone a safety net by creating a batch of miniature 'Get Out of Jail, Free' cards. These cards gave employees a free pass should they make a mistake. The cards were distributed to all 9000 employees with the assurance that if they took a risk on behalf of the company and things went wrong, they could call in the card and no questions would be asked.

This simple but ingenious move instantly signalled that employees had permission to try again. To take risks and be daring.[13] 'You can't just avoid all risk, because it will lead to entropy,' Donald explains.

One simple way to encourage bold thinking and risk-taking is to change the language we use. A colleague of mine from the Netherlands named Cyriel Kortleven has found that recasting the vocabulary of failure can make all the difference. You will never hear Cyriel talking about 'failure' but rather he encourages clients to refer to misfires and mistakes as 'nearlings'. This term describes something new that was done with the right intentions but that has not yet led to the desired result. Although it may sound like little more than semantics or wordplay, Cyriel points to example after example of clients whose thinking shifted substantially by reframing the concept of failure from being a negative to a positive thing.[14]

It all starts at the top

Boldness needs to start at the top, and this can be a challenge. Most mature organisations are led by administrators, not revolutionaries. Cultures and structures of the past tend to reward those who have played it safe enough to keep their noses clean and their record untarnished. It is these individuals who often rise to the top.

Gary Hamel picks up on this point in his book *Leading the Revolution*.

> *If you're in senior leadership and have been for 2–3 decades, ask yourself honestly: are you more willing to challenge conventions or less so? More cautious or less so? More radical or reactionary?*

Hamel suggests that senior leaders have as much scope for being bold and radical as anyone else but the problem is they have far more to unlearn. 'When it comes to business model innovation, the bottleneck is at the top of the bottle,' he observes.[15]

Most mature organisations are led by administrators, not revolutionaries.

The key message is this: people will not naturally take risks unless they are actively encouraged and incentivised to do so and they see it modelled. Removing disincentives and constraints on risk-taking is a good start, but actively fostering a daring culture of boldness from the top down is key.

ii. Build high trust and empowerment

The old adage that success has many siblings but failure is an orphan certainly rings true. When things go well, there is rarely a shortage of people willing to take credit or highlight their contribution. However, when things go awry, everyone tends to run for the door.

Worse still, a common scenario is that when a risk is taken and things go wrong, everyone stands back and points their finger at the one hapless soul who, for one reason or another, is left to shoulder all the blame. 'It wasn't our fault—we could have told you it wasn't going to work' is the common refrain.

The moment responsibility for failure is shirked or shifted, the vital role of a leader is to step in and provide 'psychological safety'. This term, defined by Harvard professor Amy Edmondson in her 2015 TED talk, is critical to ensuring that people feel confident to try new things and take innovation risks.

If the finger-pointing and blame-shifting scenario is permitted to play out unchallenged, not only will the person left holding the ball never again stick out their neck, but the same will go for everyone else in the team. The message will be received loud and clear: it could be you who is left hung out to dry next time so play it safe and don't rock the boat.

Success has many siblings but failure is an orphan.

The most powerful response to failure in a team is for everyone to step *forward* and gather around the person or group that is to blame (for want of a better word). The question then needs to be 'What can we learn from this together?' Not only does this create the very psychological safety necessary for risk-taking, but it also allows the failure lessons to be learned by everyone in a team, amplifying the benefit and insights gained.

Vice Chairman of General Electric John Rice suggests that leaders must actively support team members if they want them to take intelligent risks. 'You have to protect people who fail for the right reasons,' he says.[16]

It's a matter of trust

While a culture of trust is critical horizontally within a team, it is also important that vertical trust is communicated through empowerment. In other words, the very act of leaders empowering their people to take risks and use their judgement clearly communicates trust.

This empowerment has been a key element in Toyota's enduring success as an automaker. For almost two decades, car manufacturers such as Ford conducted benchmarks against Toyota in an effort to emulate the auto giant's success. Toyota led the market on efficiency, defect rates and innovation. Many competitors adopted Toyota's just-in-time approach to inventory, assuming that was the secret. Others tried to mimic Toyota's cultural hallmarks and habits (to the extent of mimicking the behaviour and customs of their Japanese counterparts).

However, Ford eventually discovered that one of the distinctive hallmarks of Toyota was the way in which the company empowered its people. Toyota pushed authority down to the front line in meaningful and extraordinary ways. This allowed them to unlock millions of suggestions each year for product and process improvements. At a practical level, this empowerment even meant that front-line employees had the power to stop a billion-dollar production line if they felt it necessary to do so.

iii. Give access to capital and resources

This third key to building a culture that embraces innovation risk is probably the most practical.

The bottom line is that it is pointless asking team members to generate ideas and innovate if they are not given the resources and mechanisms to do so.

When Quicken Loans founder Dan Gilbert identified the urgent need to ramp up the pace of innovation in his business, he had to confront the reality that team members with direct line responsibility were busy delivering and couldn't be expected to reinvent at the same time — a challenge he likened to asking a pilot to rebuild the plane while flying it.

As a result, Gilbert launched what became known as the company's 'mousetrap team'. This business unit had no direct production responsibilities and was charged solely with 'building a better mousetrap'. They examined every process, big or small, and, in doing so, propelled the company to new levels of efficiency, growth and client satisfaction through better internal systems.[17]

The creation of separate innovation-focused groups within organisations is not a new phenomenon. Sometimes known as 'skunk works', these breakaway groups derive their name from an independent unit of engineers created by the Lockheed Corporation in the 1950s, who were set up to work in isolation in a circus tent pitched alongside a foul-smelling plastics factory.[18]

Other businesses have also initiated splinter groups to bring about reform over the years. Xerox set up the Palo Alto Research Center (PARC)[19] and Amazon developed a Web Lab, the purpose of which is to uncover ways to improve the Amazon customer experience.[20]

More recently, Google's internal incubator, named Area 120, has been given a clear mandate to test new ideas and inventions that could become future Google products. Each Area 120 'class' has 15 teams who work to test out and prove their ideas over the course of six months. During this time, the employees are released from their normal day jobs. If projects are successful, Googlers will be allowed to continue to work on them; if not, they're invited to return to work at Google, in a different role.[21]

Naturally, the danger with developing specialised innovation teams is that it reinforces the notion that innovation and creativity are the domain of specific individuals and not the responsibility of everyone in an organisation (as we explore in chapter 12).

The challenge then is to create mechanisms to allow all employees to access the time or financial resources necessary to experiment and take innovation risks.

A number of years ago, a director at oil giant Shell began experimenting with ways to do just this. Twenty million dollars were allocated to a panel that had authority to help fund worthy ideas submitted by any employee throughout the organisation. The GameChanger initiative, as it later became known, involved a three-day kick-off innovation lab where more than 70 enthusiastic staff members were encouraged to look outside of the energy business for ideas. In addition, they were given skills for identifying and challenging long-held industry assumptions.

By the end of the second day, 240 new ideas had bubbled to the surface. This was then whittled down to 12 innovations that were nominated for funding and allocated to a work group to flesh out. Over the next 100 days, this work group was tasked with testing, refining and experimenting to determine the idea's viability before presenting back to the GameChanger funding board. Following these presentations, ideas that got the green light received on average $100 000 to create a proof-of-concept. At the end of the first GameChanger round, three-quarters of the innovations were deemed unviable while the remaining one-quarter went on to become a key part of Shell's ongoing business.[22]

Management expert and organisational theorist Gary Hamel points out that while having a central venture capital fund can be a good way to drive innovation, it is not always going to be practical. He suggests that half the challenge is that, in most companies, there is a monopsony for new ideas. In other words, there is only one buyer (in contrast to a monopoly, where there is only one seller). This one buyer tends to be a superior up the chain who has authority to grant funds and allocate resources. This naturally puts a handbrake on innovation because it often leads to political power plays rather than a contest of ideas.

To overcome this, Hamel points to the fact that in large companies there will always be hundreds of people who have some sort of a discretionary budget. If each of these individuals were given explicit permission to invest 2 to 5 per cent of their budget in any project they see as promising, suddenly internal entrepreneurs will have a vast network of 'angel' investors they can tap into for funding.[23]

∞

Every leader would do well to remember that the verbiage and aspiration to fail fast matters little if you don't have a culture and mechanisms that will enable it. Despite an appetite for risk-taking being vital to the innovation process, the negative stigma and shame associated with failure remains.

Leaders have a key role to play in being open, honest and transparent. Don't underestimate the power of owning your failures, admitting your mistakes and communicating honestly. In doing so, you will give those you lead the permission and confidence to do the same. The breakout ideas, bold thinking and big innovations you're looking for are probably lying dormant in your teams already. The light bulb is already there, waiting to be switched on. As the leader, you have your finger on the switch.[24]

Questions for reflection

∞ How comfortable are you with acknowledging mistakes and missteps?

∞ What would it take to destigmatise failure in your context?

∞ What small, incremental risks could you take in the coming weeks and months?

∞ How could you or your organisation actively incentivise boldness?

∞ How strong is the sense of 'psychological safety' in your organisation or team? What could be done to improve this?

∞ How could capital and resources be freed up to encourage experimentation and risk-taking?

CHAPTER 7

DON'T PAVE
THE CATTLE TRACK

My father-in-law recently shared a powerful metaphor he learned in his days as an IT communications manager for a large government agency.

'The biggest mistake IT technicians make when implementing new systems and hardware,' he told me, 'is to pave the cattle track'.

Realising I had never heard the term before, he went on to explain.

> *In the past when settlers and developers moved into new areas to establish suburbs or towns, they would often build roads where cattle or animals had trodden existing tracks over the years. Once these tracks turned into permanent paved roads, they would automatically become the basic grid around which houses and other infrastructure would be built.*

'The problem with this,' my father-in-law explained,

> *is that the well-trodden paths may have made sense for cattle but were rarely a sensible or appropriate route for vehicles to take — much less a grid around which a suburb could be developed.*

This short-sighted and superficial solution, he concluded, would lead to lots of problems later on.

In the IT world, paving the cattle track related to overlaying new systems and software when a radical overhaul of legacy hardware frameworks or the system itself was required.

WHAT NEEDS A FUNDAMENTAL RETHINK, NOT A SUPERFICIAL RETREAD?

Beyond the world of IT, however, I see cattle tracks constantly being paved in organisations. When looking to adapt or innovate, many businesses and leaders simply tweak the language, overhaul the branding or implement a new strategy without considering whether a fundamental rethink is required.

I remember working with some financial advisers a few years ago who were grappling with this challenge.

We had spent the afternoon looking at the theme of innovation and zeroed in on the importance of improving the experience for new clients. The first meeting between an adviser and a new client is always about establishing rapport, building trust and understanding the goals and motivations of the client. A standard component of this meeting that most advisers have used for years is the '10-why' process.

Many businesses and leaders simply tweak the language, without considering whether a fundamental rethink is required.

In case you've never experienced it, the 10-why exercise is where an adviser asks an open, leading question such as 'What is important to you when it comes to your finances?' Regardless of your response, the next question is 'And why is that important to you?', followed by 'And why is that important to you?', and so it goes on until, in theory, by the tenth 'why' question you are getting close to the client's deeply held values, motivations or fears.

I know that over the years my wife has always found this process frustrating and often patronising. Because she is an actor, I'd see her move into performer mode at about the third 'why' question and start making things up. It was a genuinely entertaining process to see where the conversation would go!

When I shared my wife's aversion to this tried-and-true approach with the group of financial advisers, many of the attendees admitted to receiving similar feedback from clients over the years, indicating that this trust- and rapport-building strategy often had the opposite effect to the one intended.

At this point, one of the attendees raised his hand and shared that a few years ago those in his practice had realised the 10-why approach wasn't working as well as it once had, so they had built an app to lead new clients through the exercise.

While I applauded the initiative, in reality this app was little more than paving the cattle track. It was a fine and more efficient way to do something ineffective—an innovation that may have felt like progress but didn't address the core innovation need.

My question for that group of financial advisers is one I often work through with clients when I am in a consulting capacity: 'What elements of your business need a fundamental rethink rather than a superficial retread?'

While retreading something outmoded and outdated can look very much like innovation (new branding, new language, new logo, etc.), these superficial enhancements will be short-term fixes at best. True innovation always approaches an opportunity or challenge by identifying the historical way things have been done (the cattle track) and considering how a new paradigm or a new path may be necessary.

THE POWER OF A NEW PARADIGM

As former business professor at the University of San Francisco Oren Harari so aptly points out, 'The electric light did not come from the continuous improvement of candles'.

In the product innovation journey of lighting, there came a point where incremental innovation was no longer going to cut it. As shown in chapter 6, failing frugally is sensible and necessary but there comes a point where revolutionary innovation is necessary. To Harari's point, creating the electric light bulb was always going to require a fundamental rethink of how light is produced.

Before we can change anything else, we really must change our mind. There is no point approaching innovation with a fixed mindset and a frame of reference bound by existing assumptions.

You'll never find new treasure using an old treasure map.

History is punctuated by great thinkers, ranging from Galileo to Thomas Edison, who posed questions others were unwilling to ask—and who saw things that others failed to see. These great men and women were able to think beyond the paradigms of their times—and dramatically changed the world as a result.

History shows us that an overreliance on established paradigms and practices can prevent mankind from taking giant leaps into the future. Remember, you'll never find new treasure using an old treasure map.

The barrage of disruptions that is about to hit us means that new mental models will be required. Paving the cattle track by perpetuating old approaches and assumptions will set any business on a collision course with irrelevance.

THE KODAK MINDSET THAT ENDED THE KODAK MOMENT

While there has been no shortage of business commentary on how and why Kodak missed the shift to digital photography, a little-acknowledged truth is that the photographics giant were actually well aware of the threat and opportunity that digital technology posed.

As far back as 1981, having invented the first forms of digital photography a few years earlier, Kodak began exploring how it could use digital to 'enhance' its traditional film businesses. While each of the film–digital hybrid initiatives Kodak devised were admirable, they were ultimately doomed to fail.[1]

A good example of this blended digital–analogue approach was the Advantix Preview camera released in the late 1990s. Featuring hybrid film–digital technology, Advantix users would still take pictures the way they always had but now there was a digital display on the back of the camera showing them the images they'd just taken. The user could then decide which photos they wanted to print and how many copies they would require.

While this seemed like a genius middle-of-the-road option to entering the digital age, and despite the $500 million spent on developing it, the

Advantix was a spectacular failure. The Advantix, it turned out, was a paved cattle track.

Kodak also made attempts to bring their traditional photo processing systems into the digital age through the Image Magic kiosks. They even formed a partnership with AOL called 'You've Got Pictures', which allowed customers to pay to have their printed photos available online for family and friends to view. However, when customers could do essentially the same things for free with Snapfish, this initiative also failed — it was simply too late to market.[2]

Another little-known foray into the digital age for Kodak was when the company acquired Ofoto in 2001. Ofoto was one of the leading online album providers at the time and had the brand tagline 'Share Memories, Share Lives'.

Kodak's goal was to let people share their photos and memories online with friends and family — a notion that could well have become the first iteration of social media if Kodak had wholeheartedly embraced the new paradigm. Reflecting on this missed opportunity, Ofoto's founder, James Joaquin, noted that whereas social media always started with the person's *life* (with photos just being a part of it), Kodak's paradigm always started and finished with the *photo* — and they couldn't make the mental shift required to see Ofoto gain traction.[3]

The reality is that if Kodak had been a startup company at the onset of the digital age rather than a publicly listed bureaucratic behemoth, they would have immediately jumped at the opportunities and possibilities that digital photography offered. However, compared with the fat margins that the traditional film business afforded Kodak, embracing digital photography could never compete financially.[4]

It is hard to overstate the missed opportunity for the company that turned memorable moments into Kodak moments. Today, more photos are taken every two minutes than in all of the nineteenth century.[5] Kodak could have driven the modern age of digital memory preservation but instead they were decimated by it because their paradigm was so anchored to the past.

While it's easy to find fault in the strategic blunders of a brand such as Kodak, even legendary innovator Apple has grappled with the challenge of being shackled by outmoded paradigms.

Despite having thoroughly disrupted the music industry with the iTunes store, Apple went on to become a prisoner of their own mental model. Although iTunes allowed consumers to pay a low price to purchase only the songs they wanted (rather than a whole album as they had done traditionally in music stores), the paradigm of music ownership became entrenched for Apple.

When Pandora and then Spotify came along with streaming services, allowing consumers to merely pay for access to music rather than paying to own it, Apple's paradigm became a shackle. They were late to the party with their own streaming solution and have been playing catch-up ever since.

THE SHIFT TO A SUBSCRIPTION MODEL

In contrast with Apple's resistance to embracing a different business mindset, iconic automaker GM has embarked on a range of recent initiatives indicative of a daring new paradigm.

One of these is their Netflix-style subscription plan for car ownership released in March 2017. Known as the 'BOOK by Cadillac' program, this auto subscription service gives members access to a fleet of cars for $1500 per month—a fee that covers all the costs of car ownership but without the liability of actually owning the asset. There are no mileage restrictions on users and no lock-in contracts for members. While initially only available in the New York metro area, the program is set to be rolled out in Los Angeles and other major markets in the near term and represents a radically new approach to car use.[6]

Electric lighting giant Philips have embraced a similar approach in responding to significant disruption. With modern LED globes now lasting for up to 50000 hours (the equivalent of running for 24 hours per day for 10 years), the traditional purchase-and-replace business model is proving much less lucrative and reliable than it once was.

As a result, Philips have begun adopting a lighting-as-service subscription model where customers can pay by the hour for the lighting they use rather than invest in the hardware up-front.

This same approach saw Rolls-Royce completely transform itself from a loss-making British manufacturer to the second biggest provider of large jet engines in the world by asking the question 'What if airlines didn't buy engines for their aeroplanes but instead paid for every hour an engine runs?'[7]

THE BLESSING OF ISOLATION

In the world of banking, it is striking that some of the most impressive innovations of recent years have emerged from China—a country often dismissed as the land of copycats and fast followers. The reason for this is that the isolation of domestic banks behind the great firewall of China has given rise to new paradigms not found in Western banks.

My colleague and banking futurist Brett King points to Alibaba and Tencent, with their respective Alipay and WeChat Pay, and suggests that these successful innovations came about due to a lack of restrictive established paradigms and legacy systems. According to King, these banks approached twenty-first-century banking challenges and opportunities with an extraordinary degree of original thinking. Unlike their Western counterparts, when Alibaba and Tencent developed their payment systems, they didn't try to patch the existing banking system but rather rethought the whole payment experience from the ground up or from 'first principles'.[8]

While in the case of Chinese banks it was technological and ideological isolation that led to fresh thinking, sometimes physical distance can have the same effect.

Research has found that the capacity for radical innovation increases proportionately with each kilometre or mile you move away from a business's head office. Experts suggests this is not only because of the echo chamber of groupthink that can exist at HQ, but also a function of the fact that people at the periphery have fewer resources and therefore need to be more creative.[9]

Embracing a new paradigm is vital if you are going to avoid innovating by paving the cattle track. As Albert Einstein observed, we can't solve problems by using the same kind of thinking we used when we created them.

MORE THAN JUST A MINDSET

While shifting your paradigm can be powerful, it's only half of the equation. Revolutionary and game-changing innovation will always require a willingness to pursue new, untrodden and creative paths practically.

Consider the world of freight and logistics. In the early 1950s, the ocean-going freight industry was in rapid decline as airfreight became more popular. Adding to the industry's challenges, costs and delivery times of sea freight were increasing sharply due to congestion at docks. This led to significant pilferage as cargo and merchandise piled up at the waterfront waiting to be loaded.

The reason for this predicament was simply that for years the ocean freight industry had focused on building faster and more fuel-efficient ships while giving little thought to the bottlenecks that arose when the ships arrived at the destination port. The solution was to entirely re-work the process of loading and stowing freight stock so that these became separate activities. This new approach meant that stock could be pre-loaded away from the dock into containers, which would then be transported to the dock only once the ship was ready to receive the cargo. The results of this process innovation were dramatic: between 1955 and 1985, freighter traffic increased five-fold while costs decreased by 60 per cent and turnaround time was cut by three-quarters.[10]

A NEW-LOOK LIBRARY

When the Woollahra City Library in Sydney's eastern suburbs embarked on a multimillion-dollar renovation a few years ago, it was clear that simply re-creating a more modern version of the old facility wasn't going to cut it.

While library design has evolved very slowly in recent decades, since the early 2000s libraries worldwide have had to ask themselves some pretty difficult questions. In the digital age, what is the purpose of a library? Certainly being a solemn and silent storehouse for printed books is no longer viable — but what could they evolve to become?

The team at Woollahra set about entirely rethinking the role and purpose of a library and ended up creating a facility four times as large as the one it was replacing. This was undoubtedly a bold move when other libraries were struggling to justify their existence and the old facility had been suffering from declining visitor numbers for years.

The new Woollahra City Library is not only aesthetically impressive, with its bright, inviting and inspiring lobby replete with an enormous vertical garden, but the daily visitor count has soared to 2500 people—up from just 400 prior to the renovation. The facility itself is almost unrecognisable as a library. While there are certainly printed books on shelves, there are also video conferencing rooms, flexible co-working spaces for local freelance professionals, workshop and seminar facilities and a Microsoft Surface technology hub.

Speaking of Microsoft, the iconic software giant is in fact the perfect example of a business that got trapped in an old paradigm and paved the cattle track better than most—only to turn things around in recent years.

MICROSOFT GETS BACK ON TRACK

Microsoft reached its peak of coolness with the release of Windows 95—people lined up for days to purchase it. The software giant's momentum seemed unstoppable—even the Empire State Building was lit in Microsoft's colours. By the end of 1997, Windows 95 ran on 86.3 per cent of PCs in the United States (by contrast, Apple's Mac OS only had 4.6 per cent market share). And yet even as Microsoft seemed untouchable, Warren Buffett sounded the alarm—worrying that the tech giant might fall prey to the very dynamics that had dethroned IBM a decade earlier.[11]

It was a prescient observation. As Josh Linkner puts it, 'Most large organisations exist to protect old ideas, not create new ones'.[12] This was certainly a trap Microsoft fell into as time went on.

The New York Times' Joe Nocera describes how this dynamic unfolded at Microsoft during the 1990s. When its Windows operating system and Office applications became enormous moneymakers, the company changed its strategy to protect the two cash cows. However, as soon as the company began defending rather than building, it became vulnerable to newer, nimbler competitors focused on creating something different, instead of 'milking the old'.[13]

So much energy was used to stop fresh innovations and instead protect the castle. Often, Microsoft embraced new technologies, such as touchscreens, smart cars, smartphones and smartwatches, significantly before Apple or Google. But the software giant repeatedly killed promising projects if they turned out to be a threat to their cash cows—the cattle tracks were so well paved they couldn't see any other paths.[14] The cost of missing the early opportunity of smartphones alone is hard to estimate, considering that by the middle of 2012 the iPhone was earning more revenue per quarter than the entirety of Microsoft.[15]

Former Microsoft executive Steve Stone recounted an experience in 1998 when programmers showed Bill Gates a prototype for a revolutionary software innovation. Gates gave it the thumbs down, saying it didn't 'look like Windows'. According to Stone, this mindset permeated the entire company, causing it to miss numerous emerging technologies.

'Windows was God,' Stone says. 'Everything had to work with Windows.'[16]

On top of this Windows obsession, many of the company's challenges during the late 1990s and early 2000s arose from the fact that the young hot shots who had built the company in the 1980s were now middle-aged managers. 'Microsoft bosses just didn't understand the burgeoning class of computer users who hadn't been born when Microsoft first opened its doors,' was how one market analyst put it.[17]

More dangerous than the fact that managers didn't understand the next generation of computer users was the fact that those in power dismissed input from this younger cohort too. A culture developed in Microsoft during the early 2000s where young company engineers were met with disinterest or resistance when they tried to communicate to their superiors the emerging trends among their peers. 'Most senior people were out of touch with the way home users were starting to use computers, especially the younger generation,' one young Microsoft developer said. As a result, when AOL moved ahead creating its instant messenger program, AIM, Microsoft trailed a full two years behind with the release of MSN Messenger.

Even once MSN was released, entrenched paradigms caused Microsoft to miss an enormous opportunity. In the early 2000s, Microsoft inadvertently found themselves working on an innovation that could have been a game-changing forerunner to Google AdWords. The development team had struck upon the idea of offering search-based advertising on its MSN portal. Despite the obvious benefits and, in retrospect, the massive boon this plan could have been, Microsoft's leaders canned the suggestion, citing concerns that it could draw people away from the lucrative banner advertisements that had become a cash cow for MSN. New paths and new options were shunned, along with the opportunities they represented.[18]

By 2010, things were looking grim for Microsoft.

Bing, the search engine they'd built to challenge Google, was burning cash. (By the end of 2012 it would end up costing the company in excess of \$6 billion.)[19] At the same time, smartphones were on the verge of surpassing the popularity of the device closest to Microsoft's heart (and bottom line) — the personal computer. Apple's iPad had just been released and was the hottest new tech gadget. All the while, Microsoft found themselves flailing — watching the future pass them by.

The company's then CEO Steve Ballmer realised that dramatic change was needed. The cattle tracks that had served the company well for years were now leading to dead ends. A key element of this shift in mindset focused on Microsoft seeking inspiration in some new places. Having spent much of the 2000s taking cues from and aiming to compete with Google and Apple, Microsoft shifted its sights to fellow Seattle-based giant Amazon — and the company's cloud computing division, Amazon Web Services, in particular.

Despite Amazon's formidable head start and market leadership in cloud-based computing, Microsoft spent billions in a catch-up effort. With key investments in new data centres and a full rewrite of its software for delivery via the web, it was clear that business-as-usual at Microsoft was over.

According to David Smith, an analyst with research firm Gartner, 'There was a realisation that the conventional wisdom about Microsoft was wrong. They saw the tremendous success that Amazon was having, and they adapted because of that'.

As a telling sign of just how far Microsoft had moved away from a Windows-focused paradigm, one of the first initiatives of the newly appointed CEO, Satya Nadella, in 2014 was to drop the Windows branding entirely from Microsoft's cloud-computing platform, Azure.

This departure was symbolic even more than it was strategic. It sent a powerful message to the market and signalled a change in Microsoft's internal culture. They were tearing up the paved cattle tracks. Dave Bartoletti, an analyst at Forrester, said the move essentially communicated that Microsoft's future business was going to be all about the cloud and that the company had to 'move away from the shackles that they were tied to in Windows'.[20]

Recent years have seen Microsoft's leaders take significant steps toward rebooting the software giant's culture. Nadella has made huge inroads in stamping out what he described as an 'unhealthy arrogance' about the company's past successes.[21] He has also been willing to cut jobs and favour innovation over existing businesses.[22]

Microsoft's spate of acquisitions since Nadella's appointment is again a clear indication of how far the company has come from its protectionist days as an organisation that shied away from buying technology. Microsoft's acquisition list is as long as it is impressive, but most significant of all was the $26 billion purchase of social networking giant LinkedIn in late December 2016.

All of this adds up to a vastly different and significantly revitalised Microsoft. As industry leader Aaron Levie reflected in December 2016: 'In three years, [Microsoft] have turned from the backwater of IT to being front and center'.[23]

THE DANGEROUS ATTRACTION OF CATTLE TRACKS

A key reason that paving the cattle track is such an easy trap to fall into is that it is typically the path of least resistance — and it is safe.

After all, if a 'paving' innovation or initiative doesn't work as well as you'd hoped, it isn't your responsibility — you didn't make the path, after all, you only built on what was already there.

Embracing new paradigms and exploring new paths is risky and, as discussed in chapter 6, many organisations have cultures that actively discourage such risk. When that is added to our natural human tendency to opt for the safe, the proven and the predictable, you can easily see why the cattle track becomes an attractive option.

Treading new paths can unsettle those around you and even offend those who've gone before you — after all, who do you think you are to improve on what has always worked?

As celebrated American writer Stewart Brand notes: 'If imitation is the sincerest form of flattery, invention is the sincerest form of criticism'. Be prepared for others to find your innovations and initiative confronting and make peace with that reality.

∞

As we round out this chapter, I want to take a big risk myself by going where most fear to tread and challenge the great genius of Albert Einstein.

Einstein is famous for having defined insanity as doing the same thing over and over again and expecting to get a different result. I'm sure you've heard this platitude repeated many a time over the years.

However, I would suggest that in this disruptive and turbulent era, insanity is the very opposite of what Einstein suggested. I firmly believe that insanity today is doing the same thing over and over again expecting to get the *same* result.

What I mean is that if you are simply repeating the same tactics, techniques and approaches that worked last year or five years ago, expecting them to be as effective today, you're going to be sorely mistaken. In fact, you'd be crazy to think they'd still work as well.

The world is changing... and fast. As such, we can't just repeat the success formulas of the past or merely tweak and improve them. Rather, staying in the game and at the cutting edge amid rampant disruption will require embracing new paradigms and exploring new paths. The cattle track of old may take you somewhere, but it's unlikely to be a place you'll want to end up.

Questions for reflection

∞ In what ways have you seen cattle tracks being paved over the years?

∞ What elements of your organisation's daily operations may need a fundamental rethink rather than a superficial retread?

∞ If you were starting from scratch or from 'first principles', what would you change in your business or organisation?

∞ Who might be a good source of input or ideas owing to the fact that they are removed from the epicentre of power in the organisation?

∞ What existing assumptions or paradigms could become shackles in the years to come?

CHAPTER 8

FOSTER HEALTHY
PARANOIA

In late 2012, just as Facebook was celebrating the milestone of having one billion users, a little red book started appearing on the desks of all its employees. The book was full of quotes and credos that captured the social media giant's core philosophy—statements such as, 'We don't build services to make money, we make money to build better services'; 'Greatness and comfort rarely coexist'; and 'Changing how people communicate will always change the world'.[1]

Capturing these sentiments was a fantastic way to ensure that the values and ethos that had made Facebook great remained front and centre as the company grew. Flicking through the pages of the little red book, however, there were two statements that stood out to me as the most remarkable. Remarkable because they are the sort of statements you rarely hear from a technology company enjoying success—much less one run by a Millennial.

The two statements were:

∞ Remember people don't use Facebook because they like us. They use it because they like their friends.

∞ If we don't create the thing that kills Facebook, someone else will.[2]

What is so inspiring about these two statements is that they powerfully capture the two characteristics of any enduringly successful organisation: *humility* and *hunger.*

When I am working with brands and organisations, I suggest that it is these two characteristics that are the most vital to cultivate and promote. And the best way to do so is by fostering healthy paranoia.

The truth is that if you have had any measure of success or notoriety, you'd do well to go into each and every day with an active awareness that you have a target painted on your back. You have competitors out there actively working to unseat your position of dominance or at least erode your market share. Furthermore, you have any number of unconventional competitors who may not even be on your radar right now but are waiting in the wings, ready to pounce.

On top of all this, you have an increasingly empowered and fickle marketplace you can't take for granted—even for a moment.

The power of healthy paranoia is that it will keep you on your A game. It is the best antidote to complacency and will ensure you identify unconventional competitive threats early on, while you are still able to adapt and respond.

There are three keys to fostering healthy paranoia that we will explore in this chapter:

1. resist the intoxicating effects of success
2. prioritise the peripheral
3. encourage diversity and dissent.

1. RESIST THE INTOXICATING EFFECTS OF SUCCESS

There are few investors who could rival Warren Buffett in his uncanny ability to pick winners.

Over the decades, Buffett has consistently outperformed the market. Yet despite this impressive track record, he has always sought to challenge his thinking and points to Charles Darwin as his inspiration in doing so.

Buffett explains how Darwin had a habit of immediately writing down any information or insight that contradicted a conclusion he had previously held. Darwin's reasoning for this was clear—unless he captured the insight quickly, his mind would naturally work to reject the discordant information in the same way a body rejects transplants. As Buffett suggests, 'Man's natural inclination is to cling to his beliefs, particularly if they are reinforced by recent experience'.[3]

Ray Dalio of the world's largest hedge-fund manager, Bridgewater Associates, is also a big believer in challenging your own assumptions. Says Dalio:

> The most powerful thing that [an investor] can do to be effective is to find people you respect who have opposite, different points of view [from yours]—and have an open-minded exchange with them about what's true and what to do about it. The more you think you know, the more closed-minded you'll be.[4]

While investors may certainly be susceptible to closed-mindedness, the reality is that all humans are prone to dismissing information, insights or threats that conflict with everything we've always known. And this tendency increases proportionately with our level of success. The greater the heights we have risen to, the more unwilling we are to question our core assumptions.

The reason for this is clear. Success tends to solidify our points of view and in many ways, this is natural. After all, if a set of assumptions and beliefs has led to triumph in the past, information or ideas outside this frame of reference will almost automatically be viewed with suspicion.

Leading Australian demographer and social researcher Hugh MacKay describes how this can easily result in closed-mindedness and tunnel vision.

> If you've adopted a rigid worldview, you tend to see everything through the filter of your convictions and, not surprisingly, you see what you're looking for. The more you use a particular theory for making sense of things, the more things seem to fit the theory.[5]

I label this dynamic 'the intoxication of success'. In examining the causal factors behind the decline of scores of businesses and brands, I found it hard to miss the role that success intoxication played.

More than merely resulting in closed-mindedness, the significant danger of success is that it can too easily lead to complacency and arrogance too.

The moment you think you've made it, you've passed it. As legendary business executive and strategist Shelly Porges observes:

> *The greatest challenge we have as we become successful is not to rest on our laurels, never feel like we've done it. The minute you feel like you've done it, that's the beginning of the end.*[6]

In order to foster a healthy sense of paranoia, it is vital to actively combat this lure of contentment and complacency. As Intel's Andy Grove was famous for saying, only the paranoid survive.

The moment you think you've made it, you've passed it.

By all means, enjoy success and celebrate milestones—but always in moderation. Examining yourself and your accomplishments with sober judgement is the key to staying humble and hungry—recognising there is always a bigger mountain to climb, always more to learn, always the chance that what worked yesterday may not work tomorrow. Toyota's mantra of 'Act like #1, think like #2' is a good example of always maintaining the paradigm and posture of a market challenger.

Like a Virgin

While Richard Branson may not exhibit the traditional hallmarks of humility, he is in fact constantly learning and always open to new ideas. He is a prolific reader and an agile thinker—always willing to change course or admit mistakes. It is this intellectual humility and appetite for growth that has kept his business empire at the cutting edge. The very act of naming his various companies and products 'Virgin' is a reminder of the humble and hungry approach Branson adopts. In his own words, the philosophy that underpins the Virgin brand is: 'I know nothing, and this will be my strength. I will develop novel solutions. You believe your experience is a strong asset, but it is really your biggest liability'.[7]

Only a posture of humility and hunger will see us able to embrace new ideas and strategies rather than arrogantly holding onto outdated or outmoded approaches. One of history's most well respected military strategists, Helmuth von Moltke, recognised this danger of arrogance. Although he always went into battle with detailed plans, von Moltke knew that a military leader had to be ready to change course once the battlefield revealed the weaknesses in his plan. 'No plan ever survived first contact with the battlefield,' he famously said.[8]

Swiss watchmakers almost miss the obvious (again)

In previous books, I have pointed to the Swiss watchmaking industry as one that was almost wiped out in the 1970s and 1980s owing to a success-borne arrogance and complacency.

When Japanese company Seiko released its Quartz-Astron watch in the late 1960s, the Swiss incumbents largely ignored the unconventional new player—dismissing Seiko's watch as a fad.[9]

The reason for such a dismissal was clear. Over the years, Swiss watchmakers had understandably developed a series of set beliefs about how watches were meant to be produced and what customers wanted in a timepiece. They confidently assumed they were the masters at creating quality watches and no-one was going to come in and tell them how to do what they did best.

This significant lack of healthy paranoia and humility had a dramatic effect. While in the early 1970s the Swiss were manufacturing half of the world's timepieces, by the mid 1980s the industry was in crisis, having shed 70 per cent of its workforce and seeing two-thirds of manufacturers close their doors.[10]

Interestingly, recent years have seen almost the same mistake being made as Swiss watchmakers have encountered a new wave of disruption in the timepiece market—smartwatches.

When smartwatches first started becoming mainstream in 2014, in a sentiment that echoed his predecessors four decades before, Francois Thiébaud, the head of Swiss watch giant Tissot, stated defiantly at a watch fair in Basel, 'We're not interested in launching a gadget watch. We like to focus on our core business instead of meandering'. The heads of rival watchmakers Patek Philippe and La Montre Hermes also went on record to suggest that smartwatches did not represent a threat for their businesses.[11]

Tellingly, these statements were made at the very time Credit Suisse released a forecast estimating the wearable electronics market would reach $US50 billion by 2017.[12]

Fast forward to that very year, and the attitudes of the Swiss had changed significantly. At the time of writing, almost every major Swiss manufacturer has embraced wearable technology in a big way. Everyone, from Alpina and Frederique Constant to Mondaine, TAG Heuer and Montblanc has released app-enabled smartwatches that combine classic Swiss design quality and cutting-edge functionality.

Even Tissot have joined the smartwatch party with the release of their own range of timepieces to rival the Apple Watch. This is certainly a dramatic about-face for a company that dismissed 'gadget watches' as strategic 'meandering' just a few years previously.[13]

A notable exception to this embrace of smartwatches is Tissot's brand sibling, Omega (also a part of the Swatch empire). Omega's chief executive, Raynald Aeschlimann still contends that smartwatches hold little appeal and make no sense for them, as the world's second largest watchmaker, to make. 'We don't build phones so why should we build a phone for the wrist?' he argues.

While it may well be that Aeschlimann's aversion to connected technology is part of a differentiation strategy, it's hard not to feel that such an attitude reflects that same naivety and complacency that brought the Swiss timepiece industry to its knees in the 1970s. Tellingly, his comments came during a two-year slump in sales for Swiss watch brands—the sharpest fall since the depths of the Seiko crisis.[14]

The iPhone's success — blessing or curse?

Despite being a key part of the very disruption affecting the timepiece industry, there are strong indications that Apple themselves are falling prey to the intoxicating effects of success. Although Apple's stock price has soared in the years since Tim Cook took the reins, the company has failed to deliver a breakthrough product on par with those that were released under Steve Jobs (including the iPod, iPhone and iPad). Apple TV has widely failed to live up to expectations, the Apple Watch has certainly been successful but not a market redefining product, and recent MacBook releases have failed to dazzle a market increasingly drawn to Microsoft's Surface Pro range.

Analysts point to the very success of the iPhone as a key reason Apple have lost their innovative edge. Widely regarded as the most successful consumer product in history, the iPhone accounts for a huge proportion of Apple's revenue and therefore dominates much of the company's focus. According to former Apple executives, the iPhone's success has 'inhibited the company's ability to develop products untethered from the phone'.

Holger Mueller, a principal analyst at Constellation Research points to Siri as a textbook example of 'leading on something in tech and then losing that edge despite having all the money and the talent...sitting in Silicon Valley'.[15] Despite being ahead of the pack at the time of Siri's launch, Apple have been late to the wider voice-activation party. Amazon have sprinted ahead, dominating the voice-activated market, releasing their Echo speaker a full 2.5 years before Apple's competing HomePod device.[16]

How to know if you're drunk on success

In his book *What Matters Now*, Gary Hamel outlines five signs that success intoxication could be setting in[17]:

1. *Defensive thinking.* When you're at the peak of an industry, it's easy to become defensive and the focus becomes on guarding and protecting rather than building — to move from being entrepreneurial to custodial. As a result, bold new ideas are viewed through the lens of how they may threaten or 'affect the base'.

2. *Inflexible business systems.* Over time the organisation becomes obsessed with continuous improvement and exploitation of what exists over what could be. Additionally, the more specialised and fixed the key assets or skills become, the less adaptable the organisation becomes. Efficiency and predictability come at the cost of agility.

3. *Fossilised mental models.* As we explored in the previous pages, closed-mindedness or a fixed paradigm is a key indication of success intoxication. What was once the 'best' way becomes seen as the 'only' way. As Nike's CEO Mark Parker suggests, 'Companies fall apart when their model is so successful that it stifles any thinking that challenges it'.[18]

4. *Abundant resources.* If necessity is the mother of invention, prosperity is the mother of complacency. Having a significant war chest of cash and resources can create a belief that ongoing dominance and success can come by outspending rivals rather than outthinking them. Abundance can also erode any sense of urgency, which can result in critical windows for taking action being missed.

5. *Contentment and entitlement.* The longer you're at the top, the harder it is to imagine that you won't always be — a sense that continued success is preordained can easily set in. Further still, mature organisations often end up being run by people who have never built a business from scratch and therefore they lack the skills and paradigm required to maintain a growth edge. Hamel likens executives of this mould to the loyal and well-mannered children of wealthy parents who come to believe they deserve a good inheritance but often lack the skills or desire to multiply that fortune.

In his book *Innovation and Entrepreneurship*, Peter Drucker describes that when key players have remained unchallenged for a long time, arrogance inevitably creeps in. Clinging to historical and increasingly dysfunctional practices, incumbents tend to ignore or even scoff at new market entrants until the more agile and responsive startups begin eroding the dominance of established players. Typically, at this point, the incumbents take action but often find that it is too late.[19]

Staying alert to the intoxicating effects of success is a vital first step to fostering healthy paranoia. As in the real world, drunkenness is always easy to identify in others but can be nearly impossible to discern in oneself. It pays to have trusted individuals around you who can offer a perspective of sobriety and objectivity.

Regardless of whether it is expressed in the form of complacency, conceit or closed-mindedness, becoming intoxicated by success will always leave organisations and leaders with a nasty hangover when they finally do wake up ... hopefully before it's too late.

2. PRIORITISE THE PERIPHERAL

One of the most formative activities of my teen years was a four-year stint as a military cadet. At an age when many adolescents tend to drift toward rebellion and individuality, being a cadet encouraged the very opposite—conformity, compliance, team dependence and resilience.

For some reason, the whole military mindset clicked for me. I quickly climbed the ranks and found myself as a unit leader. As a high-ranking cadet, one of my responsibilities at our weekly meetings was to conduct a 30-minute marching drill routine on the parade ground.

From my earliest days as a cadet, I had learned that the most important skill for marching in formation was peripheral vision. Maintaining straight-line ranks and keeping in step required a constant awareness of what was happening to your left or right without breaking the formal stance by turning your head.

As I moved into a training role, I quickly discovered that many new cadets found that using their peripheral vision was quite a challenging skill to master. After all, humans naturally recognise and focus on the things in our central range of vision. However, honing and strengthening our peripheral vision is like a muscle—it takes time and concentrated effort.

In much the same way, honing and strengthening our peripheral vision in a business context can be extraordinarily powerful, but it does take practice.

As explored in chapter 3, many of the key disruptive threats that you will need to contend with in the years to come will emerge from the periphery. As such, fostering healthy paranoia will require a constant awareness and sensitivity to what is outside your direct frame of view.

Rather than seeking out a telescope we'd be better to reach for a wide-angle lens.

I recently heard it said that many business leaders today are looking through the wrong lens when trying to identify disruption. Rather than seeking out a telescope with which we scan the horizon, we'd be better to reach for a wide-angle lens that will help us monitor the periphery.

The taxi industry in Australia offers a powerful case study on the importance of peripheral vision. While many business commentators are quick to suggest that it was a lack of foresight and innovation that left taxi operators vulnerable to the disruption of Uber, the real story is a little more nuanced.

Having worked with the taxi industry a few times in recent years, I was surprised to learn just how innovative and far-sighted they had actually been. For instance, they were the first businesses to introduce mobile credit card payment solutions in the 1980s—long before many retailers had even imagined wireless card transactions. Taxis were also the first organisation outside the military to use vehicle GPS tracking. They had even developed mobile apps for booking cars and managing payments many years before Uber came onto the scene.

That said, the industry was never expecting a technology-driven ride-sharing service to enter out of left field and upend the industry overnight. In honesty, there are few who could have predicted such an unconventional competitor could enter and so quickly dominate the market. And yet that's just what happened.

So it wasn't long-range vision but rather peripheral awareness that the taxi industry lacked. Had they been more focused on the periphery, they could have identified Uber early on rather than waiting until it became an existential threat.

THREE WAYS TO DEVELOP YOUR PERIPHERAL VISION

Develop your peripheral vision by looking outside your:

i.   industry

ii. context

iii. assumptions.

i. Look outside your industry

One of the great challenges in any established industry is that players in a sector begin to look, think and operate in a very similar way—a phenomenon often referred to as strategy convergence.[20]

The reasons for this are quite simple. Companies:

∞ tend to engage the same consulting firms to work with them

∞ hire talent from the same pool of graduates or alumni

∞ tend to read the same books and subscribe to the same journals

∞ attend the same conferences.

The result is a degree of industry groupthink where, to borrow a metaphor from horse racing, every company ends up wearing the same strategic blinkers while all assuming they are running a very individual race.

To expand your peripheral vision, you need to take your industry blinkers off. You need to look at industries entirely unrelated to your own in order to identify lessons you can learn or inspiration you could glean. You may need to read unconventional books, subscribe to unconventional magazines and attend unconventional conferences if you want to identify unconventional threats and opportunities.

> **To expand your peripheral vision, you need to take your industry blinkers off.**

Apple are the most profitable retailers in the world partly because when they went into the retail space, they didn't look to other retailers for inspiration but looked outside of the industry. In the words of Ron Johnson, who designed Apple's retail stores:

We wanted to create very distinct experiences for customers in what they perceive as a public place. More like a great library, which has natural light, and feels like a gift to the community.

Beyond library-inspired aesthetics, Apple's retail experience was also informed by a non-retail business. It was the Ritz-Carlton's approach to concierge customer service that gave rise to Apple's Genius Bar and store greeters.[21]

The key question is this: who are you looking to and benchmarking yourself against? If it is others in your marketplace or industry, you may not be looking far and wide enough to get the inspiration and insights necessary to pre-empt distruption.

ii. Look outside your context

Recent years have seen businesses spend staggering sums of money sending executive teams on technology pilgrimages to Silicon Valley. While these trips can sometimes appear to be little more than junkets, when approached well they can lead to powerful insights.

For the foreseeable future, certain locations, such as Silicon Valley and Seattle, will remain the world's engine rooms of innovation so periodic visits to get a glimpse of the technology and thinking shaping tomorrow can pay enormous dividends. Beyond getting concrete innovation ideas and inspiration, trips such as these can powerfully shift paradigms and build a healthy sense of urgency (and paranoia).

Annual technology events such as the Consumer Electronics Show held each January in Las Vegas, the annual South by Southwest festival in Austin, Texas, or TechCrunch Disrupt in New York can have a similar horizon-broadening effect.

iii. Look outside your assumptions

The third way to hone your peripheral vision is to challenge the assumptions that may have limited your frame of reference previously.

In his insightful book *How to Use Innovation & Creativity in the Workplace*, Patrick Collister suggests a range of questions to help challenge assumptions long held by an individual or group.

The first step is to identify a core assumption that seems axiomatically true — one that is even absurd to question. For example,

∞ 'Our customers would never pay more than $x for our product'

∞ 'The x and y markets would never be a viable option for expansion'

∞ 'A new player in our market would take at least x years to become a serious competitor'.

Once you have established the assumption that represents your view of what is possible, reasonable and logical, ask questions such as those Patrick Collister lays out in his book[22]:

∞ Who says this is true — what's the source of our conventional wisdom?

∞ What led me/us to draw this conclusion in the first place?

∞ Is there any evidence that this assumption is still true (or was ever true)?

∞ What would Google/Apple/McDonald's/Amazon/Virgin do in this situation?

∞ What would the unthinkable thing to do right now be?

Andy Grove famously challenged core assumptions in much this way during the 1980s when it became increasingly clear that Intel's highly successful DRAM memory-chip business was doomed. Grove turned to co-founder Gordon Moore and posed the hypothetical question, 'If we got kicked out and the board brought in a new CEO, what do you think he would do?'

Without hesitation, Moore answered, 'He would get us out of the memory business'. After a moment's reflection, Grove replied, 'Well, why shouldn't you and I walk out the door, come back and do it ourselves?' And that's what they did.[23] They in turn shifted Intel's focus from memory chips to microprocessing, and within a few years dominated this emerging technology.[24]

In the words of British philosopher and Nobel laureate Bertrand Russell, 'In all affairs, it is a healthy thing to hang a question mark on the things you have long taken for granted'.

3. ENCOURAGE DIVERSITY AND DISSENT

As we have just explored, one of the keys to fostering healthy paranoia is to combat the blinkered thinking that can result from an industry talent pool becoming specialised and homogenous over time.

Picking up on that theme, the importance of diversity and divergent perspectives in a team is hard to overstate.

Psychologist Irving Janis argues that the lack of diversity in a group insulates it from outside opinion and convinces members over time that the group's judgement on important issues must be right. These kinds of groups, Janis suggests, share 'an illusion of invulnerability and a willingness to rationalize away possible counter-arguments to the group's position'.[25]

Put simply, the last thing homogenous groups tend to be is healthily paranoid.

It's important to acknowledge that building diversity in a team or organisation doesn't happen naturally. We humans tend to surround ourselves with people who look like us, think like us and operate like us.

As a colleague of mine repeatedly tells his clients: 'Don't hire someone like you—you already know what you think'. And he's right. Bill Bernbach credits much of the extraordinary growth and success of ad agency DDB to his strategy of hiring outside the recognised talent pool of the period. While most other ad agencies were predominantly white and male, Bernbach bucked the trend and attracted a far more diverse and creative cohort.[26]

In his book *Why Good Companies Go Bad,* Donald Sull argues that conformity in leadership played a key role in the woes of companies such as Firestone Tires, Compaq and failed automaker Daewoo. Prior to their fall from greatness, Sull suggests that these companies' respective leadership teams had become 'like clones', each executive tending to reinforce a collegial point of view. In the case of Daewoo in particular, six in 10 of the company's senior management graduated from the same university, and almost one-third graduated from the same high school.[27]

Sull suggests that organisations, particularly those with longevity and success behind them, do a 'clone test' in an effort to combat such inbreeding. He encourages management teams to do a quick survey of those in leadership and ponder questions such as[28]:

∞ What is the executive team's gender breakdown?

∞ What is its average age?

∞ How many leaders rose from within the organisation?

∞ How many dress in similar ways?

∞ How many look physically similar?

∞ How many come from a similar background?

∞ How many share a common alma mater?

∞ How many socialise outside work hours?

Underscoring the importance of diversity, a recent McKinsey & Company study of 366 public companies worldwide found that companies with women and minorities in their upper ranks performed better financially. Where leadership was gender diverse, businesses were 15 per cent more likely to report returns above the average for their industry, and an even more striking link was found between business success and ethnic diversity.[29]

That said, while gender and ethnic diversity are valuable and worthy goals, it is having diversity of *perspective* rather than diversity of *profile* that matters most in fostering healthy paranoia.

The permission to speak up

Something dangerous occurs when a culture goes from being cohesive to being conformist.

While diversity is half of the solution to preventing collective blind spots, the role of dissent is equally important. After all, what is the point of having diverse perspectives if people don't feel empowered to speak up and point out threats and opportunities that others in the group have ignored or missed?

While every leader should aim to build a cohesive culture in their team or organisation, something dangerous occurs when a culture goes from being cohesive to being conformist. By the same token, team alignment is a wonderful thing—but perfect alignment forbids divergent thinking.

Peter Drucker went as far as to say that good decisions are always a function of dissenting views being encouraged and heard. 'The first rule in decision-making,' he suggested, 'is that one does not make a decision unless there is disagreement'.[30]

Naturally, for such an approach to work, a culture has to be created where junior members of staff feel safe and encouraged to 'speak truth to power'.[31]

Leaders must ensure that those who hold radically different views or bear confronting news are encouraged rather than ignored, shunned or persecuted.

There is little doubt that homogeneity in an organisation or team can be convenient and expedient. After all, it facilitates communication, makes cohesion and unity a less nuanced process and speeds up decision making. However, the trade-off is enormous. A lack of diversity leaves any team highly vulnerable—and, as in nature, lack of diversity limits your ability to adapt and change.[32]

∞

Fostering healthy paranoia is absolutely vital if you are to stay on your A game and avoid the classic pitfalls of complacency and arrogance.

As Tim Harford argues in his book *Adapt*, 'It isn't that successful individuals or organisations lack the *capacity* to innovate, but rather that they lack the *will* to do so'.[33] There is nothing like operating with an awareness that you have a target painted on your back to create the hunger and desire necessary to stay one step ahead.

Questions for reflection

∞ Inserting your own organisation's name, complete this sentence: *If we don't create the thing that kills _____, someone else will.*
How would operating with this mindset change things for you or your organisation on a daily basis?

∞ How humble and hungry would you say your organisation is?

∞ What indications of success intoxication exist in your organisation (e.g. closed-mindedness, complacency, conceit)?

∞ How could you actively prioritise the peripheral by looking outside your industry, your context or your assumptions?

∞ How could you look to promote diverse perspectives and dissenting views in decision making?

CHAPTER 9

FOCUS
ON FRICTION

When Skype's first official employee, Taavet Hinrikus, was posted to London from the company's home country of Estonia, he quickly discovered one of the perennial frustrations of expat life— getting paid.

Hinrikus's salary was still coming through his bank account in Estonia and so each month he had to go to his Estonian bank to ask it to wire his money to his bank in London. The first time he did it, he wired 1000 euros but by the time the funds showed up, four days later, the money in Hinrikus's account was a full £50 less than he had calculated based on currency exchange rates minus the £20 transfer fee. When he started asking questions, he discovered that the missing money was a result of costs that the bank charged on top of the remittance fee.

'That's what really pissed me off. [The bank] was just not being honest about it, not being transparent. I didn't think that was fair,' Hinrikus recalls.

Venting his indignation to fellow expat Estonian Kristo Käärmann, the pair hatched a plan to stick it to the banks and set up a rival foreign currency platform. The result was Transferwise—today one of the biggest and best-known fintech startups in the world.

In case you're unaware, the way Transferwise works is that it is a peer-to-peer currency-trading platform. For example, if I have AUD and want to send USD, Transferwise will match me with people who want AUD in exchange for their USD. It's a genius but simple idea that costs 0.5 to 1 per cent in transfer fees (compared to banks and traditional money transfer firms such as Western Union who charge between 5 and 10 per cent of the remittance amount). Better yet, exchanges in Transferwise occur almost instantaneously as opposed to the three to four day lag time with traditional bank wires.

Reflecting on the precedent platforms such as Transferwise have set for other fintech startups, Hinrikus predicts that by the mid 2020s, 30 per cent of financial services in the world will be owned by tech companies. Speaking at the 2016 Tech in Asia conference in Tokyo, Hinrikus had tough things to say about the banking industry. He said its business model is 'outdated' and will start 'crumbling and falling apart'. According to Hinrikus, even if banks adopt technology, they will tend to do so in order to serve their own interests and not the interests of customers. 'Customers know that,' he said. He noted that services from banks no longer suit customers and that fintech startups 'can offer cheaper, faster, and better services—options that weren't really available before'.[1]

I had to smile when I read Hinrikus's words, because it was the very week that my wife and I were transferring our mortgage from one banking lender to another. We'd already filled out countless forms and gone through the onerous account setup process where everything but our blood type needed to be verified. Then came the final step of transferring the funds in our mortgage offset account to our new bank.

I foolishly assumed that transferring the cash would be a relatively straightforward process. How wrong I was. The first hurdle was an impossibly low daily transfer limit. A note on the bank's website directed me to a three-page form I could complete and fax to the bank to increase my daily limit. The form advised me that the request would likely take one to two days to process. Alternatively, I could visit a local branch and have the limit adjusted manually. Without two days to spare (and having not owned a fax machine for well over a decade), I opted for the latter option.

Three separate trips to the bank branch over the next three days, and the transfer limit remained unchanged despite the branch manager's repeated assurances after each visit that it would only take a few hours to come into effect.

Exasperated and running out of time, I ended up transferring the money piecemeal to multiple accounts and then manually consolidating it in the new mortgage account.

I share this not as a rant but to highlight an experience that is all too common. In fact, I know you would be able to share your own remarkably similar story. We have all experienced the friction involved in dealing with businesses large and small—not to mention government departments!

Even if you are unfamiliar with the term 'friction' in a customer experience sense, you are familiar with the sensation. Friction is the stuff that makes it hard to engage with a business. It adds unnecessary complexity, frustration, cost, bureaucracy, confusion and inefficiency.

There was a time when friction was unavoidable and even an assumed part of everyday life. However, as discussed in chapter 2, if the age of empowered consumers has taught us anything, it is that friction is no longer something we need to put up with. We have options, information and a voice—which is leaving businesses that create friction increasingly unviable and threatened.

While banks are far from the only ones who have created customer friction over the years, they have done it better than most. In the merchant payments arena, banks and credit card providers have earned a fortune adding friction and cost to the transaction process and have got away with it because consumers didn't have an alternative. For instance, when you or I purchase an item at a store, the merchant is charged two broad types of fees. The first are fees paid to the merchant account providers, who act as the middlemen between the merchant and the bank. The second round of fees is the larger of the two.

> **Friction adds unnecessary complexity, frustration, cost, bureaucracy, confusion and inefficiency.**

Often referred to as 'interchange fees', these are paid directly to credit card companies. The structure of these fees is confusing—perhaps deliberately so—and varies based on the type of business the merchant runs, monthly sale volumes and the various credit card rewards programs offered by the card provider. To give a sense of just how confusing the whole setup is, Mastercard's policy document on interchange fees is more than 100 pages thick.[2]

The friction-ridden world of merchant services was the fertile ground that saw point-of-sale provider Square enter the market. Founded by legendary disruptor Jack Dorsey, Square came onto the scene in 2009 with the goal of radically simplifying the process of taking payments. Their fee structure was straightforward and their technology interface was easy to use and required minimal investment to set up.[3]

Naturally, Square represents a significant threat to the established players. However, in the words of JP Morgan's CEO, Jamie Dimon, since tech startups are 'very good at reducing the pain points' for customers they can teach traditional banks a lot.[4]

WHEN FRICTION BECOMES A FOOTHOLD

Beyond the imperative of improving consumer experience, no business or industry can ignore friction today because it is the very thing that gives disruptors a foothold. Where friction exists, so does the opportunity for a hungry new entrant to edge into the market—Transferwise and Square are both cases in point.

Considering that friction so significantly detracts from the consumer experience and can leave a business vulnerable to disruption, you'd be forgiven for wondering why businesses don't focus on addressing it more enthusiastically.

The answer? Because many businesses either fail to see friction or are actually benefitting from it in a big way.

Companies that have grown fat on the margins that friction offers will fight hard to protect their business models. When disruptors enter or technology empowers consumers with information and options, incumbents often lobby government to regulate and protect the market. Alternatively, they will make switching costs and administrative processes so onerous that consumers can't be bothered with the fuss of changing to a new competitor. At other times, the fear of the new is the key protective tactic used by incumbents: as we saw with taxi companies when they actively campaigned on the perceived dangers of ride-sharing services such as Uber.

While these ploys may work for a while, they are ultimately doomed to fail. The tide will not be held back forever. Empowered consumers will eventually grow tired of friction when frictionless alternatives abound.

THE MOST POWERFUL INNOVATION SKILL BEGINS WITH AN 'E'

Rather than waiting to deal with friction until disruptors leave you no other choice, smart organisations and leaders will adopt a more proactive approach.

Regardless of the industry or business you are in, the most important ingredient to identifying and addressing friction is *empathy*. Simply stepping into the shoes of your customers and experiencing things from their perspective can offer the most extraordinary insights—especially from an innovation standpoint.

> The most important ingredient to identifying and addressing friction is *empathy.*

Sony's legendary co-founder Akio Morita was renowned for avoiding or ignoring quantitative market research, but rather invented and innovated in response to observations of what customers did or didn't do. It was this process of stepping into the customer's world and seeing things from their perspective that was key in Morita inventing products such as the Walkman and the Discman.[5]

MAKING THE CUSTOMER THE BOSS

Innovation giant Procter & Gamble (P&G) also realised the importance of empathy following a dramatic dip in company earnings a few years ago. The financial result was the worst the company had experienced since World War II and it sent stock prices plummeting 31 per cent overnight. Against this turbulent backdrop, new CEO A.G. Lafley was tasked with turning things around.

Lafley instantly set about returning P&G's culture to one of external focus. Historically the company had been famous for making decisions based on deep customer understanding but over the years it had gradually become more inward-looking. 'We were all so busy every day,' Lafley admits:

We had our ears in our cell phones, our heads in our computer screens and we were consumed in meetings of all kinds. When you thought about it, our face was internal and our behind was facing the customer.

In an effort to address this culture, Lafley instigated a new company mantra: 'The customer is boss'. This was significant. Lafley was making it clear to staff that he as CEO was not the boss. Nor were the board of directors, the shareholders or even line managers. The only boss that mattered was the customer.

He urged staff to focus on what he called the two moments of truth for consumers: the moment they purchase a product and the moment they use it. He knew that P&G needed to learn more about both these moments of truth.

In the months that followed, staff throughout the organisation became obsessed with empathising with the customer — to the extent of spending time living with them, shopping with them and working alongside them.

Many of P&G's more legendary products in recent years came as a result of this empathy obsession. For instance, the Swiffer product range originated from watching a woman grow frustrated when she spilled coffee grounds on her kitchen floor.[6]

Empathy was similarly helpful in enabling Chinese electronic manufacturer Transsion Holdings to overtake Apple and Samsung to become the number one player in Africa's fast-growing smartphone market. Rather than approaching the African market with the same consumer assumptions that had applied in an Asian context, Transsion set out to identify the key friction points for African smartphone users.

The first key discovery they made in this process was that African consumers tended to carry around multiple SIM cards in order to avoid making expensive out-of-network calls. The second insight was that existing smartphone cameras often struggled to highlight the facial features of people with dark skin tones.

Armed with these insights, Transsion released a range of dual SIM-card smartphones that featured cameras that boosted photo clarity by allowing more light exposure.

It paid off. In 2016, Transsion had achieved 38 per cent market share in Africa and took Samsung's previous leadership position.[7]

THE POWER OF OBSERVATION

While empathy is critical for addressing the friction in a customer's daily life, it is even more critical when identifying the friction that is affecting their experience with your business.

A colleague of mine in the UK by the name of Peter Knight shares a powerful story that models this very principle.

Peter recounts the case of business strategist Mark Robb, who was working with the team at Costa Coffee a few years ago. Upon Mark's appointment, the clear brief from the company's leadership was that their outlets needed to increase per-store sales. While strategy discussions around the board table had centred on achieving this through widening food selection, adjusting coffee pricing, and updating décor and café ambiance, the key factor holding back Costa's per-store sales was something no-one imagined.

Deciding to get away from the echo chamber of HQ, Mark Robb sat himself down one day in one of Costa's busier outlets and began to simply observe the behaviour of customers.

It was about 11 am and the café was busy but not full. Mark noticed a young woman who walked in, had a quick look around and then turned around and walked straight back out the door. Assuming the customer had turned up to meet someone at the wrong place or the wrong time, Mark thought little of it. Then a few minutes later it happened again. Within 10 minutes this very same scenario of people walking in, looking around then leaving the café had occurred three times.

Intrigued as to what was going on, Mark started to ask a few questions and discovered, much to his surprise, that the reason customers were doing this had nothing to do with the coffee pricing, the food range or even the décor. Rather, the customers had work to do on their laptops and when they entered the café, they quickly scanned to see if any of the tables within reach of a power-point were available. When they discovered all the 'power-point tables' were occupied, they promptly left.

Taking this insight back to the leadership team, the decision was made to double the number of powerpoints in Costa cafés and within months sales had increased a staggering 20 per cent.[8]

Interestingly, poring over data at head office would likely have never revealed this insight. In fact, it might have resulted in leaders drawing inaccurate conclusions that may well have been counterproductive — it could have resulted in expensive overhauls of things that had no impact on the bottom line.

In reality, an over-reliance on data can often be half the problem in business. As Scott Cook, founder and chairman of accounting software giant Intuit, admits, 'For every one of our failures, we had spreadsheets that looked awesome'.[9]

In an age of empowered consumers, no business can take their market for granted.

The key message is this: in an age of empowered consumers, no business can take their market for granted. While analysing consumer data can sometimes be helpful, there is nothing as powerful as genuinely empathising with consumers in order to recognise and address the points of friction that are affecting their lives and the experience of dealing with your organisation.

THREE QUESTIONS FOR IDENTIFYING FRICTION

While empathising with and observing consumers is valuable in and of itself, if you are to successfully navigate disruption in the years to come, there are three questions you must keep front of mind when looking to identify friction:

i. What is creating frustration?

ii. What is creating inefficiency?

iii. What is creating complexity?

i. What is creating frustration?

A great example of a company identifying and addressing the frustrations friction can cause is pharmaceutical giant Novartis.

A few years ago an elderly woman who formed part of a company focus group on anti-inflammatory drugs shared her frustration about not being able to reach her back in order to apply the treatment. She explained that because she lived alone and had no-one to help her, she had resorted to smearing the gel on her shower door and rubbing her back against it. As humiliating and impractical as the improvised solution was, it was all she had found that would work.

Shocked by the revelation, the product design team at Novartis immediately got to work and invented a special applicator to be included with all future back pain gels so that people could apply them without assistance.[10]

I love this story not just because of its humanity but because it demonstrates the key question any business must ask if they are to stay one step ahead of disruption: What is frustrating our customers?

> **Smart leaders also look to identify the improvisations or 'hacks' that customers are coming up with.**

Going one step further than identifying the frustrations, smart leaders also look to identify the improvisations or 'hacks' that customers are coming up with. These can be an invaluable source of innovation insight, as Novartis discovered.

Working with a large hotel chain recently, I learned that they had discovered the value of observing the ways their customers improvised. Over the years, the hotel staff had noticed that guests would tend to slip their room key into their phone case so as not to lose it or have another item to carry. The thin plastic of the phone case meant the magnetic card could still be used to open the hotel room door, but it was far from an ideal solution.

This customer behaviour got them thinking about a way to actually turn customers' smartphones into room keys.[11] A simple but genius response to customer improvisation.

Experience is king

One of the reasons businesses cannot ignore frustration-driven friction today is that experience is king. Read any consumer review site and you'll see that the most common posts and ratings relate to a customer's experience — not simply price or quality.

Today it is the *experience* a business creates that can make or break them.

Retailers are only now waking up to this fact. While price comparability certainly matters and consumers are looking for value, as shown in chapter 2, today it is the *experience* a business creates that can make or break them.

Amazon have set the bar pretty high on a friction-free customer experience. Features such as personalised product recommendations, easy-access buyer reviews and the newly launched try-before-you buy Amazon Prime Wardrobe have transformed and permanently raised customer expectations. Added to this, Amazon's speed of delivery is matched by the speed of access. Recent data indicates that 40 per cent of online customers will abandon a website that takes more than three seconds to load. This is a significant statistic when you consider the website load-time for an average retailer clocks in at 10.9 seconds (compared to Amazon's 2.8 seconds).[12]

For Amazon, the customer experience is everything.[13]

The new normal

To reinforce a theme touched on in chapter 2, businesses today would do well to remember that a customer's most recent exceptional experience will become their new expectation of normal.

Uber are the perfect demonstration of this principle. Prior to the advent of ride-sharing, nobody got particularly frustrated with the process of booking a taxi over the phone or web and then waiting an unspecified amount of time for it to arrive.

Then along came Uber with an app that not only made booking a car quick and easy but also allowed us to track the progress of our driver as they approached—and even allowed us to give them a satisfaction rating at the conclusion of the journey. If you remember your very first Uber ride, you'll likely recall how impressed you were with the whole experience. Before you knew it, however, this level of convenience became the new standard.

Working with one of Australia's largest roadside assistance businesses a few months ago, I learned that in recent years they have overhauled their customer app so that drivers can track the assistance vehicle as they wait stranded by the side of the road. 'Uber meant customers now expect and even demand this,' the company CEO shared with me. 'In the past they didn't even know such a thing was possible, but now such a feature is simply a given'.

Become your own customer

If you want to get a clear idea of what is creating frustration-driven friction for your customers, try going beyond empathising with and observing your customers and actually *become* one.

I was working with the marketing team of a large bank recently, and a team member named Gary shared how much he learned from being a customer of the bank he worked for.

Having opened a new account, Gary tried to log in to the account only to be greeted by a pop-up window asking him to enter a security token number. Having no idea what a security token number was or how to get one, he rang his own company's customer support line. After waiting to speak to someone for well over 20 minutes, the help desk assistant informed him that he would only receive a security token number after he had logged in for the first time. 'We get this question all the time,' the help desk assistant admitted. 'I wish they'd just put a note on the website to let people know to click the button to skip the security token window for their first login.'

The next day at work, Gary tracked down the person in charge of the company's customer website and shared his experience — urging the IT team to clear up something that was a simple oversight but was causing immense frustration to the people they ought to value most — new customers.

ii. What is creating inefficiency?

Speaking with the admin manager for a large law firm recently, I was flabbergasted to hear just how stuck in the past the legal profession often is. 'In my firm,' she said, 'there is a company-wide policy that not a single email can be sent to a client without a partner reading and approving it'.

I was aghast. Every single email? 'Yep, every email,' she said.

Red tape, paperwork and bureaucracy truly are the unholy trinity of friction.

She went on to admit that staff routinely found workarounds for the rule or simply ignored it, but that, even still, the rule was significantly affecting the speed of response to clients (not to mention adding costs).

The reality is that friction in an organisation affects not only the customer's experience but also the business's efficiency.

Red tape, paperwork and bureaucracy truly are the unholy trinity of friction. And while we like to point the finger of blame at government regulators or corporate hierarchies for the red tape we get so easily bogged down by, there's every chance that the bureaucracy slowing things down most on a daily basis is entirely of our own individual making.

This is what global business advisory firm Deloitte discovered in late 2014. Researching many thousands of small- to medium-sized businesses in Australia, Deloitte found that the majority of individual managers spend up to eight hours per week complying with self-imposed red tape—at a cost, nationally, of $134 billion every year.

Failing to deal with friction-driven inefficiency will set any business or industry on a collision course with disruption.

iii. What is creating complexity?

The third driver of friction in many organisations and industries is complexity. While the world of commerce is always going to be inherently complex, many businesses and industries have exploited and expanded the complexity of their products and services in order to prop up margins and maintain control.

Take the medical billing industry for example. This highly lucrative industry pulls in $55 billion in the United States each year but its inner workings are remarkably and unnecessarily complex.[14] In the United States, for instance, customers rarely have any real idea what something will cost until they receive a bill months down the road. In an effort to address this complexity, medical billing startup Eligible has set out to make it easier for customers to know how much they are paying before they step into the doctor's office. While electronic medical claims processing is far from a new idea, existing systems are stuck in a pre-cloud and pre–data sharing age. As a result, patients have had no way of knowing in advance if their health insurance will cover a procedure or whether a more cost-effective treatment covered under their insurance plan is available. Eligible will address this gap.[15]

Striving for simplicity

If complexity adds friction, the key for any business or industry hoping to avoid being disrupted will be to strive for simplicity. This is not to say that you need to naively ignore the complex realities of life, but rather to aim to make things as simple and streamlined as humanly possible.

For many years, brand consulting giant Siegel+Gale have produced an annual Global Brand Simplicity Index that evaluates how streamlined, accessible and simple a business is to engage with. In recent years, Google have consistently taken out the number one position in the index. This should come as no surprise when you consider that the company's primary search gateway has remained extraordinarily and intentionally simple—a clean, white home page featuring no more than 30 words along with a cheery, six-character, primary-coloured logo.[16]

Another legendary brand that has gone to great lengths in recent years to radically streamline their customer experience is Disney.

Disney's new Magic Band is designed with the express purpose of removing the friction involved in a Disney vacation experience. Entry to parks is now paperless and guests are even tracked as they move throughout a theme park so a personalised experience can be created—to the point where your children can have a 'chance' encounter with their favourite Disney character and the character will know them by name. True magic, as far as any child is concerned![17]

Working with a large home loan provider recently, I challenged them to work in groups to come up with ways to actively address complexity on behalf of their customers. As each of the groups presented their suggestions, I was genuinely impressed with the calibre and quality of ideas each group had generated. One that stuck with me was to simply autopopulate home application forms on behalf of the clients.

'We have all the clients' data already and we have access to home pricing data to generate accurate property valuations sufficient for an initial credit application,' the group's spokesperson said.

So why not pre-populate the application forms for the client to get the pre-approval process underway so they can move quickly when they find their dream home? It doesn't cost us anything but it saves them time and hassle.

It wasn't rocket science, and that was part of the beauty of the suggestion.

∞

Just as it slows down objects in the physical world, friction is the most significant inhibitor to an organisation maintaining agility and momentum. Smart leaders realise that ignoring friction will not only give disruptors a foothold but that it will also significantly affect the all-important customer experience.

Dealing with friction need not be difficult or onerous. Having a good measure of empathy, a willingness to actively observe, and a commitment to keeping things simple is all it takes.

Questions for reflection

∞ In what ways could friction be creating a foothold for disruptors in your industry?

∞ What steps could you take to empathise with and observe clients and consumers?

∞ How are your customers improvising or creating shortcuts—and what could you learn from this?

∞ Which of your practices or processes have the potential to negatively affect the customer experience and create frustration?

∞ How could you simplify or streamline your business to become more efficient?

CHAPTER 10

BE DIFFERENT,
NOT BETTER

At a real estate industry conference I presented at a few years ago, the dominant theme focused on how to combat many of the disruptions explored in chapter 3. Traditional real estate agents were seeing their commissions slashed as new technology players were coming into the market offering low- or no-fee transactions. 'If we aren't careful,' the speaker before me suggested,

we're going to find ourselves in a race to the bottom on price. The consumer may feel like they're winning as prices drop but in the end, we'll see a hollowing out of the industry and everyone will lose from that in the long run.

He continued, 'If we are going to remain vital and viable as a profession, it's all about the unique value we can add as real estate agents'. He wrapped up his presentation paraphrasing Simon Sinek: 'If we do not become remarkable, we will become invisible and irrelevant'.

I was struck by the brutal honesty of this real estate agent's insights and reflected on how many other industries they applied to.

In so many sectors right now, unprecedented levels of competition (especially of the unconventional variety) mean that being clear on your differentiated value proposition is absolutely critical. As the old marketing adage goes, 'It's better to be different than better'.

When I am working with clients who are facing strong competitive headwinds, I remind them that they essentially have three choices:

1. go big
2. go boutique
3. go broke.

It goes without saying that the third option is far from a winning strategy. By the same token, achieving economies of scale and leverage by going big in order to dominate the market is rarely feasible or financially possible. And so you are left with only the second option—go boutique. Be different. Find a point of remarkableness and leverage that uniqueness to gain a competitive upper hand.

Perhaps there is no sector that needs to do this more than retail right now.

THE REMARKABLE RETAILER

As we have already discussed, online threats from the likes of Amazon have significantly undermined the value proposition of retailing. On price, Amazon will almost always win. On range, it's much the same. When it comes to the transaction, Amazon's seamless purchasing experience is hard to beat even with the most convenient in-store point-of-sale systems. And then there's convenience, with the ability to order an item on your smartphone and have it delivered within a few hours or days depending on your location. This is always going to be an appealing prospect with time-poor consumers.

Is it any wonder that Amazon accounts for one-quarter of total retail sales growth and 50 per cent of all US online sales at the time of writing? Amazon's dominance across multiple sectors is nothing short of extraordinary. They are the second largest retailer of consumer electronics in the world, and are close to becoming the largest apparel retailer in the United States, having overtaken traditional chains such as Saks, Nordstrom and Macy's in recent years.[1]

In an indication of the growing power Amazon wield, even Nike have reversed their long-held commitment to not sell through the online retailer. According to one Nike insider, it had become clear that they could 'no longer afford to ignore the online retailing behemoth' that is Amazon.[2]

In May 2017, Warren Buffett predicted that the face of retailing will look entirely different in 10 years' time. 'There will be a few things along the way that surprise us,' he said. 'The world has evolved, and it's going to keep evolving, but the speed is increasing.'

Buffett's business partner Charlie Munger went a step further in his analysis. 'It would certainly be unpleasant if we were in the department store business,' he said. Both Buffett's and Munger's comments came on the back of Berkshire Hathaway's sale of $900 million of Walmart stock—giving some indication of the billionaire investors' lack of confidence in the retail sector. 'I think retailing is just too tough for me,' Buffett admitted.[3]

Validating Buffett's concerns, recent history paints a fairly sobering picture with retailers in the United States closing stores and filing for bankruptcy at rates not seen since the recession of 2007–08.

THE DISAPPEARING DEPARTMENT STORE

Brick-and-mortar retailers in the United States announced more than 3200 store closures in the first six months of 2017, and Credit Suisse analysts forecasted that number to grow to more than 8600 for the full calendar year. By comparison, 6163 stores shut down in 2008, which had previously held the record as the retail sector's worst year. It is department stores that are feeling the pinch most, with the likes of Macy's, Sears, and JCPenney having shed nearly half a million jobs between 2001 and 2017.[4] Australian retailers are experiencing the same pressures.

Looking at the flow-on effect of this trend, analysts are predicting that 40 per cent of major shopping malls in the United States will close by the early 2020s, despite the attempts of these malls to make up for lost retail tenancies with food, entertainment and services such as doctors' surgeries and gyms.[5]

Against this rather melancholy backdrop, I believe there is hope for retailers who don't want to find themselves going broke in the coming years. The answer isn't in trying to go big and compete with the major players on price and scale. Rather, it is about finding a boutique, differentiated and remarkable value proposition.

In the case of retailing, this may mean a boutique:

∞ service experience

∞ product range.

Boutique service experiences

Retail customer service will need to go beyond simply satisfying shoppers' needs, answering their questions and executing a transaction. Retailers will need to create a multisensory experience that is worth raving about. This will mean making customers feel valued, loved and special. As highlighted in chapter 2, a customer's most recent exceptional experience will become their new expectation of normal—so delivering a remarkable service experience will be a never-ending pursuit.

Beyond enhancing the customer experience, retailers will likely see the notion of customer interaction change. Rather than having stores packed with inventory, retailers in the years to come will have shopfronts that may have only one item of each style and size for customers to try on. Once shoppers have made a purchasing decision, the item will be dispatched from a third-party location and delivered to their home or office within hours. Thus, the store becomes a showroom rather than a storeroom on display.

Nordstrom's new-format store, which opened in October 2017, gives some indication of what this will look like. The Nordstrom Local store in West Hollywood contains dressing rooms where personal stylists will help shoppers put together a new look using a 'style board' app. The store won't actually stock inventory of the items customers try on. Instead, orders will be delivered to a shopper's home. The new concept stores will also offer manicures and an in-store bar.[6]

A boutique product range

Smart retailers are recognising that simply stocking third-party brands that everyone else sells will leave you especially exposed to price wars. Having unique private-label products will allow you to compete on features and benefits rather than just price.

> **Third-party brands that everyone else sells will leave you especially exposed to price wars.**

According to BigCommerce's CTO, Brian Dhatt, Amazon is a serious threat to a certain type of retailer. Specifically, multibrand retailers such as department stores, and 'big box' outlets. The bankruptcy of Toys 'R' Us is a case in point. These businesses 'are in the most dangerous position, they have other people's products, and they can only compete on price. People who own their brand are crushing it,' he says.[7]

THREE WAYS TO BE REMARKABLE

Looking beyond the world of retail, organisations and brands across every sector will do well to find a point of differentiation or remarkableness through the following three approaches:

i.   unique positioning

ii. remarkable marketing

iii. extraordinary experiences.

i. Unique positioning

The first way to differentiate in any crowded market is to position your business in a way that others aren't. Often, this will be by adopting formats that are unusual, creative or cutting edge.

Take the example of Air New Zealand, who have established themselves as a unique brand in an industry that is often considered very beige and conservative.

Air New Zealand's unique positioning is evident from the moment you board a plane and the airline safety video begins. Rather than simply rolling through the steps necessary 'in the unlikely event of an emergency', Air New Zealand's safety demonstration videos are full-scale productions. They are quirky, irreverent and fun. But most of all, they're memorable.

Even the seat formats of Air New Zealand give an indication of how committed the company is to positioning themselves in a unique way. When Air New Zealand introduced the Skycouch a few years ago, I wondered why it hadn't been thought of earlier. This seat format allows couples travelling together to purchase three consecutive seats for a price only marginally higher than the two they are travelling in. In Air New Zealand's own words, this configuration 'creates a flexible space for whatever you want it to be—an area to relax and stretch out in, or for the kids to use as a play space. It's like having your very own couch on the plane'.

Looking at another simple but genius example of unique positioning, consider Downsize Fitness, the gym tailored to obese customers. Recognising that many overweight people are intimidated by the culture and tone of traditional gyms, Downsize Fitness limits its membership to only those who are suffering from weight loss problems. The company's positioning is that they are the gym for people who would find walking into a traditional gym confronting or embarrassing.[8]

Pursuing a point of uniqueness in the very opposite way, clothing brand Diesel have opted not to ever produce jeans for larger than a size 34 waist—compared to competitors such as Levi's who produce jeans up to size 46. Diesel's positioning is clear: they don't want to be the jeans brand for overweight middle-aged men.[9] Discriminatory? Yes. Differentiated? Absolutely.

In the ultra-competitive hotel industry, unique positioning is proving to be far more effective than competing on price alone. Consider these inventive attempts at unique positioning by hotels around the world:

∞ At London's Hub hotel by Premier Inn, guests use a hotel app to control the TV, temperature and lighting. Every room also features a local-area map that offers suggestions for meals and activities. Simply hold your smartphone camera over a location on the map and instant suggestions or recommendations will appear on your phone.[10]

∞ At the other end of the spectrum, guest rooms at Villa Stephanie in Germany's Black Forest feature a switch that will activate copper wires in the room's walls that block all radio waves and wi-fi signals (which supposedly leads to a more refreshing sleep).[11]

∞ Disney recently unveiled plans for an immersive Star Wars hotel in Los Angeles's CBD. All guests at the hotel will be given a storyline from the movie series, which they will 'live out' throughout their stay. The hotel will be modelled as a spaceship with windows looking out to 'space' and all staff will be 'cast members' in costume designed to make your stay as authentic and immersive as possible.[12]

In the technology world, Samsung's recent release of the Frame television is an elegant rethink of how TVs form part of our home's décor. Unlike traditional TV sets, the Frame is a device that is designed to look like a large artwork when it is turned off. Customers can even choose the picture on display in their frame to match their taste.[13]

Choosing to zig when the rest of the market zags, music technology stalwart Sony announced plans in June 2017 to begin producing vinyl records for the first time in three decades. Recognising a trend in young consumers' growing preference for the tactile, warm and vivid sound offered by vinyl, Sony is looking to capitalise on the renaissance of this retro music format. As a telling sign of how significant the vinyl trend has become, sales of vinyl records in the UK surpassed digital downloads in 2016 and in the United States they increased for the eleventh year in a row. In addition to returning to the production of vinyl records, Sony has also released a turntable that not only plays records, but also allows users to store the music as high-resolution digital files.[14]

The competitive advantage of being cooperative

Although seeking out or creating a unique position is powerful, sometimes the key is to identify the point of differentiation that you *already* possess and may never have leveraged.

> Sometimes the key is to identify the point of differentiation that you *already* possess and may never have leveraged.

The many mutual or cooperative businesses operating around the world are great examples of this. Although the notion of modern cooperatives and mutuals can be traced back to the mid 1800s, the reality is that many consumers still don't understand the model or recognise its value.

In a cooperative or mutual model, the entity is owned and democratically operated by members. Common cooperatives include roadside assistance businesses, mutual banks, credit unions, industry superannuation funds, insurers and a plethora of consumer buying groups.

Although eight in 10 consumers are members of mutuals or cooperatives, only 16 per cent realise they are. In fact, scarcely 30 per cent of consumers can name a single cooperative.

The reason for this is clear: many consumers simply see the name of their insurer, superannuation provider or roadside assistance company and have no idea of the business model behind it. This is especially the case for younger consumers, with 61 per cent of the under 35s reporting they've never heard of a cooperative or mutual.[15]

In my work with cooperatives and mutuals over the years, my encouragement to them has been that they in fact already have a powerful and unique positioning—it's just that often they and their members don't recognise it.

Owing to their democratic structure, cooperatives and mutuals are highly transparent and extremely accountable. Added to this, they make an enormous contribution to the community, with an average of 22 per cent of their income donated to charitable organisations. Best of all, their entire purpose of existence is to benefit members.

The value of this market positioning couldn't be any more potent in a climate where 90 per cent of consumers believe businesses are more interested in shareholder profits than customers and a similar proportion believe corporate executives are overpaid. The reality is that cooperatives and mutuals offer an alternative that most consumers would be very interested in—if only they knew what was on offer.[16]

What business are you really in?

When I am helping clients discern their unique positioning, I always begin with the all-important question 'What business are you really in?'

The power of this question is that if you engage with it thoughtfully you'll arrive at the point of your true value proposition. In my book *Winning the Battle for Relevance*, I recounted an experience of when this question significantly helped a group of business owners get their thinking unstuck.

I was presenting at a bar licensee's conference and asked the group to reflect on the business they were in. Unsurprisingly, the majority of responses centred on products and services — 'We are in the food and beverage business'. Although I understood why audience members responded the way they did, I challenged their assumptions and suggested that they were, rather, in the 'atmosphere and experience' business.

Seeing the puzzled expressions, I explained that when a customer enters a bar or restaurant and orders a glass of wine, they are aware that the price they're paying for one glass is what they'd otherwise pay for an entire bottle of the same wine at the liquor store down the road. 'So why do they willingly pay the premium?' I asked. 'Why not just buy the bottle and drink it at home?' Answering my own question, I explained that it was a bar's atmosphere and experience that added value to customers — that's what they were paying for.

This 'What business are you really in?' question has revealed some other fascinating insights with clients in recent years. I remember working with the top brass of a state police department and posing the same question to them. After some discussion, it became clear that as police officers they were in the business of 'perceived safety'.

I found the inclusion of the term 'perceived' an interesting one, but the group pointed to the fact that if the public don't *feel* safe, the work of the police isn't done. They can deal with crime and ensure community order but absolute safety is only half the battle won. From the public's perspective, a perception that they and their loved ones can feel safe going about their day and sleep well at night is where the value really lies.

In recent years this very question has set tyre giant Michelin on the path to literally reinventing the wheel. In 2014 Michelin released the world's first airless tyre, called the Tweel. Michelin North America Chairman Pete Selleck acknowledges that the new design will cost more than traditional pneumatic tyres, but that eventually it will become a dominant technology. 'Our customers don't really buy tires. What they really want to do is maintain the mobility of their vehicles'. In other words, Michelin isn't in the tyre business, they're in the 'staying on the road business' — an insight that has enabled them to be first to market with this innovative new product.[17]

The key in differentiating your market position is not to become fixated on the specific products or services you have offered in the past. Rather, by defining yourself in terms of the unique value you add, you avoid the trap of becoming a hostage of your own success and locked into business models that may have reached the end of their natural life.

> **By defining yourself in terms of the unique value you add, you avoid the trap of becoming a hostage of your own success.**

Regardless of whether you are seeking to establish a point of difference in the market or leveraging one that already exists, unique positioning is a powerful way to be different, not better, in an age of disruption.

ii. Remarkable marketing

There's nothing like thinking outside the box in order to stand out and get attention. Take the creative marketing campaign in January 2017 where AirFrance's low-cost airline, HOP!, partnered with Adidas and sports retailer Citadium to promote the airline's youth discount card. The campaign was called 'Run to Mum' and offered a €49 discount card whenever young customers purchased a pair of Adidas sneakers online. The catch was that one shoe was sent to the customer and the other shoe to their parents. The idea was to encourage customers to book a discounted flight home to collect their second shoe. (And visit their parents, of course!)[18]

In a very different example of remarkable marketing, cosmetics giant Sephora recently turned a Singapore shopping centre billboard into an unusual vending machine. Passers-by could press a button to receive a free product sample along with a coupon card allowing them to redeem another complimentary sample in a store nearby. Naturally, once the customers were in the store to pick up their second free sample, they tended to purchase other products.[19]

Or consider Spotify's advertising campaign in late 2016 designed to 'summarise' how its users had consumed music throughout the year.

Some of the more notable billboards included:

∞ Dear person who played 'Sorry' 42 times on Valentines Day—what did you do?

∞ Dear person in [New York's] Theatre District who listened to the 'Hamilton' soundtrack 5,376 times this year—can you get us tickets?

More than being irreverent and fun, this simple campaign powerfully humanised a digital brand that could otherwise easily seem devoid of any personality.[20]

Volvo sheds its conservative image

Automaker Volvo has also done a superb job of adopting remarkable marketing campaigns in recent years that have asserted the car maker as a leader in quality and innovation. The 2017 campaign slogan 'Shake the World Gently' is a perfect blend of the automaker's traditional roots of safety and reliability with a nod to the disruptive and cutting-edge technology fuelling its recent models.

This recasting of Volvo's brand began in haste with the release of the S40 model in the mid 2000s. For decades, Volvo had been known for producing solid, sturdy and reliable cars. What Volvo lacked in style or coolness, it more than made up for in safety and 'understated sensibleness'. The company had essentially positioned its cars as the automobile for 'professionals who don't need to demonstrate how successful they are by the car they drive, but who value being known for their good judgment'.[21]

With the release of the S40, Volvo set out to overhaul its image and connect with a younger demographic. As this new model exuded speed, performance, youthfulness and excitement, it needed a campaign to match.[22] In an effort to ensure that this new release hit the mark with younger car buyers, one of Volvo's TV commercials for the S40 was in the style of an Xbox video game. Another advertisement featured rap star LL Cool J promoting the car in music-video style. In addition, Volvo even developed an online mockumentary, *The Mystery of Dalaro*, which attracted more than one million hits and led to a 105 per cent jump in S40 sales within months.[23]

Naturally, marketing and brand positioning efforts such as these are a good place to start in creating a sense of differentiation but they are rarely enough on their own. It's the customer experience where the rubber really hits the road.

iii. Extraordinary experiences

Returning to the retail sector, a brilliant example of a physical retail outlet that has perfected the boutique customer experience is leather-goods store Mon Purse. Based in Sydney's upmarket eastern suburbs, Mon Purse represents what one analyst called 'the future of retail'.[24]

From the moment you walk into the Mon Purse store, the tactile experience hits you with the luxurious smell of quality leather. The uncluttered store is a stark white and features a number of desktop computers and iPads that guide customers through Mon Purse's proprietary 'bag builder' software. At each step of the process, customers can design the perfect bespoke handbag as they flick through swatches of imported calf leather in 30 colours and varying textures. They can design bags down to the finest detail using a wide array of buttons, zips, clips and clasps.

Mon Purse's bags don't come cheap and that's just the point. The positioning and marketing of the brand is deliberately exclusive. Added to this, once the bag is created, it can take up to four weeks to be built — a delay that could otherwise be seen as inconvenient but adds to the bespoke sense of craftsmanship Mon Purse is famous for.

Mon Purse's founder and chief executive, Lana Hopkins, describes the atmosphere of the store as being one of 'indulgence of fun'. But even the word 'store' doesn't sit well with Hopkins — it's designed to be more like an art gallery, she suggests.[25]

It is this visceral, multisensory and high-emotion retail experience combined with high-end technology that offers the most exciting possibilities for brick-and-mortar retail.

The Rebel sports store just down the road from Mon Purse is seeking to create a similarly visceral yet entirely different customer experience. They have designed their store to replicate a stadium, complete with wire fencing, bench seating and line markings.

More than simply employing gimmicks, Alistair Palmer of CBRE Retail Services Group suggests that retail stores will need to evolve to become 'immersive brand experience centres' offering personalised, value-added and after-sales services.[26]

The power of virtual reality

Perhaps the trend that shows greatest promise in enhancing the customer experience is virtual reality, or VR. Used creatively, it can enhance a customer's experience and differentiate a brand. The high-speed Eurostar train service linking London with destinations in France and Belgium has developed specially designed headsets that transform the roof of the train into a glass ceiling revealing an underwater world of 'sea creatures, sunken treasures and mysterious sea-scapes' as customers cross under the English Channel. Eurostar's commercial director, Nick Mercer, suggests that the VR headsets are part of the company's strategy to enhance the travel experience and encourage families to choose the train over flying.[27]

It's clear that virtual reality is here to stay and will transform the customer experience in some significant ways over the coming years. Finance companies such as Fidelity are already designing software to help you visualise your investments in 3D,[28] Yelp's Monocle feature allows users to peer through their smartphones and see information about businesses around them, and home improvement retailer Lowe's is using VR to provide do-it-yourself instruction.[29]

Underscoring the significance and potential of VR, Mark Zuckerberg predicted in 2015 that immersive 3D content would be 'the obvious next thing after video'.[30] Going one step further, Tim Cook suggested that 'VR will represent a tech trend as fundamental and revolutionary as the smartphone'.[31]

With all the big tech players, including Apple, Google, Facebook, Sony and Microsoft, investing heavily in virtual reality, Goldman Sachs estimates that it will be bigger than the TV market by 2025.[32]

∞

Campbell Soup CEO Denise Morrison recently admitted that in the face of sustained pressure from increasingly fickle consumers, 'companies and brands [such as Campbell] must differentiate themselves or risk extinction'.[33]

And she's right. As the waves of disruption continue to affect every industry and business, finding a point of difference will be critical. Whether this is through unique positioning, remarkable marketing or extraordinary experiences, in the coming years it will be more important than ever to be different rather than better.

Questions for reflection

∞ What are the key points of differentiation or uniqueness for your organisation, product or brand?

∞ What business are you really in?

∞ How could you use remarkable marketing to position your organisation uniquely?

∞ In what ways could you craft an extraordinary customer experience in order to stand out?

∞ How could VR technology enhance the customer experience in your context?

CHAPTER 11

SPARE NO
SACRED COWS

Recently I spoke at a Department of Industry conference, and following me on stage was the government minister responsible for each of the department heads in the room.

Typically, I have a good idea of what to expect when government ministers speak at conferences—and I imagine you do too. One of the odd quirks of our system of government is that portfolios are rarely awarded based on skill and experience, but rather for political expediency. As a result, an education minister often has little idea how schools function and a transport minister may have ridden in nothing but a chauffeur-driven vehicle for years.

So when government ministers address their portfolio teams, they are generally received with a polite indifference—those in the room listen dutifully while recognising that the person at the lectern knows very little about what they're saying beyond the briefing notes they've been supplied by staffers.

At this Department of Industry event, I was taken aback by the minister who, within minutes of stepping onto the platform, had captured the attention and earned the genuine respect of everyone in the room—myself included. This minister had worked in the industry.

He had well-informed and passionate views and spoke for 25 minutes without any notes about the key trends and challenges facing his portfolio. He was warm, genuine and self-deprecating. Better yet, rather than simply toeing the party line, he acknowledged key areas for improvement in the government's administering of the department and even shared a refreshingly frank insight into the culture of the public service and how it needed to change.

'Our problem in government is that we've failed to realise that every organisation needs three types of people. We need people who *start* things, we need people who *sustain* things and we need people who *stop* things,' he said.

> *Traditionally the public sector culture has been great at attracting 'sustainers'—people who can administer, manage and coordinate. We're getting better at attracting the 'starters' who have a bent toward innovation, invention and creativity. But the group we lack most are the 'stoppers'. Our bureaucracies are bloated. Our systems are dated and our programs are all too often ineffective. We need to get better at culling or stopping the old in order to make way for the new if we're going to thrive as an organisation.*

Within days of listening to this minister's address, I was reading a book that highlighted how rampant the very dynamic he spoke about was in the public sector. I learned that the last time a law was scrapped in France was in 1789—despite the fact that many regulations have questionable modern-day relevance. French schools, for instance, have to follow an 80-page document stipulating that children in day-care centres must eat one-quarter of a hard-boiled egg per meal. Even the French baguette must obey a rule that its length should not exceed 50 to 55 centimetres.[1]

Across the English Channel in Great Britain, the situation isn't any more sensible. For instance, it is still an act of treason to place a postage stamp bearing the British monarch upside down—a rule that dates back to 1848.[2]

In reality, the dynamic that this government minster described is certainly alive and well in the public sector, but it is much broader than that. For all our talk of innovation (starting) and efficiency (sustaining), I fear we have lost sight of the vital role that 'stopping' plays in maintaining an organisation's vitality and relevance.

In my book *Momentum — How to Build It, Keep It or Get It Back* I discussed one of my favourite examples of failing to stop something outdated and outmoded. For many years US military requirements stated that firing a cannon required three men — not two, not four, but always three. According to a detailed operations manual, one soldier was to hold the cannon steady, the second one loaded the ammunition, while the third soldier was to literally just stand there with nothing apparent to do. A few years ago when pressed for the reason behind this three-person rule, some military historians investigated the origin of the standard practice and discovered that originally the third man's job was to hold the horse that had dragged the cannon to the front line in case it got spooked by the sound of the cannon's explosion. Naturally, this role was necessary when the operations manual was written, as cannons were always dragged into battle by a horse.

Despite the fact that horses had been superseded by new technology many decades before, the old three-person rule stuck even though it no longer served any purpose or made any sense. It was not until relatively recently that the operations manual was updated — about 150 years after it should have been![3]

While it's easy to scoff at ridiculous examples such as this, I find that organisations of all shapes and sizes unknowingly fall into the very same trap of persisting with practices, processes and procedures that once served a purpose but no longer do.

In looking at how organisations arrive at this point, one of the models I share with clients highlights how innovations can easily become sacred cows over time.

THE MAKING OF A SACRED COW

Generally, all sacred cows or outdated practices begin their lives as an innovation. One day someone discovers a fresh way of doing things — a new technique that offers greater efficiency and effectiveness. As the innovation is implemented, it quickly becomes clear that others would benefit from it as well and so, over time, the innovation becomes considered best practice and its use is mandated and monitored across the organisation.

Then time passes — and this passage of time is the key — and new staff members are taught the best practice in induction and training programs. However, these new staff are rarely taught why the best practice was developed in the first place. Without this understanding of the *why*, new team members simply mimic the *what* and the *how* to the point where best practice becomes habitual process.

Sacred cows have a unique ability to inhibit change and prevent responsiveness to new opportunities.

As more time passes, the habitual process becomes so embedded in the organisation's ethos and culture that people follow it unthinkingly and even begin seeing it as a key part of the organisation's identity. Any efforts to challenge or change it are met with active and often militant resistance even if a compelling case can be made that new needs demand new solutions. The innovation has become a sacred cow.

Defined as 'an outmoded practice, policy, system, or strategy', sacred cows have a unique ability to inhibit change and prevent responsiveness to new opportunities.[4]

'Once managers find a process that works well enough, they usually stop experimentation and commit to what works,' explains Donald Sull in his book *Why Good Companies Go Bad.*[5]

Any business or organisation committed to navigating disruption must be equally committed to sparing no sacred cows. As times change, we must change with them. An unwillingness to dispense with vestiges of the past will quickly set you on a collision course with irrelevance.

In the words of former CEO of GE Jack Welch, 'When the rate of change on the outside exceeds the rate of change on the inside, the end is near'. Never were truer words spoken.

THREE WAYS TO IDENTIFY SACRED COWS

In order to identify sacred cows, it's valuable to understand the three common forms they take in an organisation, namely:

i.   dysfunctional processes

ii. outdated mindsets

iii. outmoded strategies or initiatives.

i. Dysfunctional processes

In my formative years growing up on the east coast of Australia, boats were an ever-present part of my childhood. One of my favourite things to do as a kid was to wander down to the wharfs and watch boats being maintained in the dry dock where they would be hauled out of the water on a giant motorised ramp.

I was always amazed to discover how vastly different boats looked above as opposed to below the waterline. Boats that looked sleek and clean while moored in the harbour were revealed as anything but once their hulls were exposed in the dry dock. Below the waterline, they were covered in thick layers of barnacles and crustaceans. My boat-enthusiast dad explained that once a year each of the boats in the harbour had to have their hulls scoured clean to remove these barnacles that would effortlessly form as the boat sat in the water. The more the barnacles grew, the heavier the boat would become — significantly impeding the boat's speed, efficiency and agility.

It's very much the same with organisations. The longer an organisation exists, the more that traditional processes, bureaucracy and red tape will naturally form. While the public-facing parts of a business can appear cutting-edge and up-to-date, it is the back end of an organisation where the dysfunctional processes can wreak the most havoc.

I was struck by the fact that Steven Mayer of private-equity giant Cerberus Capital Management recently used this very same metaphor when describing the challenges of transforming direct-selling giant Avon cosmetics.

'Avon is like a boat that's been in the water for 130 years. You have to take it out and scrape all the barnacles off,' he said.[6]

And he's right. Avon is an organisation with a lot of barnacles built up over a lot of years and the impact is clear. In recent years the company lost a huge swath of its iconic door-to-door sales representatives as it has been slow to modernise its products, capitalise on social media and fully embrace the online world.

Is the party over for party plan?

Like so many direct selling companies, years of tradition have caused Avon to become ideologically and strategically stuck.

Despite an attempt to update the company's back-end computer systems in 2013, a disastrous failed pilot in Canada resulted in Avon reverting to badly dated technology and systems for product ordering and administration.

Avon's tradition-bound distribution model has also hamstrung the company. In an age where customers can receive Amazon orders within two days, many Avon customers are still encouraged to order products through their representatives and may wait two weeks to receive supplies. While an online direct ordering process is available to customers, many representatives have opted to stick with the traditional ordering system out of familiarity or a fear that they'll lose control of their sales channel.

Returning to the themes discussed in chapter 8, it was Avon's very success in expanding into developing markets such as China and Brazil that helped mask the fundamental weaknesses in the company's North American homeland. While profits tripled from 1999 to 2004, much of this growth was from emerging markets where Avon enjoyed a first-player advantage for modern beauty products. However, within a few years the cracks began to appear and by 2011 the company had lost its crown as the world's largest direct-selling business and in 2012 alone Avon's shares lost 40 per cent of their value. In 2015, Avon was removed from the S&P 500 index and in August 2017 its market capitalisation had sunk to $1.15 billion (down from $10.25 billion in May 2013).[7]

In 2017 there was a concerted effort to revive Avon's fortunes with a redoubling of efforts to bring the company into the digital and social media age with a range of innovative and new products. Whether it's too little too late remains to be seen.

While Avon is a powerful example of a business that got stuck in traditional ways of doing things and has paid a heavy price, they are by no means the only company in their industry to have fallen prey to sacred cows and dysfunctional processes over the years.

A few years ago I was working with the executive team of fellow direct sales giant Tupperware. The company's Australian general manager at the time shared with me the angst caused when the company decided to phase out the singing of Tupperware songs at product demonstrations.

For years, Tupperware parties began with the singing of songs featuring company-themed lyrics. When the executive team decided that these songs and their accompanying 'actions' had to go, the outcry in the ranks was enormous. The GM recounted that many of the company's top demonstrators claimed it would be the end of Tupperware—even that the company would 'lose its soul'.

To their credit, the executive team held their nerve and pushed ahead with the phasing out of this very dated and dysfunctional sacred cow.

Valuable heritage or outdated tradition?

Naturally, not all traditions are bad and not all historical processes are dysfunctional. The challenge then is to determine which traditions are sacred cows and which are merely vestiges of the past that may be harmless or a positive expression of heritage.

Leading business author Robert Kriegel offers three helpful diagnostic questions to determine whether a tradition is dysfunctional or not.[8] Does it:

a. add value to the customer?

b. increase productivity?

c. improve organisational morale?

Routinely dispense with dysfunctional processes that have the potential to weigh you down, slow you down and bog you down.

If a given tradition or ritual doesn't result in a 'yes' answer to at least two of these questions, it is in all likelihood a dysfunctional process that must be dealt with if you hope to remain at the cutting edge.

In the same way that boats routinely need barnacles scoured off, organisations need to routinely and consciously dispense with dysfunctional processes that have the potential to weigh you down, slow you down and bog you down.

ii. Outdated mindsets

The second form that sacred cows take is less procedural and more psychological.

While dysfunctional processes can constrain an organisation practically, paradigms that are stuck in the past can be equally dangerous and paralysing.

I was recently interviewed by a leading retail magazine about the importance of small operators improving their point-of-sale experience. I suggested that too many small retailers are still resistant to offer electronic payment options without imposing a spend limit or surcharge. To the point discussed in chapter 9, my argument was practices such as these were a key source of friction for consumers and that retailers would do well to rethink them.

The interviewer suggested that retailers generally felt that applying surcharges was necessary due to the merchant fees imposed by banks and credit card providers. However, I challenged this assumption by pointing to the fact that transaction costs today are a fraction of what they were a few years ago and that new entrants such as Square have transformed the payment process—so retailers ought to take another look at their merchant provider and shop around.

'The bigger challenge for retailers,' I continued,

> *will be not just to revisit their merchant contracts but to fundamentally rethink their approach to customer convenience. For many retailers, convenience is seen as a privilege that customers should pay for rather than a fundamental and assumed right. This paradigm may have been reasonable 10 years ago, but it simply doesn't work with customers today.*

It was this very same outdated mindset that was responsible for discount retailer Kmart's stumble in the early 2000s. Kmart's origins as a five-and-dime store had resulted in a paradigm where customers received low prices but essentially paid for these with long checkout lines, poorly lit stores and out-of-stock items.[9] Market researcher George Rosenbaum argues that Kmart never got past the belief that 'if you give the customer something, you have to take something away such as comfort, service or convenience'.

Kmart's competitors, meanwhile, offered low prices but not at the expense of user-friendly, clean and well-stocked stores. Before long, customers came to understand that they did not have to suffer in order to save—an approach that was way outside Kmart's frame of reference.[10] The results were devastating. By 2003, Kmart in the United States was experiencing nationwide store closures, had cut almost 70 000 jobs and was posting multibillion-dollar losses.[11] The road to recovery for Kmart had to begin with a fundamental rethink of a mindset that had proven to be outdated and dangerous.

As we saw in the case of the Swiss watchmakers, to dogmatically stick with a set of assumptions that were appropriate in the past may not serve us in the future. Rejecting outright any new ideas that fail to fit into our existing assumptions can cause us to miss the very innovations that may be the key to our future success. Focused attention can become tunnel vision and niches can turn into ruts—a phenomenon known as 'inattentional blindness'.

Rethinking IP

In an inspiring example of the innovation gains that can come from abandoning outdated mindsets, consider the recent sharing of intellectual property in the automotive sector.

Automakers have long been famous for seeing their proprietary technology as a powerful source of competitive advantage that must be guarded at all costs.

In a dramatic departure from this established paradigm, in early 2015 Toyota announced that it would be offering almost 6000 patents to rival automakers for free in the hope of speeding up the development of hydrogen fuel cell cars.

At the time, Toyota's senior vice president, Bob Carter, gave an insight into the new paradigm driving the company's decision:

> At Toyota, we believe that when good ideas are shared, great things can happen. The first generation hydrogen fuel cell vehicles will be critical, requiring a concerted effort and unconventional collaboration.[12]

Ford, Renault, Nissan and Mercedes' parent company, Daimler, quickly followed suit, agreeing to share fuel cell technologies in an effort to speed up industry innovation.

David Cole, chairman emeritus of the Centre for Automotive Research, said that such moves represented a 'historic amount of collaboration'. Noting that the fuel cell's speed of development will depend on automakers sharing their IP.[13]

As legendary eighteenth-century philosopher and political activist Thomas Paine once observed, 'A long habit of not thinking a thing wrong gives it a superficial appearance of being right'.

For any organisation or industry, it is vital to examine the assumptions and paradigms that you have held onto in the past and honestly ask whether they are still constructive or relevant. After all, just as it is impossible to find new treasure using an old treasure map, it is impossible to discover new innovations and opportunities when examining the world through the prism of the past.

iii. Outmoded strategies or initiatives

As someone who spends a lot of time tapping away on my computer keyboard, I'd never given much thought to the arrangement of the very keys I was pressing. Referred to as the 'QWERTY keyboard', owing to this being the word spelt out by the six keys at the top left of the board, this standard layout dates back to 1868. At the time, typists were getting too efficient for their own good using traditional alphabetic keyboards, so, in an effort to slow typists down and avoid the resultant typewriter jams, keys were reconfigured to 'scatter' the letters to the form we all know today.

Naturally, once we moved away from using typewriters, the challenge of typewriter jams disappeared and yet the QWERTY keyboard remains—a solution to a problem that no longer exists.

While the arrangement of the letters on our keyboards is fairly inconsequential in the scheme of things, all too often organisations and businesses get stuck using outmoded strategies or initiatives that no longer solve the problem for which they were invented (or even serve no purpose at all).

In my work with clients I commonly encounter businesses that have fallen into the trap of finding ever-more efficient ways to do ineffective things. It is these ineffective and outmoded practices that are robbing them of relevance.

As times change, strategies and initiatives that have worked well in the past may no longer be as effective. It takes courage to abandon these outmoded approaches rather than allowing them to become untouchable sacred cows in the organisation's psyche.

Recognising this, recent years have seen consumer goods behemoth Procter & Gamble (P&G) announce that it would cull more than half of its brands—a bold effort to become nimbler and speed up growth. While the pruning of iconic products such as Jif peanut butter, Pringles chips, Crisco food shortening and Folgers coffee is a risk, the most striking element of this move is that it marks a departure from a strategy of aggressive expansion that has worked for P&G for decades.[14]

This strategic reorientation is tantamount to an admission from P&G's leadership that such expansion may have served them in the past but an increasingly competitive marketplace means a new paradigm was needed.[15]

The power of pruning

While sometimes it is a broad strategy that needs addressing as times change, often it is specific initiatives that need to be pruned away.

I use the word 'prune' here quite deliberately, because the skills and perspectives required to identify and address outmoded initiatives are remarkably similar to those required when pruning the garden.

Take German sporting goods company Puma for example. The early 2000s saw the company embark on a diversification push into non-core businesses and product lines, ranging from bikes to perfumes and sunglasses. After years of struggling to try and make these diversification initiatives turn a profit, Puma's leadership recently returned the company to its sportswear core business—and profitability has surged.[16]

It has been a similar story in the electronics sector with brands such as Hitachi and Panasonic. When Hiroaki Nakanishi took the reins of Hitachi amid the worst profit slump in the company's 102-year history, it was clear that pruning was required. In response, Nakanishi shed a range of product divisions, including Hitachi's mobile phone, computer parts and flat-panel TV units, to focus attention and resources. Within a year, Hitachi was back in the black to the tune of $4.35 billion.[17]

In the case of Panasonic, the company's leadership announced in May 2016 that they would be ceasing production of LCD TVs—a significant move considering Panasonic's historical dominance in the TV business. However, amid growing competition from rivals in China and South Korea, it became increasingly clear that clinging onto the TV business was simply no longer viable.[18]

LESSONS FROM LEGO

Of all the companies I have studied over the years, Lego stands out as a powerful example of a business that has thrived and remained relevant by addressing sacred cows that took each of the three forms we have explored in this chapter.

In my book *Momentum*, I explored the vital role that dispensing with sacred cows played in reviving Lego's fortunes in the mid 2000s.

The early years of the twenty-first century were a dark time for Lego. Having been rocked by the steady rise in popularity of video games in the preceding decade, the Danish toymaker was in a fight for survival and relevance in the digital age. By the end of 2003, Lego's sales had plunged by 30 per cent in one year. Worse still, the company had racked up $800 million in debt[19] and was teetering on the edge of bankruptcy.[20]

Amid this crisis, a new Lego CEO by the name of Jorgen Knudstorp was appointed in 2004. Knudstorp quickly identified that Lego needed to significantly streamline and simplify their product range and production processes. Knudstorp set about returning Lego to its range of core products and significantly reduced the complexity involved in manufacturing—reducing the number of components in Lego's product portfolio by a full 50 per cent.[21]

The results were almost immediate. By the end of 2005, Lego rebounded from a $292 million loss the previous year to a pre-tax profit of $117 million.[22] That same year, the company would post sales of $1.2 billion but, more importantly, profitability would more than triple.[23]

In addition to dispensing with outmoded products and dysfunctional processes, there were a range of outdated mindsets in the Lego business that needed addressing too.

One of these centred on the culture of closed-system design. Despite historically guarding their IP and readily suing any Lego users who infringed on it, in 2008 Lego adopted a radical new approach to product design with the launch of Lego Ideas.

This crowdsourcing site saw Lego fans accredited to use Lego's IP and submit ideas for new inventions that they could earn royalties off, should the concept make it into production.

David Gram, head of marketing at Lego's Future Lab, admits that this change in direction ruffled a lot of feathers:

When we started up our crowdsourcing site, there was complete resistance in the company. Nobody wanted an external platform. No, we have our designers, they know better. We don't want to show our competitors what we are doing, so it was a no, no.[24]

And yet the company persisted with the new direction and it began to work. In the years since the launch of Lego Ideas, a raft of new innovations, including a Lego Minecraft range, a Beatles-themed *Yellow Submarine* toy set, and Lego series inspired by NASA's brightest female stars over the years, have come to market.

Lego's recovery, in the space of just over a decade, was nothing short of breathtaking. Having addressed a long list of processes, mindsets and initiatives that had been holding the company back, in September 2014 Lego overtook Mattel as the world's biggest toymaker—an enormous accomplishment by any measure.[25] Less than a year later, Lego was named the world's most powerful brand and was voted the most popular toy of all time.[26]

> There's a good reason we humans are described as being 'creatures of habit'.

Falling sales in the first half of 2017 saw Lego's leadership embark on yet another round of pruning. In September 2017, Jorgen Knudstorp acknowledged that the company's disappointing revenue results reflected a growing bureaucracy and complexity within the business. 'We're losing momentum and we're losing productivity,' he said. 'We have built an increasingly complex organisation. This could ultimately lead to stagnation or decline'. Knudstorp plans to address this by simplifying Lego's business model and shedding 8 per cent of the company's workforce.[27] Lego is no stranger to the necessity and importance of pruning when times get tough. They've demonstrated an uncanny ability in recent years to stay one step ahead of disruption and I have no doubt they'll do it again.

∞

There's a good reason we humans are described as being 'creatures of habit'. It is in our nature to gravitate toward the predictable, the safe and the familiar. However, maintaining relevance requires us to resist every urge to get stuck in patterns and routines from the past.

Smart leaders and organisations recognise this. In turbulent and disruptive times, no sacred cow can be spared. Whether in the form of dysfunctional processes, outdated mindsets, or outmoded strategies and initiatives, vestiges of the past that may have served you well yesterday will likely prove to be a shackle tomorrow.

As best-selling business author Robert Kriegel says, 'Today's innovations are tomorrow's antiquities... Thinking that you can stay ahead by repeating the past is folly'.[28]

Questions for reflection

∞ What innovations have become best practices, habitual processes or even sacred cows in your organisation or context?

∞ What dysfunctional ways of operating may be holding your organisation back and bogging you down?

∞ Are there any outdated mindsets or assumptions that may need to be challenged or changed in order to stay relevant?

∞ What historical initiatives may need to be pruned away in the coming years in order to maintain agility?

CHAPTER 12

ADOPT A
POSTURE OF
CURIOSITY

According to David Burkus in his book *The Myths of Creativity*, 'Innovation is not an idea problem. It's a recognition problem'.

And he's spot on. Some of the best ideas for innovation, creativity and invention don't lie somewhere 'out there'. They are often right under our noses. The real skill in innovation is being able to identify and recognise the ideas that have the potential to be game changers, and the best way to do this is to adopt a posture of curiosity.

While I'm almost loathe to reference Amazon yet again — they've had more than their fair share of air time in the previous chapters — it's rather telling that Jeff Bezos' mission has always been to make Amazon 'the world's biggest laboratory'. This insatiable curiosity and commitment to experimentation is undoubtedly a key component of the online retailer's extraordinary success.

A posture of curiosity within an organisation never happens by accident. It has to be actively cultivated. As one leading innovation thinker suggests, 'While you can't bottle lightning, you can build lightning rods'.[1] In the same way, while you can't manufacture the serendipity that often accompanies great innovation, you can actively foster the sensitivity required to capitalise on insights when they present themselves.

Beyond simply encouraging team members in an organisation to be alert to great ideas that appear like a bolt from the blue, there are seven things organisations can do to actively encourage a posture of curiosity:

1. ask good questions
2. create capacity
3. observe obsessively
4. look for the unexpected
5. democratise innovation
6. leverage common creativity
7. foster fresh eyes.

1. ASK GOOD QUESTIONS

Albert Einstein once suggested that if he had an hour to solve a problem and his life depended on it, he'd spend the first 55 minutes determining the best question to ask. 'For once I know the proper question,' he said, 'I could solve the problem in less than 5 minutes'.[2]

Questions are indeed powerful and can be a great source of creativity and innovation. Take the salmon farmer who asked a simple but powerful question and came up with an unconventional solution to a persistent problem.

The common challenge this fish farmer was dealing with was the fact that farmed salmon doesn't command as high a price as wild salmon because its meat is softer. This is due to the fact that farmed salmon isn't required to swim as vigorously as fish in the wild.

Watching his fish meandering elegantly and gracefully around the pond one day, the fish farmer asked this question: What would force his fish to swim more vigorously?

The answer he came up with was as outrageous as it was outstanding. His solution was to drop a small shark into his pond.

The effect was immediate. The fish quickly learned to swim more vigorously and those that didn't ended up being shark bait. The financial cost of fish lost to the shark was more than offset by the significantly higher price he could charge at the market for his salmon![3]

In keeping with the shark theme, consider how asking a powerful question led to a significant breakthrough for swimsuit maker Speedo. In the early 2000s, a British scientist named Fiona Fairhurst was commissioned to design the fastest swimsuit ever made. Fairhurst began the process by asking the question: Where in nature is there something that is large but can swim really fast?

She settled on sharks as the ideal prototype, given their ability to swim at close to 48 kilometres an hour despite their size. In studying their physiology, Fairhurst realised that the key to a shark's speed was not having perfectly smooth skin, but rather a series of 'denticles' that propelled them through the water.

Fairhurst incorporated this insight into her design of Speedo's revolutionary Fastskin swimsuit, which was so effective in helping swimmers break records that it was eventually banned by the international swimming community.[4]

In order for an innovation-focused question to be effective, the content and intent of the question matters most. In other words, there are ways to pose questions that will unlock creativity — and vice versa.

There are three examples of the types of questions that can be helpful:

a. Imagine if...?

b. Why not...?

c. If we pretend for a moment that...?

a. Imagine if...?

This first question is powerful because the word 'imagine' has a unique capacity to broaden people's thinking beyond linear or incremental problem solving.

The example of David Hudson, who is global head of markets execution at JPMorgan Chase, is a good one. Every Monday morning, Hudson gathers his team together and poses this question: 'Imagine if you

> **The word 'imagine' has a unique capacity to broaden people's thinking beyond linear or incremental problem solving.**

had $100 million ... how would you take on JPMorgan or lessen its grip on clients?'

This role play is a powerful technique to get staff to adopt the role of disruptor or 'hacker': they are encouraged to try and break JPMorgan's business model and test it for weaknesses. The fruit of this exercise is a long list of ideas for improving the company's value proposition with clients.[5]

Or consider the example of Rick Kreiger, who stumbled upon an enormous opportunity for innovation in the healthcare sector after a bad emergency room visit. Kreiger recognised that healthcare providers were failing to deliver simple services in a convenient, affordable way. Reflecting on his experience as a patient, Kreiger asked himself: Imagine if McDonald's got into the healthcare business—how would they run things?

Recognising that the power of the McDonald's model is in its standardised systems, Kreiger went on to create a hyper-efficient and systematised kiosk-style medical clinic named QuickMedx. The business's slogan, 'You're sick, we're quick', gives some indication as to the mode of operation. Within six years, the breakout success of QuickMedx attracted the interest of CVS Caremark, who purchased the company for $200 million in 2006 and rebranded it MinuteClinic.[6]

b. Why not ...?

This second question is all about challenging long-held assumptions regarding what is possible or feasible.

A superb example of the 'why not' question comes from global furniture giant IKEA. In IKEA's early days, a marketing manager was struggling to fit furniture back into a truck at the end of a catalogue photo shoot. Watching as one attempt after another met with failure or frustration, the photographer simply asked, 'Why not just remove the table's legs?'

This simple but genius question became the seed of an idea that landed in the marketing manager's mind: Why not ship all IKEA's furniture disassembled to save on freight costs?

After sharing the idea with the rest of the executive team, it was swiftly implemented and thus IKEA's flat-pack business model was born![7]

c. If we pretend for a moment that ...?

This setup for a hypothetical scenario is extremely helpful in challenging paradigms about what is currently inconceivable (in a positive or negative sense).

Scott D. Anthony, in his bestseller *The Little Black Book of Innovation*, gives an example of how this approach could work: 'Pretend for a moment that we're legally prohibited from selling to our current customer—what would we do?'[8]

Other hypothetical questions could be:

∞ If we pretend for a moment that our biggest market disappeared, how would we respond?

∞ If we pretend for a moment that we got the green light to expand into China, what would this mean?

∞ If we pretend for a moment that Google or Facebook decided to set up in direct competition to our product at 60 per cent of the price, what would our options be?

While there's value in using this hypothetical line of questioning to expand the possibilities, the authors of a recent *Harvard Business Review* article suggest that the secret to its effectiveness lies in the fact that it places constraints on strategic responses. They say:

Executives often think that the best way to spur innovation is to remove constraints, to let hundreds or thousands of flowers bloom. Overly fragmented efforts result in nothing more than a lot of undernourished flowers. Constraints and creativity are surprisingly close friends. The more specific [the constraints], the better.[9]

2. CREATE CAPACITY

Reflecting on the essential ingredients for innovation, Professor Richard Foster of Yale University encourages businesses and leaders to make space and time for creativity. 'Don't just do something, stand there,' he implores.

Foster's advice is a timely counterbalance to the productivity-obsessed organisational cultures many of us find ourselves working in. As the

Great ideas rarely interrupt us.

old adage goes, great ideas rarely interrupt us. Powerful curiosity and deep innovation often come from the allocation of deliberate space, time and capacity. In the words of the endlessly quotable Albert Einstein, 'Creativity is the residue of time wasted'.

In their book *The Innovator's DNA*, Jeff Dyer, Hal Gregersen and Clayton Christensen highlight successful examples of companies that have set in place procedures to create capacity for innovation. Of particular note were Procter & Gamble, who have long encouraged employees to spend 75 per cent of their time working 'in the system' and the remaining 25 per cent 'on the system'.[10]

In a similar vein, the leadership at online car buying service Edmunds .com realised that one of the barriers to innovation had become the endless meetings that chewed up employees' time and creative capacity.

To remedy the situation, they implemented a new approach called 'Thinking Thursdays'. The idea behind this initiative is that all internal company meetings were to be barred for one day of the week — Thursdays.

According to Edmunds.com's director of product, Dori Merifield, Thinking Thursdays have had a dramatically positive effect on the speed and efficiency of innovation projects. 'There's more space — not just in your schedule, but in your mind,' she says.[11]

In an era where more than $37 billion is wasted every year in unnecessary meetings, according to the US Bureau of Labor Statistics,[12] perhaps it's time other companies followed the lead of Edmunds.com. Not only are full schedules costing us in terms of lost productivity but also in terms of lost capacity for creativity.

3. OBSERVE OBSESSIVELY

For years, the Japanese have promoted the idea of active observation while working in order to identify insights for continuous improvement — something often referred to as a 'Gemba walk'.

Regardless of what you call it, the value of intentional observation is enormous — and not just in identifying friction, as discussed in chapter 9. Observation is also a powerful tool for creativity and innovation.

I love the example of a Virgin Atlantic employee who one day observed a section of empty kerb space at Heathrow Airport and got to thinking about how this space could be used to better serve customers. Off his own initiative, the employee sought permission from airport authorities to use the space and proposed a plan for Virgin to build a kerbside check-in kiosk—at the time, the first of its kind.[13]

Or take the example of Frank Stephenson, the chief designer at supercar maker McLaren. One day, Stephenson was examining the design of a British fighter jet and noticed that it didn't have windscreen wipers like ordinary planes. While most of us would observe this and think little more of it (if we noticed the absence of wiper blades at all), Stephenson's curiosity was piqued.

After doing some research, he discovered that the plane's windscreens use high-frequency sound waves, similar to those used by dentists to remove plaque from patients' teeth, to keep water off. 'I was told that it's not a coating on the surface but a high-frequency electronic system that never fails and is constantly active. Nothing will attach to the windscreen,' he reveals.

> Observation is a powerful tool for creativity and innovation.

Stephenson turned his attention to how this same technology could be applied to McLaren's racing cars to improve a vehicle's aerodynamics. McLaren successfully implemented it in the 2015 P1 hypercar release.[14]

Connecting the unconnected

Frank Stephenson's experience with the fighter jets underscores an important principle for curiosity and creativity—that of 'associational thinking',[15] or making connections between unconnected things.

Steve Jobs pointed to how powerful but surprisingly simple associational thinking is when he admitted that 'Creativity is just connecting things. When you ask creative people how they did something, they feel a little guilty because they didn't really do it, they just saw something'.[16] Easy for Steve Jobs to say, perhaps!

Examples of this process of observing the connection between unconnected things abound: Fujifilm launched a wildly successful cosmetics company named Astalift in 2006 after making the discovery that the anti-UV technology they'd used to help prevent ageing in photos worked as effectively on skin.[17]

One of the keys to observing the connection between unconnected things is to avoid the trap of overspecialisation, which can lead to tunnel vision. You will see everything through the lens of what you already know or, worse yet, fail to notice anything outside the scope of your existing knowledge.

Attesting to this fact, a *Harvard Business Review* article from November 2014 argued the best ideas often come from observing things outside your industry or area of specialisation. For example, when a study on the safety gear of carpenters, inline skaters and roofers was conducted by three European economics professors, they found that the groups formulated better gear-improvement ideas for the other fields than they did for their own.[18]

4. LOOK FOR THE UNEXPECTED

Building on the importance of observation, often creativity and breakthrough innovation is merely a function of being alert to luck and serendipity. There are many powerful examples of staying alert to the unexpected, including that of Honda, who broke into and dominated the American off-road motorbike market by sheer accident.

Originally the company had set its sights on entering the on-road motorcycle market, but were met with persistent setbacks. Frustrated by the relentless failures, one of the US-based Honda executives, Kihachiro Kawashima, headed off-road in the hills behind Los Angeles one Saturday afternoon. Quickly, his Supercub bike started attracting the attention and interest of other riders.

In the months that followed, many of these bystanders began ordering their own Supercubs. Back at head office in Japan, the company leaders were so focused on the on-road market that they failed to recognise the growing orders for off-road bikes. Eventually the sales quantities became impossible to ignore and the executives woke up to the enormous opportunity that had been staring them in the face the whole time. They shifted their attention to off-road models and the rest is history.[19]

Opportunities often come disguised as anomalies

Honda's experience illustrates an important principle for creativity and innovation: the best ideas are often outliers or anomalies that are so unexpected that they're easy to miss. The key lesson for any organisation or leader is to stay alert to unexpected results and disconfirming evidence.

> The best ideas are often outliers or anomalies that are so unexpected that they're easy to miss.

History is full of examples of breakthrough innovations that only came about because someone was alert to the unexpected. Consider examples such as cornflakes, microwave ovens, Post-it notes, the Walkman, Teflon, nylon, Rogaine, kitty litter, Velcro, skateboards, to name a few.[20] Even the consumer sensation Craisins came about accidentally when someone at the Ocean Spray corporation discovered one day that leftover cranberry skins actually tasted quite good.[21]

The challenge for established businesses is to create systems that allow for the unexpected. In most businesses, unexpected successes usually go unnoticed because traditional reporting mechanisms aren't designed to detect them and feed them back to decision makers.

Along similar lines, Scott D. Anthony warns leaders to avoid the trap of separating the research functions of a business from decision makers—especially if the research is outsourced to a third-party company.

The problem with separating research and decision making is that researchers are wired toward summarising, synthesising and simplifying their findings. While this makes for trends that are easy to digest and communicate, this summation process almost always discounts or ignores data that doesn't conform to the expected results or lie within a few standard deviations of the mean. However, it's those very anomalies and outliers that can matter most as they may well be nascent trends that deserve attention or demand further examination.[22]

Such anomalies are 'outside the box' so if organisations and individuals are too busy measuring only what fits their existing hypothesis or assumptions, they may well miss opportunities that lie just beyond the frame of view. The cost of missed opportunities can be enormous. In the words of a client of mine: 'You've got to think outside the box or you'll soon be buried in one'. Overly dramatic, perhaps, but no less true when it comes to the critical importance of creativity in innovation and relevance.

In a more measured assessment, a former vice president of Monsanto, S. Allen Heininger, suggested that staying alert to the unexpected is a critical ingredient to business longevity and survival. According to Heininger, if a business is to succeed in the long run, it has no option but to remain 'alert to serendipity'.[23]

5. DEMOCRATISE INNOVATION

Many organisations unconsciously subscribe to a form of innovation apartheid. Sometimes this is driven by a misplaced belief that creativity is a special skill or ability possessed by gifted individuals. Other times, organisational structures create the notion that only those with certain titles or levels of authority are entitled to innovate.

The irony of this notion is that my work with countless organisations over the years has left me with little doubt that the best people to offer ideas and suggestions for innovations are frontline team members who interact with customers and competitors every day of the week. By virtue of the fact that they work 'at the coal face', these individuals glean perspectives and insights that those on the upper floors of corporate head offices rarely will.

In the words of Greg Lindon, who has been instrumental in the design of Amazon's customer interface:

> *In my experience, innovation can only come from the bottom. Those closest to the problem are in the best position to solve it. Everyone must be able to experiment, learn, and iterate. Position, obedience and tradition should hold no power.*[24]

While we celebrate visionary and highly visible innovators such as Jeff Bezos, Elon Musk, Richard Branson and Steve Jobs, it's important to remember that innovation is not the domain of a 'ruling elite'.

Smart leaders and organisations are recognising that there is tremendous power in unlocking the creative potential of everyone in an organisation. In the next chapter, we explore how the very structure of organisations can help facilitate this. However, before we can shift power structures, we must address the paradigms that sit behind them.

Henry Ford once famously asked, 'Why is it that whenever I ask for a pair of hands, a brain comes attached?'[25] Like many of his contemporaries, Henry Ford wanted employees that operated like robots: predictable, compliant and efficient. In reality, many leaders today are locked into the same paradigm—although very few would be so bold as to verbalise it in the way Ford did.

However, it is the latent human characteristics of creativity, curiosity and imagination possessed by every member of an organisation that can be the most important source of competitive advantage.

Innovation is everyone's job

A great example of a business that has recognised this in recent years is the household appliance manufacturer Whirlpool. A few years ago, Whirlpool recognised that they were rapidly losing ground to competitors. They had done all the right things: they'd improved efficiency in manufacturing, they'd consolidated their various brands, and they'd embarked on a global expansion to capitalise on growing markets. However, the core of Whirlpool's issue was a cultural one where innovation was not occurring at a rate necessary to keep pace with the market.

To address the problem, the company's leadership decided to embark on an exercise in cultural transformation by casting a new five-word internal vision: 'Innovation comes from everyone, everywhere'.

This marked a significant change in the way that company employees viewed their role and responsibilities. Creativity and innovation was now everybody's job and not just the domain of leadership or the R&D department. Within a few years, Whirlpool had transformed itself from a traditional manufacturer to a customer-focused enterprise producing some of the most innovative products in the industry.[26]

One of the more significant breakthroughs that came from this new democratised approach was an innovation that quickly became a multibillion-dollar business.

The genesis of this particular innovation came from a series of observations that Whirlpool staff made when doing research in users' homes. The historical assumption was that Whirlpool's target market was women. However it occurred to a team of Whirlpool employees that there is one room that is generally a man's domain — and one that had been largely ignored by companies over the years. That room? The garage.

Working from this insight, Whirlpool developed an innovative garage organisation system that they released under the brand name Gladiator Garageworks.

New thinking at the NHS

An even more impressive example of democratised innovation can be seen in the UK's lumbering National Health Service. Widely regarded as one of the most bureaucratic and unbending health services in the world, from deep in the ranks of the NHS's 1.7 million employees came a spark of innovation a few years ago that quickly became a wildfire.

Two women buried in the NHS bureaucracy became frustrated with the lack of progress and innovation they saw around them and in January 2013 set out to create a small movement known as the 'Day of Change'.

This initiative saw an online platform established where employees would make pledges for how they could change the NHS and improve patient care. The initial goal was that the Day of Change would attract 65 000 pledges from across the organisation, but this number quickly blew out to more than 185 000.

The flow-on effect in subsequent years has been extraordinary, with the Day of Change shifting the focus on ownership of innovation down to the individual and encouraging employees everywhere to be actively looking for ways to change the NHS for the better.

The NHS experience highlights that cultural change is not enough in democratising innovation — ensuring that innovation becomes an organisation-wide focus also requires more pragmatic steps to address bureaucratic roadblocks.

Look out for the clay layer

Reflecting on the challenges Toyota was facing in keeping up in a fast-paced age, the automaker's president, Akio Toyoda, pointed to the fact that it was hard for information from the front lines to filter up to him. 'Even if the information reaches me,' he said, 'by the time it does, it's probably outdated'.[27]

This dynamic I often refer to as the 'clay layer' exists in many organisations. The term describes how those in the lower echelons of an organisation often have the best ideas for improving performance, productivity or profitability, yet their ideas and insights typically fail to come to the attention of those who could act on them in a timely fashion—if at all.

Why? Because a 'clay layer' of middle management gatekeepers stifle such innovations in order to preserve and protect the status quo.

This aspect of bureaucracy played a key role in Nokia's demise as a leader in the mobile phone business. A full seven years before the iPhone's release, Nokia's research team developed mobile phones with colour touch screens, mapping software and e-commerce functionality.

A few years later, Nokia designed a wireless-enabled tablet computer long before the iPad was even imagined. And yet, according to former Nokia chief designer Frank Nuovo, many cutting-edge innovations such as these never made it to market due to a dysfunctional corporate culture. Nuovo describes how, in addition to being fragmented by internal rivalries, Nokia's research efforts were disconnected from the company's operations departments that were responsible for bringing devices to market—resulting in missed opportunities that cost the company dearly.[28]

> **The best ideas already exist in an organisation – in the hearts, minds and perspectives of its people.**

Innovation really must become everyone's job. As the old adage tells us, none of us is as smart as all of us. The faster leaders can shift out of the 'innovation apartheid' mode, the sooner they'll realise that the best ideas already exist in an organisation—in the hearts, minds and perspectives of its people.

6. LEVERAGE COMMON CREATIVITY

A colleague of mine recently posted a brilliant but anonymous quote on Facebook that has stuck with me ever since: 'Collaboration is not about gluing together existing ideas. It's about creating ideas that didn't exist until everyone entered the room'.

I love that insight because it is so true. There is something magic that happens when groups of diverse and curious individuals come together around issues. I've seen so many cases where a creative synergy develops when ideas and solutions form that none of the group could have come up with individually.

While the notion of brainstorming is far from unfamiliar, the reality is that many corporate brainstorming sessions are far from effective. I bet you've experienced this personally.

To understand the keys to making common creativity work, it's worth understanding where the notion of brainstorming originated. The original idea was created by Alex Osborn of global ad agency BBDO (he is actually the O in the name). The original purpose for brainstorming sessions was to address the tendency in ad agencies (and many other businesses) for people to be hesitant to share ideas for fear of ridicule or reprisal. The idea was to create an environment where people felt safe to share any and all ideas with a view to allowing the collective creativity of a group to steer discussions towards options and insights that would otherwise never have seen the light of day.

Experienced ad man Patrick Hollister suggests that good facilitation is key to ensuring that brainstorming truly unlocks the collective creativity of a group. He outlines a range of principles for facilitating group brainstorming sessions that I believe are relevant in any business context:[29]

∞ The facilitator must go into a brainstorming session from a position of strength. They must be sufficiently experienced and well-regarded so as to be held in high esteem by the group. That said, the facilitator's personal power must not be so great that they dominate, stifle or control the discussion.

∞ The facilitator's primary job is to ensure that every person has the chance to be heard and to monitor the tone of discussions.

The first hint of sarcasm and criticism needs to be dealt with swiftly if discussions are to stay open and constructive. Ground rules and penalties must be established for non-conforming behaviour (such as a time-out or a five-dollar 'cynicism fine' that gets donated to charity). It needs to be established at the outset that titles, status and reputation (good or bad) are left at the door.

∞ The facilitator needs to have a clear plan beforehand as to where they want the session to go. Good brainstorming is not simply a stream-of-consciousness exercise but needs to be directed by a clear sense of *why* the group has come together, *what* the problems they're seeking to address are, and *how* they'll know when they have achieved the outcome. To this last point, it's important to clarify that the goal is to come up with dozens of good ideas at most (not hundreds).

∞ The structure of a brainstorming session is also important. Hollister suggests a general rule of thumb where the first 10 per cent of time is dedicated to setting the purpose and ground rules for the meeting. The next 50 per cent of the session is spent generating ideas, followed by 25 per cent of session time discussing the ideas and voting on ones that deserve further attention or expansion. The final 15 per cent of the session is about deciding on a set of clear actions for moving forward. Notice that good brainstorming is not just about idea generation but a plan for taking action. Hollister's recommendation is that brainstorming sessions go for no more than two hours and that the group size be no more than eight people.

∞ The final and most important aspect of a facilitator's role is that they remain absolutely neutral. All ideas suggested are captured and evaluated by the group — not filtered by the facilitator. Even if someone in the group has a ludicrous idea, it's important the facilitator captures it because a failure to do so will be perceived as a criticism or rejection that'll quickly dissuade others from sharing.

Leveraging the common creativity of a group through facilitated brainstorming sessions is not rocket science and yet many organisations miss the opportunity it represents. Do it well, though, and you will quickly find yourself sifting through ideas that never existed before the group came together. And among those ideas could well be the gold nugget of your next breakthrough innovation.

7. FOSTER FRESH EYES

In 1997 when Naval Commander Michael Abrashoff took command of the *USS Benfold*, it was a significant appointment in many ways. Not only was Abrashoff the youngest leader to assume such a high-ranking post, but being appointed to lead the worst-performing US Navy ship in the Pacific Fleet must have seemed like a recipe for failure. Morale on the *USS Benfold* was at an all-time low and this was coupled with a woeful safety record and skyrocketing expenses.

Amazingly, at the 12-month anniversary of Abrashoff's appointment, the story couldn't have been more different. The *USS Benfold* had become the top performing ship in the region despite having no additional funding, no investment in updated technology and the very same crew that had been aboard a year earlier.

The secret to this turnaround had been to rethink the way crew members approached their roles. Abrashoff saw little sense in highly skilled crew members spending their time doing $10 per hour jobs when $100 per hour jobs needed their attention.

He grouped the ship's thousands of tasks into two broad categories: non-value-added chores and mission-critical work. He then set about actively seeking the input and ideas of crew members about how to shift the focus from the first category to the second.

A common complaint that immediately surfaced was the time and funds dedicated to continuously painting the ship—a task that took a full eight months of every year and cost hundreds of thousands of dollars. Sailors also complained that much of the requirement for painting was driven by rust and cracking caused by bolts and fasteners that tarnished the paint as they rapidly corroded. One day, a sailor came forward with a novel suggestion for addressing the problem: replace all the standard-issue bolts and fasteners with ones made from stainless steel.

This had never been tried before but Abrashoff decided to give it a go. The full replacement cost totalled $25 000 but would result in cost savings each year of well over ten times that amount.

Not only did this simple innovation free up sailors from doing the menial and non–value adding chore of painting, but it proved to be such a success that central command ordered every ship in the fleet follow suit and swap to stainless steel bolts.[30]

What strikes me most about this story is the fact that the size of the military bureaucracy could easily have prevented the sailor from making the simple suggestion he did. It would have been understandable if he'd dismissed the idea when it occurred to him, assuming 'surely someone has tried this at some stage—it's so obvious after all'. And yet, because of the culture Michael Abrashoff fostered, the sailor felt confident enough to make the suggestion—a suggestion that Abrashoff was in turn brave enough to take a risk with and implement.

The benefit of not knowing any better

This case study beautifully illustrates the power of fresh eyes. The perspective of those who 'don't know any better' owing to their inexperience, unfamiliarity with the status quo or lack of authority should be prized above all else.

The simple reason for this is that those with fresh eyes will invariably see what the experts fail to pick up on because they are too close to the situation.

Added to this, people with fresh eyes will often see the 'obvious' solution to complicated problems that have confounded the experts for years.

> **Those with fresh eyes will invariably see what the experts fail to pick up on because they are too close to the situation.**

Take the example of a young man by the name of Massoud Hassani. Having grown up in Kabul, Afghanistan, Hassani was well aware of the issue of landmines in his homeland. While experts had spent years trying to figure out a way to clear fields of deadly hidden mines, Hassani came up with an idea that was as simple as it was brilliant despite his lack of experience or formal qualifications.

Watching how tumbleweeds freely blew across the ground, Hassani devised an artificial tumbleweed made up of 200 bamboo rods with plastic feet called a 'Mine Kafon' ('mine exploder' in his native language). These Mine Kafons were heavy enough to trigger mines but light enough to be blown by the wind and flexible enough to withstand multiple blasts per unit. In the years since its creation, Hassani's ingenious invention has saved countless lives around the world.[31]

It was a similar story with 18-year-old Mexican man Julian Rios Cantu, who recently invented a bra that can detect early signs of breast cancer in the wearer.

Fitted with over 200 sensors, this 'auto exploration bra' only needs to be worn by users for one hour per week. The sensors monitor the texture, colour and temperature of the wearer's breasts, synching this data with a smartphone app via Bluetooth. The bra's heat sensors, for instance, are able to detect blood flow, which often indicates areas where blood may be feeding cancer cells.

Cantu's invention was motivated by his own mother's gruelling battle with breast cancer and by the fact that mammograms are difficult and expensive to access in Mexico. (There are only 9.5 mammography machines per million people in the country.)

While Cantu's invention is remarkable in its functionality and impact, the more remarkable thing is that it took an 18-year-old without a medical degree or experience in cancer treatment to come up with it.

Whether it is a new staff member who has just joined the team or a young person who hasn't yet 'learned their place', the beauty of those with fresh eyes is that they have no trouble thinking outside the box because they don't yet know what the box even looks like. More importantly, people with fresh eyes are blissfully unaware of how things have 'always been done'. As *The Forgotten Plague* author Frank Ryan suggests, 'Solutions often lie in unexpected places where only beginners might bother to look'.[32]

In previous chapters we have explored the various innovation mistakes that saw Microsoft largely miss the opportunities of social media, smartphones and search-based advertising. However, recent years have seen Microsoft address the insular and rigid culture that has held them back in the past.

Symbolic of how much Microsoft has changed, the company's 2015 annual executive retreat marked a significant departure from tradition. This retreat was new CEO Satya Nadella's first in the top job and he used the gathering of 180 of Microsoft's top leaders to make it clear that things were changing. Unlike previous retreats, Nadella controversially invited the heads of companies Microsoft had recently acquired to be a part of the retreat. This move was met with resistance from a number of the established leaders who felt the presence of these newcomers breached the established protocol of these exclusive events.

Nadella responded to the concerns and complaints head on:

> We're doing this because of the insights they bring. We did not get everything right about our culture, especially around learning from others. Otherwise, why would we miss big trends?[33]

Not all of Microsoft's executive team saw Nadella's move as an affront. Scott Guthrie, executive vice president of the Microsoft Cloud and Enterprise Group, who joined the company in 1997, affirmed the change: 'In the past, Microsoft assumed you had to be at the company 10 or 20 years to be in a leadership role,' he says. 'We consciously have recognised, "No, actually, that's wrong". We want to have people that have only been here six months'.[34]

While experience and longevity can be of value, the perspective of fresh eyes is hard to ignore. In the words of Alan Kay, who fathered the personal computer while based at Xerox's Palo Alto Research Center: 'Perspective is worth 80 IQ points'.[35]

And he's right: a fresh way of seeing things is often more valuable than sheer intelligence or significant experience.

Crowdsourced creativity

While leveraging the input of new entrants to an organisation can be a great way to harness fresh perspectives, a crowdsourced model of using social media to gain fresh insights can be equally powerful.

Companies such as Starbucks and discount airline JetBlue have made extensive use of social media in recent years for generating ideas. Surprisingly, McDonald's have been relatively late to the party, only recently establishing a dedicated team to monitor various social platforms. Paul Matson, McDonald's director of social and digital engagement, admitted this oversight, saying that, for a brand that gets mentioned on social media every one or two seconds, 'We seemed deaf and mute'.[36]

More than simply monitoring social media in order to respond to unhappy customers or try to manage their reputation, McDonald's quickly discovered that social media could be a powerful source of ideas and innovation. The launch of McDonald's all-day breakfast menu in October 2015 came about in response to Millennials who were complaining on social media about the fact they couldn't get breakfast items after 10.30 am.[37]

Organisational theorist James G. March argues that in order for knowledge to develop and grow, there must be a constant influx of the naive and the ignorant. In his book *The Wisdom of Crowds,* James Surowiecki agrees. 'Bringing new members into the organisation, even if they are less experienced and less capable, actually makes a group smarter.'[38]

Unfortunately, encouraging fresh perspectives from newcomers is generally low on the agenda for many organisations and leaders. More often than not, when a new person comes into a business, they tend to be implicitly told to sit in the corner, look and learn, and watch 'how things are done around here'. Then only once they know 'how things are done' can they offer any input or suggestions. In essence, new entrants are given their own custom-fit mental blinkers through a process called 'induction' (more appropriately known as 'indoctrination') and by the time their input or suggestions are sought they no longer have fresh eyes at all.

If you're in leadership, I strongly urge you to make the most of the people in your organisation or business who have fresh eyes — either due to their age or lack of experience. Furthermore, consider *deliberately* bringing people into your organisation who have experience in a different context. You'll be amazed what they see and the ideas they come up with. In the words of legendary futurist Alvin Toffler, old information looked at through new perspectives makes new information.

∞

In global research conducted in early 2015, it was found that a full 67 per cent of businesses lack the internal culture required to drive innovation.[39] Even when the will and desire for innovation exists, it's the supporting culture and mindset that are critical to seeing creativity and inventiveness flourish in any organisation.

As such, deliberately adopting a posture of curiosity by implementing all or some of the strategies we've discussed throughout this chapter will be key to driving the innovation necessary to stay one step ahead of disruption.

Questions for reflection

∞ How could you incorporate the habit of asking strategic questions in your role or context (e.g. imagine if…, why not…, if we pretend for a moment that…)?

∞ What steps could you take to create capacity for innovation and experimentation?

∞ How could you actively observe customers in order to gain insights and ideas?

∞ How could you become more alert to serendipity and luck?

∞ How could you create a culture where innovation becomes the responsibility of everyone in the organisation?

∞ In what ways could you leverage common creativity through crowdsourced ideas and brainstorming activities?

∞ What steps could you take to leverage the perspectives and insights of those with fresh eyes?

CHAPTER 13

THINK LIKE A STARTUP

In the early 2000s Jack Welch famously challenged his executive team to imagine themselves as technology startups entering the marketplace to challenge GE's various business units. In this exercise, which he dubbed 'Destroy Your Business.com', he encouraged each business unit to think about how they could kill their own products and revenue models using web-based resources and emerging models.

After each executive had presented their cannibalisation strategy, Welch asked the business leaders to go beyond hypotheticals and actually apply the thinking, tactics and technologies they had contrived to their own real-world businesses. It was a transformational experience for GE.[1]

More than a stunning example of the very healthy paranoia discussed in chapter 8, this visionary exercise was an effort to instil a startup mentality in a group of leaders who were in anything but startup mode—each of them was responsible for sprawling enterprises, billion-dollar budgets and many thousands of employees.

While many large businesses might use the *Lean Startup* language inspired by Eric Ries's best-selling book, fostering a startup *mentality* can be easier said than done. Nevertheless, doing so is vitally important if you are to thrive in this age of disruption.

In many ways, startups naturally exhibit many of the key mindsets and approaches we have explored in recent chapters. By virtue of their size, naivety and enthusiasm, startups tend to be humble and hungry—always looking for the big breakthrough and working tirelessly on every opportunity that comes their way. They are also ruthlessly customer-centric and friction-focused. The absence of historical baggage means there are no cattle tracks to pave, and slim margins along with small cash reserves mean that healthy paranoia tends to be a permanent condition.

However, in addition to the characteristics we have explored so far, the startup mentality is one characterised by three crucial qualities:

1. agility and responsiveness
2. action-orientation
3. a purpose-driven and entrepreneurial culture.

1. AGILITY AND RESPONSIVENESS

Large and mature organisations tend to be inertial at their core. In nature, as it is in business, size is almost always inversely related to agility.

> In nature, as it is in business, size is almost always inversely related to agility.

So is it possible for large businesses and mature organisations to mimic the agility and responsiveness of a nimble startup?

London Business School professor Gary Hamel suggests that, while this is challenging, it is definitely possible.

Sharing the stage with Gary at a conference in Singapore recently, I was fascinated to hear about the work he'd been doing in recent years helping large businesses shed the lumbering weight of inertia.

As one of the world's leading authorities on transforming large institutions, Gary is under no illusions as to how difficult the journey to agility can be. Even in the face of crisis or disruption, many incumbents will instinctively hunker down and stubbornly resist or fight the change—even to the point of lobbying governments to hold back the tide rather than adapting to it.

He suggests that the core challenge is that many large organisations don't have agility in their DNA. Trying to remedy this is like trying to get a dog to walk on its hind legs:

> If you dangle a treat in front of Bowser's nose, you may coax him into taking a few, halting steps on his hind feet, but the moment you turn your back, he'll be down on all fours again. That's because he's a quadruped, not a biped. Walking upright isn't in his DNA. Similarly, most companies don't have adaptability DNA in their corporate genome.[2]

To address this, efforts akin to gene therapy are required. What's necessary is a re-work of the way power, information and authority are distributed in an organisation. Mindsets need to be examined, assumptions challenged and systems reset.

Rethinking the role of control

Of all the psychological and practical shifts that large organisations need to make, it is the transition away from a hierarchical and bureaucratic management model that will prove most critical to achieving agility.

While talk of network-based business structures is far from new, and despite the rhetoric of empowerment and decentralisation, most leaders and large organisations cling to nineteenth-century management models. Although a rigid bureaucratic approach may promote discipline, alignment, consistency and predictability, these benefits all come at the cost of the very agility and responsiveness required to win in the twenty-first century.

There are of course exceptions to the rule. Companies such as ING, W.L. Gore, Haier, Nucor, Kyocera, Michelin and GE Aviation offer powerful examples of how large organisations can operate with systems and cultures typically belonging to much smaller entities.

In my book *Winning the Battle for Relevance*, I explored the brilliant example of W.L. Gore in pioneering a decentralised management model.

By any metric, W.L. Gore is an impressive business. Since the company's inception in 1958, it has never once made a loss. It is consistently ranked as one of the 'best places to work' and is an innovation powerhouse boasting more than 7500 registered patents to date.[3]

And yet, despite all these conventional measures of success, it is W.L. Gore's unconventional strategy for achieving them that is most extraordinary. Unlike every one of their competitors, no employee at W.L. Gore has a title. There are no bosses and no formal hierarchy. As a result, there is a free flow of ideas and innovation, resulting in an agile culture. All employees are 'owners' of the company, which creates a powerful sense of accountability and responsibility.

W.L. Gore's approach to appointing and evaluating leaders is equally unusual. Leaders are not chosen based on experience, longevity or even skill but based on the feedback and views of colleagues. The basic test of leadership is this: Are others willing to follow you?

Every employee is subject to a review process where they are evaluated by 20 to 30 peers and each employee will, in turn, evaluate 20 to 30 of their colleagues. The criteria for peer rankings is based around contribution to the company, how well you work with others, and how aligned your personal values are to the organisation's values. You only evaluate and are evaluated by employees you know and the results of these rankings are vitally important as they drive leadership opportunities and even your pay packet.

Beyond a culture of decentralised power, W.L. Gore's structure supports and reinforces a non-hierarchical model.

Business units and plants are kept deliberately small (no more than 250 to 300 people) and are clustered together on larger campuses based around function—for example, research, manufacturing and sales operate near each other.[4]

Although W.L. Gore has no EVPs, SVPs or VPs, the company does have a CEO; her name is Terri Kelly. Kelly acknowledges that while W.L. Gore's approach to management can be time-consuming, the trade-off is that it creates powerful buy-in and commitment.

In reflecting on how transferable the W.L. Gore model is for other businesses, Kelly suggests that other organisations could easily replicate the success of W.L. Gore's model but would need to first ask themselves some important questions such as:

∞ *What behaviours have been rewarded and reinforced in the past?* These will have created a series of unconscious expectations that need to be addressed.

∞ *Do you have a culture that genuinely believes in and encourages the contributions of individuals?* While most organisations espouse the importance of empowerment, many prize conformity above individuality.

∞ *Does your culture foster a collaborative spirit or is your culture one of competition and protectionism?* A true collaboration culture is always focused on ideas and outcomes rather than who gets the credit.

∞ *What motivates your leaders and what do they value?* If it is titles, power and preferential treatment, any attempts to challenge these sources of reward will be met with active and/or passive resistance.

According to Kelly, the biggest roadblock to moving away from a hierarchical model is generally a company's leaders:

You have to evaluate your leadership model. Our model requires leaders to look at their roles differently. They're not commanders; they're not lynchpins. Their job is to make the rest of the organisation successful. They have to give up power and control to allow this chaotic process to happen.[5]

Kelly says that while shifting to a decentralised model can be a challenging transition culturally, it is one worth making. She points to the fact that younger generations are looking for empowerment and a sense of meaning in their work. They want to know what they're working towards and to have sense of how their contribution is making a difference. Further still, they expect to work in a collaborative environment where information is shared freely. 'If an organisation doesn't have these things, you won't be able to attract [young] talent, and you certainly won't be able to retain it,' she says.[6]

Higher-order thinking at Haier

If there's one country where you'd expect the decentralised leadership ethos of W.L. Gore to be met with resistance, it would be China. Owing to its centralised Communist paradigm, you could easily imagine the notion of removing titles and empowering employees throughout an organisation to be a stretch for a Chinese business.

And yet leading Chinese electrical appliance manufacturer Haier is in fact a shining example of a decentralised and agile workplace structure.

Invoking Immanuel Kant, Haier's chairman, Zhang Ruimin, says,

> We encourage employees to become entrepreneurs because people are not a means to an end, but an end in themselves. Our goal is to let everyone become their own CEO — to help everyone fully realise their potential.[7]

This is more than mere rhetoric. Ruimin has been steadily transforming Haier's culture into one of genuine empowerment and self-direction over recent years.

Today, Haier's 40 000 staff are broken up into 2500 microbusinesses or microenterprises consisting of no more than 15 people. Each microenterprise has its own P&L and is accountable to achieve certain success metrics.

In contrast with the company's prevailing national culture, the entire business only has three leadership levels: CEO, platform team leaders and microenterprise members. The transition to this simple leadership structure did not come without its challenges. Haier lost 10 000 middle managers in the process — some of whom were made redundant, while others struggled to adjust mentally to their diminished authority and opted to leave.

From an agility and innovation standpoint, Haier's structure is extraordinary. The prevailing mindset from the chairman down is that the customer pays employees — not the company. This is reinforced by a notion of 'zero-distance' between the company and the customer, where real-time market feedback and input is sought actively.

Haier's Air Cube is a great example of an innovative product that was developed in response to consumer feedback and input. The Air Cube is a filter system that purifies the air in your home — ridding it of more than 250 common pollutants. What's most remarkable about this product, however, is how it came about. The genesis of the Air Cube was an idea generation platform where more than 800 000 customers had shared suggestions identifying their pain points and frustrations with existing products in the market. The Haier team used this feedback in every aspect of the Air Cube's design.

Although it's possible that crowdsourced product design like this could occur in even the most hierarchical organisation, in the case of Haier it's clear that the rate of innovation has required both internal and external responsiveness — a level of agility that traditional structures simply couldn't facilitate.

Looking at Haier's internal culture, one of the key drivers of innovation is the fact that every microenterprise can contract with any other microenterprise within the business. More than simply contracting services, this also allows microenterprises to raise venture capital for new projects from other business units — on the proviso that those seeking to raise funds invest some of their own money too. This has essentially created an internal venture capital pool within Haier and has led to a range of breakthrough innovations in recent years, including the tremendously successful gaming computer, Thunderobot.[8]

Bludgeoning bureaucracy in the banking sector

Founded in 1871, Svenska Handelsbanken may have a rich heritage but is anything but stuck in the past.

For years, it has been a shining example of what is possible when a large business takes the concept of empowerment and decentralisation seriously. Operating 840 branches in 25 countries and with a workforce of 12 000 people, Svenska Handelsbanken would have every reason for opting to retain power and control centrally. However, they don't.

Each one of the bank's branches has an extraordinary amount of control over how they engage with their local market. Branches have their own website and make decisions about marketing initiatives, staffing levels and employee salaries. Most remarkably, individual branches even set pricing for banking products such as loans at the local level.

While such local variance can pose challenges for brand consistency, the payoff is that local branches are extraordinarily adaptable to local needs and are accountable for their results. Almost all customer communications originate from a local branch rather than head office, which results in a tone that is personal, relevant and authentic.

Although the running costs of a branch are higher for Svenska Handelsbanken than comparable banks, the costs of lower central administration, bureaucracy and middle management at head office more than make up for it. And the proof is in the results. Svenska Handelsbanken have outperformed every one of their European banking peers since 1971. An astonishing feat by any standard.

Looking at one final example, GE Aviation has adopted a similar structure of decentralised power by eliminating shop-floor foremen across their 83 factory sites. GE's 26 000 production employees now work within self-managed teams and the result has been a marked increase in efficiency and effectiveness. Interestingly, GE's experience is in line with the findings of a recent study conducted by the University of Iowa, which found that factory workers who supervise themselves tended to outperform workers in more traditional hierarchies.[9]

Smaller and smarter

In addition to empowering employees, improving motivation and driving accountability, this shift to a smaller network model of business can also prove beneficial to the quality of thinking and creativity. As Steve Jobs observed, 'The quality of work resulting from a project is inversely proportional to the number of people involved in the project'.[10] Large and bureaucratic organisations tend to stifle creativity — after all, for ideas to get traction they need to survive the 'death by a thousand cuts' that often occurs as they make their way up the chain.

It's for this reason that Google have limited their average team size to fewer than seven individuals[11] and Jeff Bezos has used the 'Two Pizza Team' rule to ensure that work groups at Amazon never get any larger than 10 people — or small enough to be adequately fed by two large pizzas.[12]

Too good to be true?

While it's tempting to dismiss this model of shifting authority from central bureaucracies to networks of startup-esque business units as something that 'would never work in our business', I'd challenge this assumption. If big banks, a Chinese multinational and an industrial manufacturer can adopt this agile model, I'd argue the biggest barriers to embracing it are not pragmatic but rather the paradigm-bound and power-driven.

One important clarification to make is that control in itself isn't bad and need not stifle agility or innovation. After all, businesses need quality control to ensure safety, reliability and efficacy. However, control will limit both agility and responsiveness when it becomes a tool of power. It will also communicate a lack of trust and discourage the sort of revolutionary thinking necessary to adapt to disruption.

Regardless of whether an organisation adopts a wholesale model of decentralisation as we've explored in the previous pages, what's clear is that every business and leader must examine whether their culture, systems and power structures are fit for the future. After all, if the desire for control, predictability and order comes at the cost of agility and responsiveness, this may be too high a price to pay.

2. ACTION-ORIENTATION

As we have discussed previously, a dangerous dynamic can develop when a business matures. The entrepreneurial, adventurous spirit that got the company off the ground can give way to a focus on conservation, administration and maintenance.

Added to this, large companies can be easy places to hide. You can have the facade of being busy but produce very little. It's easy to fill your day attending meetings, writing reports and crafting beautiful strategy documents but actually not get much done.

This is simply not possible in startup businesses. It's all hands on deck and if someone isn't producing, it'll become clear very quickly.

For any organisation, the key is to cultivate the action-orientation, hunger and drive that are characteristic of startups. After all, innovation is more than just planning, analysing and strategising—it's about *doing*. In the words of Thomas Edison, 'If you're not sweating, you're not innovating'.[13]

In addition to analysis paralysis, large and successful organisations can often suffer from what Scott D. Anthony calls 'the Curse of Abundance'. The extensive resources of incumbents can erode a sense of urgency to act. 'Large companies,' he said, 'are often patient for results. The deep pockets of incumbents allow them to follow wrong strategies for longer. They keep throwing bodies against a problem'.[14]

ANZ, one of Australia's oldest banks, is in the process of transitioning away from the hierarchical model of old and becoming ruthlessly action- and outcomes-oriented. According to ANZ chief executive Shayne Elliott, the goal is to take a leaf out of the books of Haier and W.L. Gore and 'take an axe to the bank's hierarchies and bureaucracy'. Elliott's goal is to 'shift the workforce into "agile" teams, mimicking the way businesses such as Google, Facebook and Spotify operate' in order to act on opportunities and launch new products faster.

In the new structure, the bank will be re-organised into teams of 10-person 'squads' that will group together into 'tribes'. Beyond the limiting of a team's size and the adoption of new language, ANZ will also overhaul the company's approach to leadership and authority. Squad and tribe leaders will be appointed based on their adaptability and capacity to work across multiple teams rather than their tenure or career experience.

Instead of having departments that are heavily specialised around internal banking functions, teams will be organised around customer outcomes.

Day-to-day activities will change too. Team members will be asked to view project delivery timelines as six-week sprints, while their accountability for activity and progress will be gauged in daily stand-up meetings.

ANZ will be the first major Australian company to make such a drastic change to work practices and it doesn't come without its dangers. In the process of moving away from the traditional command-and-control hierarchy, risk management and regulatory compliance will remain vital—especially for a bank.[15]

To foster the action-orientated urgency of a startup, try shortening the horizons of deliverables and making teams accountable for daily or weekly progress as the ANZ bank are doing with their humans-week sprints. Add some competition and incentives into the mix and watch people's action-orientation shift into overdrive.

Naturally, action-orientation driven by shorter work horizons can foster dangerous short-term-ism if you're not careful. To combat this, leaders must always keep a longer term view, ensuring that the frenetic pace of experimentation, innovation and execution in the ranks stays aligned and strategic.

3. A PURPOSE-DRIVEN AND ENTREPRENEURIAL CULTURE

Startups tend to spring up in response to a gap, a need or an opportunity. Processes, power games and traditions aren't relevant—it's all about solving a problem or achieving a result as quickly and effectively as possible. As such, entrepreneurial skills such as inventiveness, curiosity and experimentation are key.

However, the longer a business or organisation exists, the easier it is for this entrepreneurial spirit to take a backseat.

In Walter Isaacson's biography of Steve Jobs, Jobs described how difficult it can be for large businesses to maintain an entrepreneurial and adventurous culture as they mature.[16] Dyer, Gregersen and Christensen describe a similarly dangerous dynamic in their book *The Innovator's DNA*. They explain how in the early days of any venture, discovery skills (such as exploration, innovation and creativity) are more highly valued than delivery, execution or management skills. However, as the company flourishes, this priority is reversed. Entrepreneurs are replaced by professional managers who have proven skills in delivering results but are not necessarily good at creating new ideas.[17]

While an organisation's leaders need to remain in entrepreneur mode as a business grows, they also need to foster a culture of entrepreneurialism in the people they lead.

Unfortunately, the bureaucratic system prevalent in most mature organisations has never been very good at promoting the innate creativity, curiosity, passion and imagination of human beings. The founder of the bureaucratic system, Max Weber, suggested that 'Bureaucracy develops more perfectly the more it succeeds in eliminating all the purely personal, irrational, and emotional elements which escape calculation'. In other words, the very things that make us entrepreneurial.

The bureaucratic system has never been very good at promoting the innate creativity, curiosity, passion and imagination of human beings

Online shoe and clothing retailer Zappos offers a great example of a mature business that has recaptured its startup roots. Recent years have seen the company move to abandon traditional authority structures and place the onus on employees to manage themselves. Zappos' CEO, Tony Hsieh, points out that the key benefit of this is that employees no longer have to seek permission to try new and innovative things as they once did. While the transition to the decentralised model has worked wonders, Hsieh admits that the company did lose a number of people who were somewhat institutionalised in the old structure and couldn't cope with the newfound freedom.[18]

Beyond changing structures, Zappos have ensured that a clear sense of purpose permeates the organisation. The company has built a powerful culture based on purpose over profits — one that inspires employees to bring their full, creative and entrepreneurial selves to work.[19]

An organisation of entrepreneurs

Over the years, many have built on Abraham Maslow's famous hierarchy of needs in order to understand the nature of human motivation. Drawing inspiration from the work of Maslow, Gary Hamel[20] and others, I'd propose the hierarchy shown in figure 13.1 when it comes to an organisation's employee paradigm.

Figure 13.1: employee paradigm hierarchy

Level 1: Compliance

This lowest level of human motivation focuses on having employees do as they are told. A set of prescribed rules and procedures are established and employees are encouraged to act but not think. Output is measured and monitored in order to achieve efficiency and predictability. At this level, employees are much like robots and bring very little of themselves into the workplace. They will work hard as long as they are being monitored and will generally do only as much as is required and no more. The ideal employee in level one organisations is **Efficient**.

Level 2: Competence

This second level is where employees are encouraged to work hard but to think as well as act. Intelligence and skill are valued and encouraged. Employee competence is key and skill training is a priority. However, employees are encouraged to develop skills in specialised but not general areas. Work tends to be siloed. The ideal employee in level two organisations is **Effective**.

Level 3: Commitment

At the third level, employees are incentivised to work hard and proactively find solutions to problems. However, such initiative is still restricted to siloed areas of specialty. This can lead to an 'it's not my job' culture, where employees apply themselves but only in their designated area and only as long as incentives exist. The ideal employee in level three organisations is **Engaged**.

Level 4: Creativity

Level four is where things get interesting. This is where the intellectual and emotional skills of employees are drawn out. Conventional wisdom is challenged, out-of-the box thinking is encouraged, and dissenting views are heard and acted upon. Employees know that their input is valued and so they seek out new information, new approaches and innovations that go well beyond their area of responsibility. Systems of accountability ensure that creativity doesn't turn into chaos or anarchy. The ideal employee in level four organisations is **Entrepreneurial**.

Level 5: Calling

At this top level, employees take full ownership of the vision. An overarching sense of purpose compels people to go above and beyond—the *individual's* sense of purpose is connected to the *organisation's* sense of purpose. Team members bring their whole selves to work and take work with them—always talking about, dreaming about and imagining how to advance the cause. The ideal employee in level five organisations is **Evangelistic**.

∞

Looking at the hierarchy shown in figure 13.1, I'd challenge you to reflect on which level of the employee paradigm pyramid your organisation is at. In contrast, which level do you imagine reflects the employment paradigm of a healthy startup business?

Interestingly, while many startups begin their lives at level 5, this is generally not sustainable as a company grows—after all, very few employees are going to be as zealous about the cause as a company's founders.

Over time, healthy and sustainable startups aim for level 4—the entrepreneurial employee paradigm.

In contrast, many large and mature businesses have organisational cultures and employee paradigms that more closely reflect levels 3, 2 or even 1. In these organisations, employees

Organisations need to be filled with individuals who are empowered, motivated and inspired to operate like entrepreneurs.

may be efficient, effective or even engaged, but in the disruptive years ahead this is not going to be enough.

A level-4 employee paradigm needs to be the goal. Organisations need to be filled with individuals who are empowered, motivated and inspired to operate like entrepreneurs.

As discussed in the preceding chapters, the most potent and creative innovations will likely come from everyone and anyone in an organisation. The key point, though, is that enduringly successful businesses will need team members who don't just bring their hands to work but also their heads and their hearts.

∞

As LinkedIn's co-founder Reed Hoffman suggests, Silicon Valley is a mindset, not a location. In much the same way, what sets startups apart from other businesses is not their size or context, but rather the paradigm with which they operate.

In order to think like a startup, leaders and businesses must have a relentless focus on creating structures that foster agility, responsiveness and action-orientation. Added to this, the entrepreneurial skills of curiosity, experimentation and creativity must be prized above all else.

Questions for reflection

∞ In what ways is your organisation's size or longevity coming at the cost of agility and responsiveness?

∞ What would some of the barriers be to moving to a decentralised model of power? And what do you suspect the benefits of this move might be?

∞ Who would feel threatened by a shift away from a hierarchical model of control?

∞ How could you actively limit the size of work teams and the time horizons of projects?

∞ At what level is your organisation in the employee paradigm pyramid? What steps could you take to foster a level 4 culture of entrepreneurialism?

CONCLUSION

Amid all these discussions about disruption and how to navigate it, I am mindful that you could well be feeling apprehensive at this point. After all, when you consider the turbulent times that lie ahead, it can seem confronting and even a bit terrifying.

In a recent TED talk, the great disruptor Elon Musk admitted that addressing this fear is a key motivator for all he is building and creating: 'I'm not trying to be anybody's saviour,' he said. 'I'm just trying to think about the future and not be sad'.[1]

Like Musk, I wholeheartedly believe the future is something to be excited about and hopeful for. The future may be confronting and uncertain, but it truly is an amazing time to be alive.

That said, the macro trends we've explored in this book can seem enormous and overwhelming to the point where we may feel that our role as individuals is minimal at best. However, nothing could be further from the truth. The role of the individual in helping brands, organisations and our world navigate the changes ahead cannot be underestimated.

A story I stumbled across recently highlighted this point very powerfully.

Shortly before the ill-fated *Titanic* set sail from Southampton on her maiden voyage, a last-minute crew change saw Second Officer David Blair replaced by Charles Lightoller — a change that almost certainly saved Blair's life, but which contributed to the loss of more than 1500 souls in the frigid waters of the Atlantic.

Blair's inadvertent role in the *Titanic* disaster has only come to light in recent years. As it turns out, when he was removed from his post, David Blair took with him the only key to the locker holding binoculars for the *Titanic*'s lookout tower. He had intended to pass this key on to his replacement, but in his haste to disembark before it set sail, this never happened.

As a result, those in the *Titanic*'s crow's nest lookout were left without binoculars and had to rely on their eyesight alone. In an inquiry following the tragedy, one of those manning the lookout on the night of the sinking, Fred Fleet, revealed that if he and his colleagues had had binoculars, there was no doubt they would have seen the iceberg soon enough to have averted disaster. As one expert noted, 'This is the key that could have saved the *Titanic* had it not left the ship'.[2]

The lesson here is powerful and perennially relevant. Organisations and institutions the world over are facing disruptions of a scale and significance we have never seen before. Like the icebergs lurking on the horizon on that fateful night in April 1912, these disruptions pose an extraordinary and existential threat.

But we all as individuals have a role to play in navigating the disruptions that lie ahead. No matter your level of experience, education or authority, it is your perspective, your insights and your ideas that may well be the key to preparing now for what's next.

And so as we sail into the uncharted waters that lie ahead, I want to wish you all the very best. Be brave and be bold. Embrace change before you are left with no other choice. Make failure your friend and avoid the trap of retreading that which needs rethinking. Embrace the paranoia that will keep you humble and hungry, focus obsessively on friction and strive to be different from, not better than, the competition around you. Remember that no sacred cows can be spared, get comfortable with a posture of curiosity, and approach the world with the entrepreneurial spirit and sense of purpose that any startup does.

As Elon Musk suggests, the future need not be viewed with fear or foreboding. Fortune does favour the prepared, and so now is the time to gear up and get ready.

To draw this book to a close, there is no better insight to leave you with than a caution first given 2500 years ago by the great Chinese philosopher Lao Tzu. 'Resisting change,' he said, 'is like trying to hold your breath. Even if you succeed, it won't end well'.

Such simple, profound and timely wisdom for thriving in this age of disruption.

APPENDIX A: THE DISRUPTIBILITY INDEX

HOW PRONE TO DISRUPTION ARE YOU?

In order to gauge how prone to disruption your business or organisation currently is, consider the 18 statements below and rate how true each of them is for you by circling the numbers along the scale from 1 to 5 provided:

1. **We operate in a market dominated by a small number of large operators.**

   NOT TRUE   1 – 2 – 3 – 4 – 5   VERY TRUE

2. **Profit margins on our products and services are generous.**

   NOT TRUE   1 – 2 – 3 – 4 – 5   VERY TRUE

3. **There is strong cohesion and unity within the team and we generally agree with each other's point of view.**

   NOT TRUE   1 – 2 – 3 – 4 – 5   VERY TRUE

4. **Government regulations and high setup costs are significant barriers to entry for new competitors.**

   NOT TRUE   1 – 2 – 3 – 4 – 5   VERY TRUE

5. The organisation is run by seasoned leaders who have significant leadership experience.

NOT TRUE   **1 – 2 – 3 – 4 – 5**   **VERY TRUE**

6. We make decisions based on data-driven insights and research rather than gut feel or intuition.

NOT TRUE   **1 – 2 – 3 – 4 – 5**   **VERY TRUE**

7. Consumers in our market find it difficult to change providers owing to the complexity and cost of doing so.

NOT TRUE   **1 – 2 – 3 – 4 – 5**   **VERY TRUE**

8. We have a strong heritage and many years of success behind us.

NOT TRUE   **1 – 2 – 3 – 4 – 5**   **VERY TRUE**

9. Our business systems and processes are proven and predictably effective.

NOT TRUE   **1 – 2 – 3 – 4 – 5**   **VERY TRUE**

10. We have significant financial and people resources at our disposal.

NOT TRUE   **1 – 2 – 3 – 4 – 5**   **VERY TRUE**

11. Much of our bread-and-butter revenue comes from high-skill, repeat and routine work.

NOT TRUE   **1 – 2 – 3 – 4 – 5**   **VERY TRUE**

12. We have experienced very few significant failures and strategic missteps in recent years.

NOT TRUE   **1 – 2 – 3 – 4 – 5**   **VERY TRUE**

13. Long-term projects and initiatives are well-resourced and clearly mapped out.

NOT TRUE   **1 – 2 – 3 – 4 – 5**   **VERY TRUE**

14. We routinely engage professionals to conduct formal market research with our customers.

NOT TRUE   **1 – 2 – 3 – 4 – 5**   **VERY TRUE**

15. Our proprietary assets or intellectual property are a key source of competitive advantage.

NOT TRUE   **1 – 2 – 3 – 4 – 5**   **VERY TRUE**

16. We regularly attend industry conferences and subscribe to all the leading trade journals/publications.

NOT TRUE   **1 – 2 – 3 – 4 – 5**   **VERY TRUE**

17. We have highly skilled individuals and teams that focus on innovation and research and development.

NOT TRUE   **1 – 2 – 3 – 4 – 5**   **VERY TRUE**

18. Quality control and performance metrics are closely monitored to ensure efficiency and effectiveness.

NOT TRUE   **1 – 2 – 3 – 4 – 5**   **VERY TRUE**

Now tally up the circled ratings you have given for each statement to determine your disruptibility score:

- ∞ 18–36 — minimally prone to disruption
- ∞ 37–54 — moderately prone to disruption
- ∞ 55–72 — highly prone to disruption
- ∞ 73–90 — extremely prone to disruption.

If you are like most of my clients, this result is likely a surprising one. Such is the paradoxical nature of the disruptive age we are entering. The very habits, practices and paradigms that may have been a strategic advantage in the past could well leave you vulnerable in the years to come.

However, even if you are only minimally or moderately prone to disruption, it pays to stay vigilant. The speed and pace of change means that a secure position today may not remain so for long.

APPENDIX B: THE SOCIETAL IMPLICATIONS OF AUTOMATION

In chapter 1 we looked at how big data, artificial intelligence (AI) and widescale automation will transform businesses and industries, but it is also valuable to widen the scope and explore some of the broader implications of these trends for society at large.

Take privacy, for instance.

The old adage stands true: nothing in life is truly free. With recent years seeing more software, online tools and apps made available to us at no charge, what we've failed to realise is that we *have* in fact paid for these benefits—and the currency has been our data. A good rule of thumb to remember is that in the digital age, if you are not paying for a product, you *are* the product.[1] In other words, the data and privacy you give away is where the value exchange occurs.

> In the digital age, if you are not paying for a product, you *are* the product

If you wear a device that monitors your sleep, exercise or the number and type of calories you consume, it won't be long before your insurance company will offer you a discount on your premium if you agree to share this data with them.[2]

While this may seem innocuous enough, it's what companies do with this data (and who they onsell it to) that we would be smart to pay attention to.

Our privacy can easily be violated. Look at AccuWeather, a popular weather app. In August 2017 it was revealed that the app was collecting private location data without users' permission. AccuWeather was then providing this data to a third-party data monetisation firm — even if the user had location sharing settings disabled on their smartphone.[3]

In another alarming example of what may become commonplace in the years ahead, a United States Senate Commerce committee revealed in 2013 that an American company named Medbase200 had sold lists of families with specific illnesses, including AIDS and gonorrhoea, to pharmaceutical companies. Even more despicable, they also advertised lists of rape victims at a price of $79 per 1000 names, and similar databases of domestic violence victims.[4]

While privacy legislation in various countries around the world aims to protect our data and identity, we are entering an age where legislation will struggle to keep up with the rate of technological advancement — especially when AI gets involved.

In a landmark case, the UK's data protection watchdog recently ruled that Google's AI lab DeepMind failed to comply with privacy laws in a data-sharing deal struck with the NHS. The agreement had given the DeepMind lab access to 1.6 million NHS patient records across three hospitals without the patients' prior knowledge.

Why was the NHS sharing data with DeepMind in the first place, you may ask? It was all in order to develop a new app called Streams, which would send an alert to a clinician's smartphone if a patient's condition deteriorated. It also allows clinicians full visibility on a patient's medical records to see where patients are being looked after.

The level of data shared with DeepMind was such that information on whether a patient was HIV-positive, had ever overdosed on drugs or had had an abortion was made readily available.

The UK's information commissioner, Elizabeth Denham, said after the court ruling:

> There's no doubt the huge potential that creative use of data could have on patient care and clinical improvements, but the price of innovation does not need to be the erosion of fundamental privacy rights.[5]

And this will be the balance we will need to keep aiming for in the years to come. With our data becoming more valuable, useful and powerful than ever, protecting our privacy and anonymity will perhaps become more important and more difficult to achieve than ever before.

Look no further than the recent case of US retailer Target overstepping the privacy mark to see why.

When Target's data scientists discovered that there was a strong correlation between early stage pregnancy and the purchase of a range of 25 health and cosmetics products, they decided to put these insights to use. When a customer's transaction history indicated the purchase of a certain number of these 25 products, the company's marketing machine swung into action, bombarding the customer with pregnancy-related advertising.

Beyond running the risk of possibly being insulting or presumptuous, Target's strategy proved disastrous for one teenage customer who suddenly began receiving pregnancy-themed advertising mailed to her home. When her father contacted store management, irate at the inappropriateness of sending such mail to his teenage daughter, it was left to his daughter to break the awkward news. In reality, a national retail store's data department knew she was pregnant long before any of those closest to her had any clue.[6]

WILL YOUR JOB BE TAKEN BY A ROBOT?

Beyond infringements of privacy, it is the impact that automation will have on jobs and professions that is perhaps most significant.

You've likely read the headlines regarding how many million jobs will be taken by robots, or what percentage of professions will disappear in the coming years. While some of these predictions are deliberately crafted for dramatic effect, they may well be close to the mark.

The most thorough and widely reported research looking at the potential of automation-led job losses in the coming years was conducted in 2013 by researchers at Oxford University. These researchers found that as many as 47 per cent of total United States employment had a 'high risk of computerisation' by the early 2030s[7] — more than 64 million jobs in all.[8]

In one sense, concerns about the impact of automation are nothing new. In 1931, John Maynard Keynes famously warned about widespread technological unemployment 'due to our discovery of means of economizing the use of labor outrunning the pace at which we can find new uses for labor'.[9]

In 1949, an internationally renowned MIT mathematician named Norbett Wiener predicted in *The New York Times* that technological automation would ultimately lead to 'an industrial revolution of unmitigated cruelty' which would 'reduce the economic value of the routine factory employee to a point at which he is not worth hiring at any price'.[10]

Sharing these concerns, in the mid 1960s US President Lyndon B. Johnson established the National Commission on Technology, Automation, and Economic Progress to examine the impact of technology on the economy and employment.[11]

What's most extraordinary about these concerns and predictions is that they were issued at a time when automation technology was positively primitive by today's standards — in the 1960s, for instance, 'computers' were still people, not machines.

This is half the challenge of predicting the ramifications of automation in the years to come — it is almost impossible to imagine the impact of technologies that are still in their infancy. Reflecting on this theme in a 2014 address, Bill Gates stated that 'Automation threatens all manner of workers, from drivers to waiters and nurses. I don't think people have that in their mental model'.[12]

In other words, we have almost no paradigm for imagining the world that will exist in the 2030s and 2040s — much less which of today's professions and industries will even still exist.

Millions of jobs and countless professions are set to disappear in the coming few decades. The question is, which will they be, and how can you ensure you don't find yourself in the firing line? Service industries and white collar jobs have been less affected by automation throughout history, but this is beginning to change.

The occupations set for obsolescence

The Oxford researchers who predicted 47 per cent of jobs would disappear arrived at this figure by analysing more than 700 different occupations. They identified a range of professions that were most prone to automation, including[13]:

∞ telemarketers and phone support workers

∞ tax preparers, bookkeepers and accountants

∞ insurance appraisers (especially in the auto industry)

∞ umpires, referees and other sports officials

∞ legal secretaries and paralegals

∞ waiters, hosts and hostesses

∞ real estate agents and brokers

∞ secretaries and administrative assistants

∞ couriers and messengers

∞ sewers

∞ watch repairers

∞ library technicians.

Other experts have added to this list with predictions of disruption-prone professions of their own. Digital media futurist Amy Webb predicts at least five career fields are 'ripe for disruption' very soon[14]:

∞ retail cashiers

∞ marketers

∞ customer service and support workers

∞ journalists

∞ lawyers.

Perhaps this fifth profession comes as a surprise. After all, surely an occupation as highly skilled as law would be safe from automation?

Think again.

AI is already transforming how discovery and research functions in legal cases are being done. Gone are the days where an attorney would sit in front of a computer monitor scanning a continuous stream of documents (up to eight in an hour) determining they were 'relevant' or 'not relevant' to a specific case. Now AI-powered software can scan millions of documents in the blink of an eye and determine which are the relevant ones.[15]

Going beyond simple word searches, this technology can isolate relevant legal concepts that may seem unrelated to the search parameters.

Courts too are beginning to embrace the age of AI. Family courts have recently been trialling an AI system called 'Split Up', which assesses the distribution of assets after separation. Larry Kamener of the Boston Consulting Group suggests that although robots will not replace judges any time soon, the

> combination of a judge's expertise and a computer's ability to process and analyse information can let judges make better decisions. A.I. could even draft judgments for review by a judge.[16]

Journalists may also seem an odd inclusion on Webb's list, owing to the creative nature of their work. However, sophisticated algorithms are already writing articles so human-sounding that readers cannot tell the difference between a piece written by a human journalist and one written by a computer.

According to Kristian Hammond, co-founder of a company that specialises in automated narrative generation, by the mid 2020s, 90 per cent of news will likely be generated by an algorithm.[17]

DISRUPTION-PROOF PROFESSIONS

Looking on the bright side, the Oxford researchers didn't just identify vulnerable jobs but also a range of professions that were deemed as highly unlikely to be automated. These included:

∞ mental health and substance abuse social workers

∞ choreographers

∞ physicians and surgeons

∞ psychologists

∞ human resources managers

∞ computer systems analysts

∞ anthropologists and archaeologists

∞ marine engineers and naval architects

∞ sales managers

∞ chief executives

∞ recreational therapists

∞ audiologists

∞ dentists.

While listing specific occupations that could be susceptible to or safe from automation is of value, MIT academics Daron Acemoglu and David Autor suggest that we would do well to evaluate how disruption-prone a profession is by examining it across two broad axes: cognitive vs manual, and routine vs non-routine.[18]

According to Acemoglu and Autor, professions and industries in the top left quadrant (non-routine and manual) such as hairdressers will fare well in the age of automation. On the other hand, cognitive and routine professions such as cashiers, mail clerks and bank tellers will be especially prone to automation.

CAREER ADVICE IN THE AGE OF AUTOMATION

Working with a group of CEOs recently, I was struck by the fact that the questions that kept arising from the audience didn't relate to their businesses or workforces but rather their own families. Midway through discussions, one of the CEOs raised her hand and with a distinct tone of concern asked: 'I have two teenage daughters—what study and career advice would you recommend I offer them in light of all this?'

I loved the raw honesty of the question as it brings back into sharp focus the fact that we're not talking about macro trends but individuals—the very people we love and care about most.

My response was that in addition to pursuing any profession that is both non-routine and manual, there are four specific skills and capabilities that will put any human in good stead to remain relevant in the age of automation:

1. creativity
2. instinct
3. perception
4. social/emotional skills.

1. Creativity

While creativity has been the sole domain of humans through history, AI is quickly encroaching, with learning algorithms mastering the art of musical composition, creative writing, graphic design and even new product engineering.[19] However, the elements of creativity that rely on our ability to synthesise unrelated ideas and construct something new or unexpected will remain a uniquely human skill for a long time yet. Added to this, our ability to craft humour, employ irony and explore the spiritual and metaphysical dimensions of life will not be replicated by a machine any time soon. After all, machines do not have a soul and it is the soul of a human out of which true creativity springs forth.

For the foreseeable future computers will remain devices especially good at answering questions, but not posing them. This means that entrepreneurs, inventors, scientists and creators of all kinds who can figure out what problem or opportunity to tackle next, or what uncharted territory to explore, will continue to be highly valuable.[20]

Machines do not have a soul and it is the soul of a human out of which true creativity springs forth.

Bearing this in mind, it's likely we will see a resurgence in the value of a traditional liberal arts education and its credo of 'learning how to think' in the years to come.[21]

2. Instinct

The value of our gut feeling, as humans, is hard to overstate. After all, our intuition plays a vital role in decision making—even if we fail to recognise it. I bet you can think of a good decision you have made at some stage in your life merely based on gut instinct. You had no data or logic by which you could discern the best path to pursue; you just knew it was right. Conversely, I suspect you can pinpoint poor or even disastrous decisions you have made in life because you relied on logic and went against your gut.

Machines are always dependent on the code they have been given or the data they are fed—neither of which allow for the very human instincts that are so critical when operating in a complex, uncertain and unpredictable world.

Gerd Gigerenzer in his book *Gut Feelings* underscores the important and often undervalued role of instinct in decision making:

> *In my scientific work, I have hunches. I can't explain always why I think a certain path is the right way, but I need to trust it and go ahead. I also have the ability to check these hunches and find out what they are about. That's the science part. Now, in private life, I rely on instinct. For instance, when I first met my wife, I didn't do computations. Nor did she.*[22]

Albert Einstein also argued in favour of placing value on human instincts: 'The intuitive mind is a sacred gift and the rational mind is a faithful servant. We have created a society that honors the servant and has forgotten the gift'.[23] In a twenty-first-century context, I would add that we have created machines that excel in modelling the servant but have little hope of emulating the master.

3. Perception

As MIT professors Erik Brynjolfsson and Andrew McAfee point out, computers are extraordinarily good at pattern recognition within their frames—but their skills advantage evaporates the moment they need to operate outside of these frames. Put simply, one of our key advantages as humans is our ability to employ multiple senses, which gives us a much broader scope for perceiving the world around us than any computer can achieve.

Cooks, gardeners, repairers, nurses, carpenters, dentists and home health aides all require significant amounts of multisensory perception, complex communication and large-frame pattern recognition—things we humans do best.[24] Our senses of touch, sight, hearing and smell significantly surpass the perceptive abilities of our digital equivalents and this is unlikely to change any time soon.[25]

Global retail giant Zara is a good example of a business that values the instincts and perceptions of their human staff over data-driven insights. When deciding what clothes to make, Zara doesn't look to computer modelling or analytics, rather they rely on their staff to discern and observe what customers are wearing and buying — looking for clues as to what the 'next hot thing' will be. Once staff have made suggestions, Zara's legendary production facilities are configured to be able to transform the suggestion from concept to product within five weeks. If it sells, they then mass produce and roll the item out more broadly.[26]

4. Social/emotional skills

Beyond our ability to create, intuit and perceive, it is our uniquely human capacity to care, empathise and connect emotionally that is perhaps our greatest and most enduring advantage over robots.

We are social and emotional beings and no humanoid robot will ever be able to truly replicate our high-touch abilities. Again, the soulless nature of machines will always mean their interactions with us will be cold and calculated, no matter how lifelike the technology becomes.

Jeff Bezos has famously said that great innovations lie in the unchanging elements of human existence. 'Don't ask me what will change. Ask what will not change,' he says.

The great unchangeables in life are clear: We want to be loved, known, to communicate, to care and be cared for. We crave connection and community.[27]

Nineteenth-century American writer and philosopher Elbert Hubbard said, 'One machine can do the work of fifty ordinary people. No machine can do the work of one extraordinary person'.[28]

He is right of course. The key message is that what defines 'extraordinary' is changing. The extraordinary individuals of the future will be so because of the degree to which they possess and harness the four human capabilities above. So if you are considering the smartest career choice for you or those you love, look for the ones that allow you to leverage your creativity, instinct, perception and social/emotional skills and you're likely to be on a safe wicket.

THE END OF MIDDLE CLASS AND MIDDLE MANAGEMENT?

While there will certainly be winners in the coming age of automation, people whose jobs will be not only safe but perhaps more lucrative than ever, even these 'safe' jobs will be unevenly distributed and far fewer in quantity. The World Economic Forum's Klaus Schwab highlighted this reality when he compared Detroit in 1990 with Silicon Valley in 2014. He pointed to the fact that in 1990, the three biggest companies in Detroit had a combined market capitalisation of $36 billion, revenue of $250 billion and 1.2 million employees.

In contrast, in 2004 Silicon Valley's three biggest companies had a market cap of $1.09 trillion, generating approximately the same revenues but with 10 times fewer employees than their Detroit counterparts two decades earlier.[29]

While this comparison could be deemed overly simplistic, what it does highlight is that those who will most be affected in the coming age of automation will be the very group that has also driven economic growth in recent decades: the middle class and those in middle management.

Since 2004, for instance, the average number of people employed full-time in the finance departments of large companies has declined 40 per cent as online tools have revolutionised account keeping. In the case of telco giant Verizon, automation of finance processes has seen 200 back-office locations close in recent years and finance department costs slashed by 21 per cent.[30] How pleased the finance department would be to see numbers like this—if they hadn't come at the cost of the department itself!

As a demonstration of how middle management will be affected by the age of automation, consider the example of San Francisco–based software company Good Data. By using Amazon's cloud services, Good Data can perform data analysis for its more than 6000 clients with a staff of just 180 people. In the past, each of these 6000 client companies would have required a team of at least five to perform the same analysis. So you do the maths 30 000 employees have been replaced by just 180 aided by automation technology.[31]

THE BRIGHT FUTURE OF AUTOMATION

I'm mindful that all this talk of countless millions out of work can make for less than inspiring reading. While the trends and possibilities we've explored in the past few pages are melancholy at best, there is some good news.

According to Accenture and Frontier Economics, AI has the potential to double annual economic growth by 2035 in 12 key economies that, together, generate more than 50 per cent of the world's economic output.[32] This need not seem entirely surprising when you consider that it takes the average person only 11 hours of labour per week to produce as much as they could produce in 40 hours in 1950, owing to technological advances over that time period.[33]

It's been also estimated that two-thirds of the shift away from automatable tasks will be driven by people changing the *way* they work, not losing their jobs entirely. The upshot of this is that automation will see workers rely more on their brains and personalities than on physical labour. By 2030, machines will likely take over roughly two hours of the repetitive manual tasks we currently do each week. This will allow for a greater focus on the interpersonal, instinct-driven and creative tasks that we humans do best.[34] Research from McKinsey questions the whole notion that AI will eliminate entire professions, but that rather it will simply remove the repetitive and mundane roles within existing jobs.[35]

In another sanguine assessment, the author of *Eat People*, Andy Kessler, suggests in *The Wall Street Journal* that

> *Technology always creates more jobs than it destroys. Steam engines destroyed jobs ... but enabled an explosion of manufacturing. Cars killed trolleys but enabled hundreds of millions of new jobs. Yes, some people are left behind. But as society gets wealthier, we can help them catch up.*[36]

To give an idea of just how many opportunities new technology can open up, consider how many new jobs and how much new wealth Apple's App Store has created since its inception in 2008. Within seven years of its launch, the App Store was generating $100 billion in revenues: more than the entire film industry.[37]

So while we've talked a lot about jobs and professions that will disappear in the coming years, it bears mentioning that scores of new professions will also be birthed—ones with titles we can scarcely imagine—including[38]:

∞ 3D organ printer technician

∞ neural augmentation specialist

∞ bio-identity manager

∞ neuromarketing manager

∞ tele-presence events manager

∞ virtual worlds entertainment producer

∞ amnesia surgeon

∞ chief experience officer

∞ energy harvester

∞ terabyter.[39]

Beyond economic growth and new professions, some of the brightest thinkers of our age point to the fact that widescale automation of professions through AI and robotics may well be the most significant shift in the way we humans have defined and derived value for many centuries.

The question celebrated writer and economic theorist Scott Santens poses is one worth pausing to reflect on: 'No one should be asking what we're going to do if computers take our jobs—we should all be asking what we get to do once freed from them'.[40]

Santens' question echoes a similar sentiment expressed by the great economist Adam Smith in 1776:

> The man whose whole life is spent in performing a few simple operations, of which the effects are perhaps always the same, or very nearly the same, has no occasion to exert his understanding.[41]

Put more simply, as robots free us from doing much of what we've described for centuries as 'normal everyday work', will we humans have the capacity to become more human and less robotic?

This is in fact the other end of the spectrum from the social Armageddon scenario most often painted. Could it be possible that the age of automation sees us adapt as humans to no longer define ourselves by our work—while at the same time ushering in a new age of productivity and prosperity? Work satisfaction is bound to increase as machines take over a greater share of dull routine jobs done by typically low-skilled workers. If current automation trends continue, low-skill workers will take on more stimulating and satisfying human tasks at work, and as many as 62 per cent of them will be happier in their jobs by 2030 compared with today.[42] Could automation even see the working week shortened, much as it was reduced from 7 to 5 days in the last century?[43]

A BALANCED PERSPECTIVE

While this utopian view is certainly an attractive notion and even a worthy goal, I suspect the reality of transitioning to a widely automated economy is going to be a bumpy ride. As possibly the most informed thinkers in this space, economists Erik Brynjolfsson and Andrew McAfee suggest, 'Technological progress is going to leave behind some people, perhaps even a lot of people, as it races ahead'.[44] We humans do have an amazing capacity for adaptability, but will we adapt fast enough?

Past senior adviser for innovation to the US secretary of state Alec Ross is concerned that we won't: 'Previous waves of digital-led globalisation and innovation drew enormous numbers of people out of poverty in low-cost labor markets—the next wave could do the opposite'.[45]

This is of special significance for young people, of whom 70 per cent are entering roles and occupations that are highly vulnerable to computerisation.[46]

Former US Treasury Secretary Lawrence Summers is concerned about this very point: 'If current trends continue, it could well be that a generation from now a quarter of middle-aged men will be out of work at any given moment'. From his standpoint, 'providing enough work' will be the major economic challenge facing the world.[47]

Note that Summers describes this as an *economic* challenge rather than a social or ideological one. That is significant because employees are, among others things, consumers. Wholesale job losses won't just have an impact on the social fabric of our communities but also on the very engine room of our economy.

In his book *The Rise of Robots*, Martin Ford recounts an often-told story about an interaction between Henry Ford II and Walter Reuther, who was the head of the United Auto Workers Union at the time. Touring a recently automated car manufacturing plant, the Ford Motor Company CEO taunted Reuther, asking, 'Walter, how are you going to get all these robots to pay union dues?' Reuther came right back at Ford, asking 'Henry, how are you going to get them to buy your cars?'[48]

The simple but important message is this: machines do not consume.

It's important to note that consumer spending by individuals makes up at least two-thirds of GDP in the United States and roughly 60 per cent in many developed countries. Jobs are the mechanism by which this purchasing power is distributed.[49]

SO WHAT IS THE BEST RESPONSE?

All this begs an important question: if we're going to see many millions of people out of work and a corresponding impact on consumption and GDP, what can we as a society start doing now to prepare?

Minds much greater than mine have been giving this a lot of thought in recent years. Some suggest a proactive strategy akin to Roosevelt's Depression-era New Deal may be necessary. By identifying the industries and workers most at risk of being disrupted by automation, governments could partner with employer groups and industry associations to offer job retraining and upskilling.[50]

While this is no doubt an admirable idea, the question is whether the disrupted employees and industries are capable of or willing to embrace the scale of upskilling that'd be required to keep pace. Also, with the strong possibility of a lower aggregate number of jobs on offer in the years to come, retraining people for roles that simply may not exist seems a little shortsighted.

Brynjolfsson and McAfee suggest a range of interesting ideas for recasting economic and social norms in an automated age. These range from designating certain categories of work that can only be performed by people (such as caring for babies and the elderly) to implementing a 'Made by Humans' brand that indicates a product was hand-crafted.[51]

At a more fundamental level, some suggest that the age of automation may well require us to implement an idea that's been thrown around over the years but never taken seriously—that of Universal Basic Income, or UBI.

UBI is essentially a program by which everyone would receive an equal amount of money each year that would ensure a minimum standard of living without removing the incentive to work.

This notion was first proposed in 1797 by English-American political activist Thomas Paine, in his pamphlet 'Agrarian Justice'. Later proponents included philosopher Bertrand Russell and Martin Luther King Jr.

While UBI may sound like a borderline socialist policy, it's worthwhile noting that economists and politicians from even the conservative far right have been advocates over the years—including the likes of Milton Friedman and Friedrich Hayek.[52] Conservatives have tended to endorse UBI on pragmatic rather than idealistic grounds, as it would preserve key elements of capitalism while addressing the reality that, as technology advances, some people can't make a living by offering their labour.[53] Despite unilateral support at various points over the past two centuries, no government has ever been willing or able to go from idea to implementation with UBI. The coming years will likely force our hand.

BEYOND THE ECONOMICS

As we bring this discussion to a close, there is one final facet of the societal implications of widescale automation we must consider: the non-economic value of work.

While we may be able to use automation to increase our economic productivity and quality of life, this will come at a cost. Certainly some of that cost can be ameliorated by compensating people whose jobs and professions are disrupted, and that is well and good.

However, what this purely economic focus ignores is the fact that being productive and gainfully employed is about far more than economics.

Work brings dignity to an individual's life. It creates the social bonds that hold our society together. It gives us a sense of purpose.[54] It brings a rhythm and structure to our days, weeks and lives. It also keeps us out of trouble.

As Voltaire famously observed, 'work saves a man from three great evils: boredom, vice and need'. We may be able to address the economic need that being out of work creates, but dealing with boredom and vice are issues that cannot be solved economically.

In a similar vein, Daniel Pink in his book *Drive* suggests that the three key motivations in life are mastery, autonomy and purpose. There are few things that create these things like doing work — even if it is menial and low-skilled.

∞

The coming age of widescale automation will have far-reaching effects on every facet of human life. While there will certainly be a number of benefits, it'd be naive or foolish not to consider the costs as well. I am confident that humans will adapt to this new normal but I am certain that the social transition ahead will be a challenging one for many.

The important role governments and civic leaders will play in forging new paths and imagining new possibilities cannot be overstated. The fabric of our society will be tested and many economic and philosophical assumptions of old will need to be challenged. But we must confront these challenges together and resist the trap of allowing a form of 'survival-of-the-fittest' Darwinism to recast the social order. To do this could well spell disaster for us all.

As the great Greek philosopher Plutarch observed, 'an imbalance between rich and poor is the oldest and most fatal ailment of all republics'. Just as the Luddites did in the late eighteenth century, each of us will need to fight to ensure that the gains created by automation are enjoyed by all.

ACKNOWLEDGEMENTS

Writing this book has been a truly fascinating experience. As someone who spends his life absorbed in the future, the research that went into these pages revealed some trends and forecasts that even I found staggering.

Like any significant undertaking, this book has been far from a solo effort. I have been surrounded by many brilliant individuals who regularly challenge and sharpen my thinking. Special mention to Dave Kuhn, Toby Zerna and Sam Haddon who do this better than most.

Thanks to Leanne Christie and the team at Ode Management for their constant support and encouragement. You really are world class.

Thanks also to Lucy, Chris and the team at Wiley along with my superb copy editor Allison Hiew and proofreader Shelia Kumar. You have each helped make this book more cohesive and compelling than it otherwise would be.

A big thank you to my wonderful wife, Hailey, and my little boy, Max, for your patience and grace as I worked long hours to meet tight publishing deadlines. I love you both more than I can say.

Finally, thanks to the many thousands of clients and audience members whose stories and experiences have informed both my thinking and the content of this book. I am forever in your debt.

REFERENCES

INTRODUCTION

1. Urban, T. 2015, 'The A.I. Revolution: The Road to Superintelligence', *Wait but Why* blog, 22 January.

2. Hamel, G. 2002, *Leading the Revolution*, Penguin, New York, p. 123.

3. Collister, P. 2017, *How to Use Innovation and Creativity in the Workplace*, Pan Macmillan, London, p. 160.

4. Szczerba, R. 2015, '15 Worst Tech Predictions of All Time', *Forbes*, 5 January.

5. Wallop, H. 2008, 'Bill Gates and Sir Alan Sugar Made Some of Worst Technology Predictions of All Time', *The Telegraph*, 9 December.

6. Ibid.

7. 2016, 'Foot in Mouth: 33 Quotes from Big Corporate Executives Who Laughed Off Disruption When It Hit', *CB Insights* blog, 14 December.

8. Hamel, G. 2002, *Leading the Revolution*, Penguin, New York, p. 123.

9. Bort, J. 2015, 'Retiring Cisco CEO Delivers Dire Prediction', *Business Insider*, 9 June.

10. 2015, 'Picking the Next Disruption', *Business Spectator*, 27 July.

11. Sasse, B. 2017, 'The Challenge of Our Disruptive Era', *The Wall Street Journal*, 21 April.

12. Rothkopf, D. 2017, *The Great Questions of Tomorrow*, Simon & Schuster, New York, p. 5.

13. Ibid., p. 10.

CHAPTER 1

1. Hamel, G. 2012, *What Matters Now*, Jossey-Bass, San Francisco, p. 120.

2. Kessler, A. 2017, 'Bill Gates vs. the Robots', *The Wall Street Journal*, 26 March.

3. Coran, M. 2017, 'Luddites Have Been Getting a Bad Rap for 200 Years', *Quartz*, 30 April.

4. Schwab, K. 2016, *The Fourth Industrial Revolution*, Penguin, London, pp. 6–8.

5. Ross, A. 2016, *Industries of the Future*, Simon & Schuster, New York, p. 154.

6. Ford, M. 2015, *Rise of the Robots*, Basic Books, New York, p. 86.

7. Ross, A. 2016, *Industries of the Future*, Simon & Schuster, New York, p. 153.

8. Rothkopf, D. 2017, *The Great Questions of Tomorrow*, Simon & Schuster, New York, p. 18.

9. Schwab, K. 2016, *The Fourth Industrial Revolution*, Penguin, London, p. 26.

10. Clancy, H. 2014, 'How GE Generates $1 Billion from Data', *Fortune,* 11 October.

11. Ferguson, A. 2016, 'Internet of Everything Coming to Change Our Lives', *The Sydney Morning Herald,* 30 July.

12. 2015, 'Picking the Next Disruption', *Business Spectator,* 27 July.

13. Ross, A. 2016, *Industries of the Future*, Simon & Schuster, New York, pp. 193, 194.

14. Brynjolfsson, E. & McAfee, A. 2017, 'The Business of Artificial Intelligence', *Harvard Business Review*, July.

15. Ford, M. 2015, *Rise of the Robots*, Basic Books, New York, p. 92.

16. Ibid.

17. Brynjolfsson, E. & McAfee, A. 2014, *The Second Machine Age*, Norton, New York, p. 141.

18. Brynjolfsson, E. & McAfee, A. 2017, 'The Business of Artificial Intelligence', *Harvard Business Review*, July.

19. Urban, T. 2015, 'The A.I. Revolution: the Road to Superintelligence', *Wait but Why* blog, 22 January.

20. Ford, M. 2015, *Rise of the Robots*, Basic Books, New York, p. 234.

21. Rothkopf, D. 2017, *The Great Questions of Tomorrow*, Simon & Schuster, New York, p. 29.

22. Turner, A. 2016, 'Google I/O: Chatty Assistant at Core of New Messaging App Home Control Centre', *The Sydney Morning Herald,* 19 May.

23. Brynjolfsson, E. & McAfee, A. 2017, 'The Business of Artificial Intelligence', *Harvard Business Review*, July.

24. Ibid.

25. 2014, 'How Google Cracked House Number Identification in Street View', *MIT Technology Review,* 6 January.

26. Ross, A. 2016, *Industries of the Future*, Simon & Schuster, New York, p. 28.

27. Kanter, Z. 2015, 'Autonomous Cars Will Destroy Millions of Jobs and Reshape the US Economy by 2025', *Quartz,* 13 May.

28. Ibid.

29. della Cava, M. 2017, 'Self-Driving Electric Vehicles to Make Car Ownership Vanish', *The Australian Financial Review,* 9 May.

30. Hirschauge, O. 2015, 'Are Driverless Cars Safer Cars?', *The Wall Street Journal,* 14 August.

31. Ramsay, M. 2016, 'Baidu to Test Drive Autonomous Cars in the U.S.', *The Wall Street Journal,* 16 March.

32. Thompson, C. 2015, 'How Cars Could Become Obsolete Within 30 Years', *Business Insider,* 30 June.

33. Colias, M. 2017, 'GM Tries a Subscription Plan for Cadillacs', *The Wall Street Journal,* 19 March.

34. Mims, C. 2017, 'How Self-Driving Cars Could End Uber', *The Wall Street Journal,* 7 May.

35. Camhi, J. 2017. 'Transportation and Logistics Briefing', *Business Insider,* 23 August.

36. Mims, C. 2016, 'Driverless Cars to Fuel Suburban Sprawl', *The Wall Street Journal,* 20 June.

37. Biba, E. 2016, 'Driverless Cars Will Improve Our Cities, Our Stress Levels and Our Waistlines', *The Australian Financial Review,* 6 February.

38. Constine, J. 2017, 'Val.ai lets self-driving cars bid for parking spots', *TechCrunch,* 15 May.

39. Kanter, Z. 2015, 'Autonomous Cars Will Destroy Millions of Jobs and Reshape US Economy by 2025', *Quartz,* 13 May.

40. Santens, S. 2015, 'Self-Driving Trucks Are Going to Hit Us Like a Human-Driven Truck', *Medium,* 17 May.

41. Kanter, Z. 2015, 'Autonomous Cars Will Destroy Millions of Jobs and Reshape US Economy by 2025', *Quartz,* 13 May.

42. Scism, L. 2016, 'Driverless Cars Threaten to Crash Insurers' Earnings', *The Wall Street Journal,* 29 July.

43. Ibid.

44. Ford, M. 2015, *Rise of the Robots,* Basic Books, New York, p. 183.

45. Spector, M. & Ramsay, M. 2016, 'U.S. Proposes Spending $4 Billion to Encourage Driverless Cars', *The Wall Street Journal,* 16 January.

46. Corfield, G. 2017, 'Kill Animals and Destroy Property Before Hurting Humans, Germany Tells Future Self-driving Cars', *The Register,* 24 August.

47. Kanter, Z. 2015, 'Autonomous Cars Will Destroy Millions of Jobs and Reshape US Economy by 2025', *Quartz,* 13 May.

48. Biba, E. 2016, 'Driverless Cars Will Improve Our Cities, Our Stress Levels and Our Waistlines', *The Australian Financial Review*, 6 February.

49. Berman, D. 2013, 'Daddy What Was a Truck Driver?', *The Wall Street Journal*, 23 July.

50. Ibid.

51. Davies, A. 2016, 'Uber's Self-Driving Truck Makes Its First Delivery', *Wired*, 27 October.

52. 2015, '2020 Technology Landscape', *Citrix Technology Office*, April.

53. Lee, A. 2017, 'Alipay Rolls Out World's First "Smile To Pay" Facial Recognition System at KFC Outlet in Hangzhou', *South China Morning Post*, 1 September.

54. 2015, '2020 Technology Landscape', *Citrix Technology Office*, April.

55. Taylor, K. 2016, 'Carl's Jr.'s CEO Predicts a Future of Restaurants with No Workers and Zero Human Interaction', *Business Insider*, 19 March.

56. Brandon, J. 2017, 'Walmart Will Scan for Unhappy Shoppers Using Facial Recognition', *VentureBeat*, 9 August.

57. Schwab, K. 2016, *The Fourth Industrial Revolution*, Penguin, London, p. 63.

58. Yeates, C. 2015, 'Rise of the Robots Highlights Grey Areas in Financial Service Advice Rules', *The Sydney Morning Herald*, 20 September.

59. 2013, 'Digital Darwinism: Thriving in the Face of Technology Change', The Association of Chartered Certified Accountants.

60. Ross, A. 2016, *Industries of the Future*, Simon & Schuster, New York, p. 40.

61. Cummins, C. 2016, 'Robots Are the New Frontline Receptionists', *The Sydney Morning Herald*, 6 October.

62. Ross, A. 2016, *Industries of the Future*, Simon & Schuster, New York, p. 39.

63. Ibid, pp. 15–17.

64. 2016, 'Amazon Plans for Giant Airship Warehouses Revealed', *The Guardian*, 30 December.

65. Boyle, M. 2017, 'Wal-Mart Applies for Patent for Blimp-Style Floating Warehouse', *Bloomberg*, 19 August.

66. Ford, M. 2015, *Rise of the Robots*, Basic Books, New York, pp. 16, 17.

67. Ibid, pp. 5, 6.

68. Brynjolfsson, E. & McAfee, A. 2014, *The Second Machine Age*, Norton, New York, p. 142.

69. Glaser, A. 2017, 'Virginia Is the First State to Pass a Law Allowing Robots to Deliver Straight to Your Door', *Recode*, 1 March.

70. Parsons, J. 2017, 'Retailers Must Move Fast to Avoid Amazon Trainwreck', *The Australian Financial Review*, 27 January.

71. Schwab, K. 2016, *The Fourth Industrial Revolution*, Penguin, London, p. 15.

72. Ford, M. 2015, *Rise of the Robots*, Basic Books, New York, p. 160.

73. Schwab, K. 2016, *The Fourth Industrial Revolution*, Penguin, London, p. 121.

74. Ford, M. 2015, *Rise of the Robots*, Basic Books, New York, pp. 152, 153.

75. Ross, A. 2016, *Industries of the Future*, Simon & Schuster, New York, pp. 32, 33.

76. Medix 2015, 'Top 10 Implantable Wearables Soon to Be in Your Body', *WTVOX*, 27 October.

77. Hannah, F. 2016, 'Robots Taking Our Jobs? Yeah, but Only the Crap Ones', *The Sydney Morning Herald*, 2 April.

78. Ge, C. 2017, 'Alibaba, Tencent See A.I. as Solution to China's Acute Shortage of Doctors', *South China Morning Post*, 12 July.

79. Ibid., pp. 32, 33.

80. Warhurst, L. 2016, 'Robot Performs Cancer Operation in a NZ First', *Newshub*, 16 November.

81. Bishop, T. 2017, 'Amazon Unveils $20 Dash Wand with Alexa for Voice-Enabled Grocery Ordering and Home Controls', *GeekWire*, 14 June.

82. Dunn, J. 2017, 'Amazon's Alexa Has Gained 14,000 Skills in the Last Year', *Business Insider*, 6 July.

83. 2017, 'Break Through the Hype — Uncover the Reality of A.I.', *Oracle + Bronto*, July.

84. 2017, 'Chatbots Will Save Business $8B a Year', *Which-50*, 9 May.

85. Haridy, R. 2017, 'Lingmo Language Translator Earpiece Powered by IBM Watson', *New Atlas*, 12 June.

86. Brynjolfsson, E. & McAfee, A. 2014, *The Second Machine Age*, Norton, New York, p. 23.

87. 2015, '2020 Technology Landscape', *Citrix Technology Office*, April.

88. Brynjolfsson, E. & McAfee, A. 2014, *The Second Machine Age*, Norton, New York, p. 231.

CHAPTER 2

1. King, M. 2015, 'Real Estate Agents Are on the Endangered List', *The Advocate*, 11 September.

2. Wilkins, G. 2016, 'Disruptor Sets Sights on Real Estate Industry', *The Sydney Morning Herald*, 1 August.

3. King, M. 2015, 'Real Estate Agents Are on the Endangered List', *The Advocate,* 11 September.

4. Ibid.

5. Courtenay, A. 2015, 'Start-up Invents Shazam for Property', *The Sydney Morning Herald,* 22 July.

6. Morrison, K. 2014, '81% of Shoppers Conduct Online Research Before Buying', *Adweek*, 28 November.

7. Perez, S. 2017, 'Cortana Can Now Do Price Comparisons When You're Shopping Online', *TechCrunch*, 9 June.

8. Townsend, T. 2017, 'Google Lens Is Google's Future', *Recode,* 19 May.

9. Rothkopf, D. 2017, *The Great Questions of Tomorrow*, Simon & Schuster, New York, p. 39.

10. Kash, R. & Calhoun, D. 2010, *How Companies Win*, HarperCollins, New York, pp. 2–3.

11. Ibid.

12. Perry, K. 2014, 'Hotel Guests "Fined" for Leaving Bad Review on TripAdvisor', *The Telegraph,* 18 November.

13. 2013, 'It's (Almost) All About Me', *Deloitte Australia,* July.

14. Alexander, H. 2016, 'Health Insurance Companies Encourage Consumers to Rate Doctors on New Website', *The Sydney Morning Herald,* 29 July.

15. Canton, J. 2015, *Future Smart*, Da Capo Press, Philadelphia, p. 163.

16. Collister, P. 2017, *How to Use Innovation and Creativity in the Workplace*, Pan Macmillan, London, p. 14.

17. Rothman, W. 2014, 'MakerBot Unveils a 3-D Printer Nearer to $1,000', *The Wall Street Journal,* 6 January.

18. Columbus, L. 2015, '2015 Roundup of 3D Printing Market Forecasts and Estimates', *Forbes,* 31 March.

19. Ibid.

20. Ibid.

21. Schwab, K. 2016, *The Fourth Industrial Revolution,* Penguin, London, p. 163.

22. Ford, M. 2015, *Rise of the Robots,* Basic Books, New York, pp. 177, 178

23. Ibid., p. 180.

24. Murphy, M. 2016, 'We're Closer to a Future Where We Can 3D Print Anything', *Quartz,* 5 April.

CHAPTER 3

1. Truman, C. 2015, 'The Fall of Singapore', *historylearningsite.co.uk*, 19 May.

2. Ho, S. 2013, 'Battle of Singapore', *Infopedia*, 19 July.

3. Truman, C. 2015, 'The Fall of Singapore', *historylearningsite.co.uk*, 19 May.

4. Ho, S. 2013, 'Battle of Singapore', *Infopedia*, 19 July.

5. Rapier, G. 2017, '13 Quotes From Bosses Who Mocked Technology and Got It (Very) Wrong', *Inc*, 15 June.

6. 2016, 'Foot in Mouth: 33 Quotes from Big Corporate Executives Who Laughed Off Disruption When It Hit', *CB Insights* blog, 14 December.

7. Ibid.

8. Schwab, K. 2016, *The Fourth Industrial Revolution*, Penguin, London, pp. 51, 52.

9. Lardinois, F. 2017, 'Google Launches Its A.I.-Powered Jobs Search Engine', *TechCrunch*, 20 June.

10. McGregor, J. 2014, 'eHarmony Wants to Match You with the Perfect Boss', *The Washington Post*, 8 August.

11. Bensinger, G. & Nicas, J. 2016, 'Uber to Put 100 Autonomous Volvo SUVs on Road in Pittsburgh', *The Wall Street Journal*, 18 August.

12. Houser, K. 2017, 'Lab-Grown Meat Is Healthier. It's Cheaper. It's the Future', *Futurism*, 21 February.

13. Linkner, J. 2014, *The Road to Reinvention*, Jossey-Bass, San Francisco, pp. 80–2.

14. Terlep, S. 2017, 'Gillette Faces New Attack from Old Razor Rival', *The Wall Street Journal*, 24 May.

15. 2016, 'Foot in Mouth: 33 Quotes from Big Corporate Executives Who Laughed Off Disruption When It Hit', *CB Insights* blog, 14 December.

16. Rapier, G. 2017, '13 Quotes from Bosses Who Mocked Technology and Got It (Very) Wrong', *Inc*, 15 June.

17. Perez, S. 2017, 'Comcast's "Instant TV" service for Cord Cutters Could launch by Year-end', *TechCrunch*, 27 July.

18. Flint, J. & Ramachandran, S. 2017, 'Netflix: the Monster That's Eating Hollywood', *The Wall Street Journal*, 24 March.

19. Flint, J. & Fritz, B. 2017, 'Disney Channels: Children Are Tuning Out', *The Wall Street Journal*, 4 July.

20. Ramachandran, S. 2017, 'As Streaming Services Amp Up, Not All TV Channels Make the Cut', *The Wall Street Journal*, 14 May.

21. 2017, 'Updates from VidCon: More Users, More Products, More Shows and Much More', Official *YouTube* blog, 22 June.

22. Nicas, J. 2017, 'YouTube Tops 1 Billion Hours of Video a Day, on Pace to Eclipse TV', *The Wall Street Journal*, 27 February.

23. Lee, V. 2017, 'Hasbro Shares Its Content Strategy Behind Launching a Brand on YouTube', *Think with Google*, June.

24. Anthony, S. 2017, *The Little Black Book of Innovation*, Harvard Business School Publishing, p. 90.

25. Ibid.

26. Sheahan, M. et al. 2016, 'Porsche CEO: an iPhone Belongs in Your Pocket, Not on the Road', *Business Insider*, 1 February.

27. Etherington, D. 2017, 'Tesla Now Worth More Than GM, Making It the Most Valuable U.S. Automaker', *TechCrunch*, 4 April.

28. Lee, M. 2012, 'Tesla Stores Challenges Auto Dealerships', *Union-Tribune San Diego*, 26 October.

29. Shankleman, J. & Warren, H. 2017, 'Solar Power Will Kill Coal Faster Than You Think', *Bloomberg*, 16 June.

30. Caughill, P. 2017, 'As Cost Plunges, Solar Power Is Ready to Surpass Coal', *Futurism*, 18 June.

31. Shankleman, J. & Warren, H. 2017, 'Solar Power Will Kill Coal Faster Than You Think', *Bloomberg*, 16 June.

32. Dzieza, J. 2015, 'Why Tesla's Battery for Your Home Should Terrify Utilities', *The Verge*, 13 February.

33. Ibid.

34. Sweet, C. & Higgins, T. 2016, 'Tesla CEO Elon Musk Aims to Make Solar Panels as Appealing as Electric Cars', *The Wall Street Journal*, 28 October.

35. Musk, E. 2017, 'The Future We're Building — and Boring', *TED Talk*, April.

36. Badger, E. 2015, 'Who Millennials Trust, and Don't Trust, Is Driving the New Economy', *The Washington Post*, 16 April.

37. Hartmans, A. 2017, 'Airbnb Now Has More Listings Worldwide Than the Top Five Hotel Brands Combined', *Business Insider*, 11 August.

38. Ross, A. 2016, *Industries of the Future*, Simon & Schuster, New York, p. 91.

39. Redrup, Y. 2017, 'Airbnb Books Flight Centre Deal Amid Corporate Travel Boom', *The Australian Financial Review*, 27 June.

40. Statt, N. 2016, 'Airbnb Is Transforming Itself from a Rental Company into a Travel Agency', *The Verge*, 17 November.

41. Zaleski, O. & De Vynck, G. 2016, 'Airbnb Is Building a Flight-Booking Tool', *Bloomberg*, 19 December.

42. Perez, S. 2017, 'Facebook Adds a Travel-Planning Feature Called City Guides', *TechCrunch*, 3 March.

43. Strutner, S. 2016, '7 Google Flights Tricks That Are Better Than Any Travel Agent', *The Huffington Post*, 18 October.

44. Whitehouse, K. 2015, 'Silicon Valley Is Coming Warns JP Morgan CEO', *USA Today*, 9 April.

45. McEnerny, T. 2015, 'Millennials to Wall Street: Cute Bank Branch... Dad', *DealBreaker*, 2 June.

46. Ibid.

47. Ibid.

48. Hamel, G. 2002, *Leading the Revolution*, Penguin, New York, p. 146.

49. Ross, A. 2016, *Industries of the Future*, Simon & Schuster, New York, p. 76.

50. Schwab, K. 2016, *The Fourth Industrial Revolution*, Penguin, London, p. 19.

51. Galland, D. 2017, '5 Industries That Blockchain Will Likely Disrupt by 2020', *Forbes*, 29 March.

52. Eyers, J. 2016, 'Blockchain and How It Will Change Everything', *The Sydney Morning Herald*, 6 February.

53. Schwab, K. 2016, *The Fourth Industrial Revolution*, Penguin, London, p. 63.

54. Eugenios, J. 2015, 'Your Bank Account: the Next Thing to Go Obsolete', *CNN Money*, 8 June.

55. 2016, 'Millennials, Mobiles & Money', *Telstra Corporation*.

56. Ross, A. 2016, *Industries of the Future*, Simon & Schuster, New York, p. 86.

57. Perez, S. 2017, 'You Can Now Send and Request Money in Gmail on Android', *TechCrunch*, 14 March.

58. Letts, S. 2014, 'Digital Disruption Could Cost Australian Banks $27 Billion a Year', *ABC News*, 4 July.

59. Karabell, Z. 2015, 'The Uberization of Money', *The Wall Street Journal*, 6 November.

60. Demos, T. 2016, 'Square's Newest Offering: Bank Loans', *The Wall Street Journal*, 24 March.

61. Rudegeair, P. 2017, 'Jack Dorsey's Square Inc. May Soon Loan You Money', *The Wall Street Journal*, 27 June.

62. Demos, T. 2016, 'Square's Newest Offering: Bank Loans', *The Wall Street Journal*, 24 March.

63. Rudegeair, P. 2017, 'Jack Dorsey's Square Makes a Move into Banking', *The Wall Street Journal*, 6 September.

64. Benner, K. 2017, 'Inside the Hotel Industry's Plan to Combat Airbnb', *The New York Times*, 16 April.

65. Schlesinger, L. 2017, 'Airbnb Took from Us, We Will Take from Them', *The Australian Financial Review*, 5 May.

CHAPTER 4

1. Terlep, S. 2016, 'Millennials Are Fine Without Fabric Softener; P&G Looks to Fix That', *The Wall Street Journal*, 16 December.

2. Terlep, S. 2016, 'Millennials Change the Complexion of the Beauty Business', *The Wall Street Journal*, 3 May.

3. Dent, H. 2009, *The Great Depression Ahead*, Simon & Schuster, New York, p. 43.

4. 2016, 'Millennials, Mobiles & Money', *Telstra Corporation*.

5. Barton, C. et al. 2012, 'The Millennial Consumer — Debunking Stereotypes', *The Boston Consulting Group*, April.

6. Virmani, P. 2014, 'Note to India's Leaders: Your 150m Young People Are Calling for Change', *The Guardian*, 8 April.

7. Ford, K. 2016, 'The Population of People Under the Age of 30 Is Set to Explode — and the World Isn't Ready', *Business Insider*, 13 August.

8. Boitnott, J. 2014, '5 Reasons Why Content Marketing Fails for Millennials', *Inc*, 24 September.

9. Abramovich, G. 2016, '15 Mind-Blowing Stats About Millennials', *CMO*, 1 July.

10. Ibid.

11. Ibid.

12. Ibid.

13. Tredgold, G. 2016, '29 Surprising Facts That Explain Why Millennials See the World Differently', *Inc*, 2 May.

14. Ifeanyi, K. 2017, 'Viacom's New Study Is a Marketer's Blueprint for Millennials', *FastCompany*, 19 April.

15. Ibid.

16. Ibid.

17. Ibid.

18. Mulligan Nelson, E. 2012, 'Millennials Want to Party with Your Brand but on Their Own Terms', *AdAge*, 2 August.

19. Antonow, Z. 2017, '41 Revealing Statistics About Millennials Every Marketer Should Know', *Ascend*, 6 June.

20. 2015, '2015 Global Contact Centre Benchmarking Report', *Dimension Data.*

21. Mitchell, S. 2016, 'Retailers Embrace Digital Ahead of Millennial Tsunami', *The Sydney Morning Herald*, 9 June.

22. Radfar, C. 2017, 'Autonomous Cars Will Bring a Moveable Feast of Products and Services', *TechCrunch*, 2 July.

23. Safdar, K. 2016, 'Target Goes after Millennials with Small, Focused Stores', *The Wall Street Journal*, 4 October.

24. 2017, 'Who Are the Millennial Shoppers? And What Do They Really Want?', *Accenture Outlook.*

25. Dudar, H. & Green, J. 2012, 'Gen Y Eschewing V-8 for 4G Threatens Auto Demand', *Bloomberg*, 7 August.

26. Biba, E. 2016, 'Driverless Cars Will Improve Our Cities, Our Stress Levels and Our Waistlines', *The Australian Financial Review*, 6 February.

27. Ibid.

28. Ibid.

29. Hagerty, J. 2016, 'Harley-Davidson Tries to Rejuvenate Motorcycle Sales', *The Wall Street Journal*, 12 January.

30. Ayers, J. 2016, 'How Banks Can Tackle Millennial Skepticism', *TechCrunch*, 2 November.

31. Back, A. 2016, 'A Future for Bricks-and-Mortar Banking', *The Wall Street Journal*, 30 May.

32. Ayers, J. 2016, 'How Banks Can Tackle Millennial Skepticism', *TechCrunch*, 2 November.

33. Ibid.

34. 2016, 'Millennials, Mobiles & Money', *Telstra Corporation.*

35. Lee, T. 2013, 'Top 10 Trends of the Next Generation of Travel: the Millennials', *Hotel Online*, April.

36. Ibid.

37. Germano, S. 2014, 'A Game of Golf? Not for Many Millennials', *The Wall Street Journal*, 1 August.

38. Ibid.

39. Boitnott, J. 2014, '5 Reasons Why Content Marketing Fails for Millennials', *Inc*, 24 September.

40. Fromm, J. 2011, 'Millennials and Cause: Seven Things We Learned from 5,493 People', *Barkley*, 24 October.

41. 2016, 'Millennials, Mobiles & Money', Telstra Corporation.

42. 2015, '2015 Millennial Survey', Deloitte.

43. Ibid.

44. 2015, 'Generations in the Workplace: the Big Shift', Lehigh University, 2 March.

45. 2015, '2015 Millennial Survey', Deloitte.

46. Ibid.

47. Ibid.

48. Waters, C. 2017, 'Angry, Young Accountants Lead Exodus from Big Firms', *The Sydney Morning Herald*, 31 March.

49. Ibid.

50. Huang, D. & Gellman, L. 2016, 'Millennial Employees Confound Big Banks', *The Wall Street Journal,* 8 April.

51. Ibid.

52. Drucker, P. 1985, *Innovation and Entrepreneurship*, HarperCollins, New York, p. 92.

CHAPTER 5

1. Brynjolfsson, E. & McAfee, A. 2014, *The Second Machine Age*, Norton, New York, p. 20.

2. Anthony, S. 2017, *The Little Black Book of Innovation*, Harvard Business School Publishing, pp. 89, 90.

3. Ibid., p. 91.

4. Hamel, G. 2002, *Leading the Revolution*, Penguin, New York, p. 137.

5. Ibid., p. 126.

6. Ibid., p. 129.

7. Yoo, T. 2017, 'Barclays' Boss Thinks His Bank Is Too Big to Be Challenged by Fintech Startups', *Business Insider,* 4 May.

8. Kharpal, A. 2017, 'Bank Branches Will Be "As Common As a Blockbuster" Store, Ex-Barclays CEO Antony Jenkins Says', *CNBC*, 27 June.

9. Ramachandran, S. & Trachtenberg, J. 2012, 'End of Era for Encyclopedia Britannica', *The Wall Street Journal*, 14 March.

10. Hamel, G. 2012, *What Matters Now*, Jossey-Bass, San Francisco, p. 122.

11. Rigby, R. 2011, *Business Thinkers Who Changed the World*, Kogan Page, London, p. 1.

12. Hastings, R. & Andreessen, M. 2017, 'Tech and Entertainment in the Era of Mass Customization', *a16z Podcast,* 25 February.

13. Bailey, M. 2017, 'Seek and Hudson Back Slingshot Accelerator for Disruptive Workplace Ideas', *The Australian Financial Review,* 6 February.

14. Kargas, C. 2014, 'Adapting to Survive and Thrive', *Transportation Evolution Institute,* 16 October.

15. Hullinger, J. 2015, 'This Is the Future of College', *Fast Company,* 18 May.

16. Ibid.

17. Dodd, T. 2015, 'University of Adelaide Is Phasing Out Lectures', *The Australian Financial Review,* 28 June.

18. Ibid.

19. Dodd, T. 2015, 'Universities Should Be Like Netflix and Allow Binge Learning', *The Australian* Financial *Review,* 27 October.

20. Gettler, L. 2012, 'Focused on the Negatives', *Management Today,* April.

21. Mourdoukoutas, P. 2017, 'Corning Beats Apple', *Forbes,* 9 July.

22. Christensen, P. & Raynor, M. 2003, *The Innovators Solution,* Harvard Business School, pp. 40, 41.

23. Hamel, G. 2012, *What Matters Now,* Jossey-Bass, San Francisco, pp. 64–9.

CHAPTER 6

1. Schwab, K. 2017, 'What Designers Can Learn from the Museum of Failure (Yes, It Exists)', *Fast Company,* 6 June.

2. Wilczek, F. 2017, 'The Power of Learning by Doing', *The Wall Street Journal,* 18 January.

3. Kriegel, R. & Brandt, D. 1997, *Sacred Cows Make the Best Burgers,* Time Warner, New York, p. 6.

4. Sull, D. 2003, *Why Good Companies Go Bad,* Harvard Business School, pp. 33, 34.

5. Collister, P. 2017, *How to Use Innovation and Creativity in the Workplace,* Pan Macmillan, London, pp. 34, 35.

6. Linkner, J. 2014, *The Road to Reinvention,* Jossey-Bass, San Francisco, pp. 61–3.

7. Collins, J. & Hansen, M. 2011, *Great by Choice,* HarperCollins, New York, pp. 78–80.

8. Hamel, G. 2012, *What Matters Now,* Jossey-Bass, San Francisco, p. 124.

9. Ibid., p. 125.

10. Williams-Grut, O. 2015, 'An "Uber Moment" Is Heading for the Banking Industry', *Business Insider*, 27 November.

11. Anthony, S. 2017, *The Little Black Book of Innovation*, Harvard Business School Publishing, p. 65.

12. Krupp, S. 2015, '6 Strategies Great Leaders Use for Long-Term Success', *Business Insider*, 19 May.

13. Kwoh, L. 2013, 'Memo to Staff: Take More Risks', *The Wall Street Journal*, 20 March.

14. Kortleven, C. 2016, *Less is Beautiful*, p. 161.

15. Hamel, G. 2002, *Leading the Revolution*, Penguin, New York, p. 153.

16. Rice, J. 2013, 'Failure Has to Be Acceptable', *The Wall Street Journal*, 25 February.

17. Linkner, J. 2014, *The Road to Reinvention*, Jossey-Bass, San Francisco, p. 75.

18. Harford, T. 2011, *Adapt*, Farrar, Straus and Giroux, New York, p. 242.

19. Ibid., p. 11.

20. Dyer, J., Gregersen, H. & Christensen, C. 2011, *The Innovator's DNA*, Harvard Business School, p. 166.

21. Perez, S. 2017, 'Google Unveils Advr, an Experimental Area 120 Project for Advertising in VR', *TechCrunch*, 28 June.

22. Hamel, G. 2002, *Leading the Revolution*, Penguin, New York, pp. 271, 272.

23. Hamel, G. 2012, *What Matters Now*, Jossey-Bass, San Francisco, p. 128.

24. Collister, P. 2017, *How to Use Innovation and Creativity in the Workplace*, Pan Macmillan, London, p. 150.

CHAPTER 7

1. Carroll, P. & Mui, C. 2008, *Billion Dollar Lessons*, Penguin, New York, p. 5.

2. Ibid., pp. 94–5.

3. Anthony, S. 2017, *The Little Black Book of Innovation*, Harvard Business School Publishing, p. 69.

4. Carroll, P. & Mui, C. 2008, *Billion Dollar Lessons*, Penguin, New York, p. 103.

5. Brynjolfsson, E. & McAfee, A. 2014, *The Second Machine Age*, Norton, New York, p. 126.

6. Colias, M. 2017, 'GM Tries a Subscription Plan for Cadillacs', *The Wall Street Journal*, 19 March.

7. Osterwalder, A. & Pigneur, Y. 2010, *Business Model Generation*, Wiley, New Jersey, p. 141.

8. Chan, P. 2017, 'QR Codes—the Catalyst for Mobile Payment in China', *Medium,* 4 June.

9. Hamel, G. 2002, *Leading the Revolution*, Penguin, New York, p. 264.

10. Drucker, P. 1985, *Innovation and Entrepreneurship*, HarperCollins, New York, pp. 62–3.

11. Eichenwald, K. 2012, 'Microsoft's Lost Decade', *Vanity Fair,* August.

12. Linkner, J. 2014, *The Road to Reinvention*, Jossey-Bass, San Francisco, p. 58.

13. Nocera, J. 2012, 'Has Apple Peaked?', *The New York Times*, 24 September.

14. Ovide, S. 2013, 'Next CEO's Biggest Job: Fixing Microsoft's Culture', *The Wall Street Journal*, 25 August.

15. Ibid.

16. Eichenwald, K. 2012, 'Microsoft's Lost Decade', *Vanity Fair,* August.

17. Ibid.

18. Anthony, S. 2017, *The Little Black Book of Innovation*, Harvard Business School Publishing, p. 225.

19. Ibid.

20. Day, M. 2016, 'How Microsoft Emerged from the Darkness to Embrace the Cloud', *The Seattle Times,* 12 December.

21. Eichenwald, K 2012, 'Microsoft's Lost Decade', *Vanity Fair,* August.

22. Ovide, S. 2014, 'Microsoft Bucks Trend as Sales Defy Expectations', *The Wall Street Journal*, 23 October.

23. Ibid.

CHAPTER 8

1. England, L. 2015, 'Here's What's Inside the Little Red Book That Is Placed on the Desk of Every Facebook Employee', *Business Insider,* 29 May.

2. Ibid.

3. Zweig, J. 2013, 'Lesson from Buffett: Doubt Yourself', *The Wall Street Journal*, 5 May.

4. Ibid.

5. MacKay, H. 2011, 'Where There's Faith, So Too Doubt', *Sydney Morning Herald*, 26 December.

6. Kriegel, R. 1991, *If It Ain't Broke … Break It!*, Time Warner, New York, p. 74.

7. Larreche, J. 2008, *The Momentum Effect*, Wharton School Publishing, New Jersey, p. 51.

8. Anthony, S. 2017, *The Little Black Book of Innovation*, Harvard Business School Publishing, p. 63.

9. Thompson, J. 2009, '1969: Seiko's Breakout Year', *Watchtime*, 20 December.

10. Ibid.

11. Koltrowitz, S. 2014, 'Smart Watches? Not at This Time, Say Wary Swiss', *The Sydney Morning Herald*, 31 March.

12. Ibid.

13. Gretler, C. 2017, 'Swatch Takes on Google, Apple with Watch Operating System', *Bloomberg*, 17 March.

14. McSpedden, B. 2017, 'Hold the Phone: Connected Watches Not the Answer for Omega', *The Australian Financial Review*, 12 February.

15. Mickle, T. 2017, 'I'm Not Sure I Understand — How Apple's Siri Lost Her Mojo', *The Wall Street* Journal, 7 June.

16. Ibid.

17. Hamel, G. 2012, *What Matters Now,* Jossey-Bass, San Francisco, pp. 107–9.

18. Linkner, J. 2014, *The Road to Reinvention*, Jossey-Bass, San Francisco, p. 28.

19. Drucker, P. 1985, *Innovation and Entrepreneurship*, HarperCollins, New York, p. 85.

20. Hamel, G. 2002, *Leading the Revolution*, Penguin, New York, p. 49.

21. Garrison, M. 2013, 'What Apple Learned from a Luxury Hotel', *Marketplace*, 31 December.

22. Collister, P. 2017, *How to Use Innovation and Creativity in the Workplace*, Pan Macmillan, London, p. 158.

23. Galant, G. 2016, 'If We Got Kicked Out and the Board Brought In a New CEO, What Do You Think He'd Do?', *Medium*, 22 March.

24. Collins, J. & Hansen, M. 2011, *Great by Choice*, HarperCollins, New York, pp. 139, 140.

25. Surowiecki, J. 2004, *The Wisdom of Crowds*, Anchor Books, New York, pp. 36–7.

26. Collister, P. 2017, *How to Use Innovation and Creativity in the Workplace*, Pan Macmillan, London, p. 95.

27. Sull, D. 2003, *Why Good Companies Go Bad*, Harvard Business School, pp. 44–57.

28. Ibid., pp. 44–57.

29. Lublin, J. 2015, 'Study Links Diverse Leadership with Firms' Financial Gains', *The Wall Street Journal*, 20 January.

30. Ibid., p. 233.

31. Ibid., p. 236.

32. Hamel, G. 2012, *What Matters Now*, Jossey-Bass, San Francisco, p. 123.

33. Harford, T. 2011, *Adapt*, Farrar, Straus and Giroux, New York, p. 242.

CHAPTER 9

1. Balea, J. 2016, 'Transferwise: Banks Are Greedy — That's Why They're Losing Out to Fintech Startups', *Tech In Asia*, 13 September.

2. Ross, A. 2016, *Industries of the Future*, Simon & Schuster, New York, p. 80.

3. Ibid.

4. Whitehouse, K. 2015, 'Silicon Valley Is Coming Warns JP Morgan CEO', *USA Today*, 9 April.

5. Anthony, S. 2017, *The Little Black Book of Innovation*, Harvard Business School Publishing, p. 116.

6. Ibid., pp. 95–7.

7. Lin, L. & Strumpf, D. 2017, 'Two Simcards and Better Selfies: How China's Smartphones Are Taking on Apple', *The Wall Street Journal*, 8 June.

8. 2017, 'What Are the Drivers?', *The Property Academy Four-I Newsletter*, Issue 110.

9. Anthony, S. 2017, *The Little Black Book of Innovation*, Harvard Business School Publishing, p. 169.

10. Larreche, J. 2008, *The Momentum Effect*, Wharton School Publishing, New Jersey, p. 22.

11. Higginbotham, S. 2015, 'Hilton Will Let Hotel Guests Use Their Smartphones as Their Room Keys', *Fortune*, 12 August.

12. Flanders, C. 2017, 'Amazon Will Train Australians to Expect Far More', *The Australian Financial Review*, 2 August.

13. Young, Y. 2017, 'Why Can't My Bank Be More Like Amazon?', *The Globe and Mail*, 4 August.

14. Buhr, S. 2017, 'Eligible Founder Katelyn Gleason's Plan to Upend the Billion Dollar Medical Billing Industry', *TechCrunch*, 25 March.

15. Ibid.

16. Kortleven, C. 2016, *Less is Beautiful*, p. 115.

17. 2015, '2020 Technology Landscape', *Citrix Technology Office*, April.

CHAPTER 10

1. Mitchell, S. 2016, 'Drums Are Beating as Amazon Sets Up Shop', *The Australian Financial Review*, 21 December.

2. Germano, S. & Stevens, L. 2017, 'Nike to Sell Some Items Directly to Amazon', *The Wall Street Journal*, 21 June.

3. Peterson, H. 2017, 'Warren Buffet Has Confirmed the Death of Retails as We Know It', *Business* Insider, 9 May.

4. Ibid.

5. Fung, E. 2017, 'The Mall of the Future Will Have No Stores', *The Wall Street Journal*, 12 June.

6. Kapner, S. 2017, 'Nordstrom Tries on a New Look: Stores Without Merchandise', *The Wall Street Journal*, 10 September.

7. McDuling, J. 2017, 'Amazon in Australia Is An Enormous Opportunity for Some', *The Australian Financial Review*, 21 April.

8. Kortleven, C. 2016, *Less is Beautiful*, p. 71.

9. Collister, P. 2017, *How to Use Innovation and Creativity in the Workplace*, Pan Macmillan, London, p. 172.

10. Kronsberg, M. 2016, 'Are High-Tech Hotels Alluring — or Alienating?', *The Wall Street Journal*, 28 April.

11. Ibid.

12. Kumparak, G. 2017, 'Disney Is Opening An Immersive Star Wars Hotel Where Each Guest Gets a Storyline', *TechCrunch*, 15 July.

13. Dunn, J. 2017, 'Samsung's Gorgeous New TV Double as Artwork — Here's How It Looks in Person', *Business Insider*, 2 July.

14. Gale, A. 2017, 'Groovin': Sony to Press Its First Vinyl Records Since 1989', *The Wall Street Journal*, 29 June.

15. Denniss, R. & Baker, D. 2012, 'Who Knew Australians Were So Co-Operative?', *The Australia Institute*, October.

16. Ibid.

17. Kim, S. 2014, 'Michelin Reinvents the Wheel with Airless Tire', *ABC News*, 22 November.

18. 2017, 'The Future of Customer Experience', *TrendWatching*.

19. 2017, 'The Future of CX', *Medium*, 9 June.

20. Smith, K. 2016, 'The Ten Best Marketing Campaigns of 2016', *Brandwatch*, 16 December.

21. Drucker, P. 1985, *Innovation and Entrepreneurship*, HarperCollins, New York, p. 80.

22. Van den Bergh, J. & Behrer, M. 2011, *How Cool Brands Stay Hot*, Kogan, Philadelphia, pp. 131, 132.

23. Ibid.

24. Armitage, C. 2016, 'Future of Sydney's Retail and Online Shopping', *The Sydney Morning Herald*, 17 May.

25. Ibid.

26. Ibid.

27. Amey, K. 2017, 'Eurostar Launches Virtual Reality Headsets So Its Passengers Can Explore the Ocean as They Cross the English Channel', *Daily Mail*, 14 July.

28. 2015, '2020 Technology Landscape', *Citrix Technology Office*, April.

29. 2017, 'Break Through the Hype — Uncover the Reality of A.I.', *Oracle + Bronto*, July.

30. Mims, C. 2015, 'Virtual Reality Isn't Just About Games', *The Wall Street Journal*, 2 August.

31. Statt, N. 2017, 'Tim Cook Says Augmented Reality Is a Big Idea Like the Smartphone', *The Verge*, 10 February.

32. Ferguson, A. 2016, 'Internet of Everything Coming to Change Our Lives', *The Sydney Morning Herald*, 30 July.

33. Hufford, A. 2017, 'Campbell Soup Contends with a Choosier Customer', *The Wall Street Journal*, 27 August.

CHAPTER 11

1. Kortleven, C. 2016, *Less is Beautiful*, p. 31.

2. Ibid.

3. Linkner, J. 2014, The *Road to Reinvention*, Jossey-Bass, San Francisco, p. 77.

4. Kriegel, R. & Brandt, D. 1997, *Sacred Cows Make the Best Burgers*, Time Warner, New York, p. 1.

5. Sull, D. 2003, *Why Good Companies Go Bad*, Harvard Business School, pp. 25–9, 35.

6. Terlep, S. 2017, 'Avon Freshens Up in a Bid to Win Back Middle America', *The Wall Street Journal*, 21 March.

7. Ibid.

8. Kriegel, R. & Brandt, D. 1997, *Sacred Cows Make the Best Burgers*, Time Warner, New York, p. 17.

9. Turner, M. 2003, *Kmart's 10 Deadly Sins*, Wiley, New Jersey, pp. 100–1.

10. Ibid., pp. 100–1.

11. Ibid., p. 8.

12. Undercoffler, D. 2015, 'Toyota Opens Patents on Hydrogen Fuel Cell Technology to Competitors for Future of Automobile Industry', *The Sydney Morning Herald*, 7 January.

13. Ibid.

14. Anthony, S. 2017, *The Little Black Book of Innovation*, Harvard Business School Publishing, pp. 216, 217.

15. Ng, S. 2014, 'P&G to Shed More Than Half Its Brands', *The Wall Street Journal*, 1 August.

16. Emmerentze Jervell, E. 2016, 'Lego CEO Sees Potential for Brand in Digital Products', *The Wall Street Journal*, 8 December.

17. Wakabayashi, D. 2012, 'Hitachi President Prods Turnaround', *The Wall Street Journal*, 10 May.

18. 2016, 'Panasonic Pulls Plug on LCD TV Panels in Japan', *The Japan Times*, 31 May.

19. Robertson, D. 2014, *Brick by* Brick, Random House, New York, p. 98.

20. Ibid., p. 70.

21. Ibid., p. 114.

22. Ibid., p. 283.

23. Ibid., p. 216.

24. Durkin, P. 2015, 'How Brick-Headed Consultants Almost Killed Lego, and It Rebuilt to Be 2015's Most Powerful Brand', *The Australian Financial Review*, 13 October.

25. Min-Jung, K. 2012, 'Feature of the Month: Lego', *Beyond Magazine*, August.

26. Robertson, D. 2013, *Brick by Brick*, Crown Business, New York, p. 3.

27. Weinberg, C. 2017. 'Lego Cuts 1,400 Jobs as Sales Slump on Weak Batman Demand', *Bloomberg*, 5 September.

28. Kriegel, R. 1991, *If It Ain't Broke … Break It!*, Time Warner, New York, pp. 2, 69.

CHAPTER 12

1. Hamel, G. 2002, *Leading the Revolution*, Penguin, New York, p. 289.

2. Rothkopf, D. 2017, *The Great Questions of Tomorrow*, Simon & Schuster, New York, Introduction.

3. Collister, P. 2017, *How to Use Innovation and Creativity in the Workplace*, Pan Macmillan, London, p. 142.

4. Anthony, S. 2017, *The Little Black Book of Innovation*, Harvard Business School Publishing, p. xvi.

5. Son, H. 2017, 'JPMorgan's Moonshot Man Wants to Help Wall Street Fire Its Traders', *Bloomberg*, 7 June.

6. Anthony, S. 2017, *The Little Black Book of Innovation*, Harvard Business School Publishing, pp. 129, 130.

7. Dyer, J., Gregersen, H. & Christensen, C. 2011, *The Innovator's DNA*, Harvard Business School, p. 150.

8. Anthony, S. 2017, *The Little Black Book of Innovation*, Harvard Business School Publishing, pp. 33, 34.

9. Anthony, S. et al. 2015, 'The 6 Most Common Innovation Mistakes Companies Make', *Harvard Business Review*, 23 June.

10. Dyer, J., Gregersen, H. & Christensen, C. 2011, *The Innovator's DNA*, Harvard Business School, pp. 221, 222.

11. Feintzeig, R. 2016, 'No Meetings Allowed: It's Thinking Thursday', *The Wall Street Journal*, 12 September.

12. Kortleven, C. 2016, *Less is Beautiful*, p. 27.

13. Hamel, G. 2002, *Leading the Revolution*, Penguin, New York, p. 18.

14. Hall, S. 2013, 'Mclaren to Axe Windscreen Wipers: Report', *The Sydney Morning Herald*, 19 December.

15. Anthony, S. 2017, *The Little Black Book of Innovation*, Harvard Business School Publishing, pp. 33, 34.

16. Ibid., p. xvi.

17. Ibid., p. 162.

18. Chandra, A. 2015, 'How to Help Innovation Grow Up at Your Organisation', *Fast Company*, 18 May.

19. Christensen, C. 2000, *The Innovator's Dilemma*, Harper Collins, New York, pp. 174, 175.

20. Kriegel, R. 1991, *If It Ain't Broke … Break It!*, Time Warner, New York, pp. 155, 156.

21. Kwoh, L. 2012, 'You Call That Innovation?', *The Wall Street Journal*, 23 May.

22. Anthony, S. 2017, *The Little Black Book of Innovation*, Harvard Business School Publishing, p. 204.

23. Kriegel, R. 1991, *If It Ain't Broke … Break It!*, Time Warner, New York, pp. 155, 156.

24. Linden, G. 2006, 'Early Amazon: Shopping Cart Recommendations', *Geeking with Greg* blog, 25 April.

25. Hamel, G. 2002, *Leading the Revolution*, Penguin, New York, p. 261.

26. 2006, 'Case Studies on Innovation', IBS Case Development Centre, p. 20.

27. Kubota, Y. 2016, 'Behind Toyota's Late Shift into Self-Driving Cars', *The Wall Street Journal*, 12 January.

28. Troianovski, A. & Grundenberg, S. 2012, 'Nokia's Bad Call on Smartphones', *The Wall Street Journal*, 18 July.

29. Collister, P. 2017, *How to Use Innovation and Creativity in the Workplace*, Pan Macmillan, London, pp. 150–5.

30. Linkner, J. 2014, *The Road to Reinvention*, Jossey-Bass, San Francisco, pp. 77, 78.

31. Ibid., p. 66.

32. Ibid., pp. 42, 43.

33. Greene, J. 2016, 'Look Who's Back! Microsoft, Rebooted, Emerges as a Tech Leader', *The Wall Street Journal*, 16 December.

34. Ibid.

35. Hamel, G. 2002, *Leading the Revolution*, Penguin, New York, p. 125.

36. Jargon, J. 2016, 'McDonald's Turns to Social Media to Draw Millennials', *The Wall Street Journal*, 13 October.

37. Ibid.

38. Surowiecki, J. 2004, *The Wisdom of Crowds*, Anchor Books, New York, pp. 30, 31.

39. Jacks, T. 2015, 'Australian SMEs Failing the Innovation Test, Says Microsoft', *The Australian* Financial *Review*, 17 March.

CHAPTER 13

1. Ashkenas, R. 2012, 'Kill Your Business Model Before It Kills You', *Harvard Business Review*, 2 October.

2. Hamel, G. 2012, *What Matters Now*, Jossey-Bass, San Francisco, p. 131.

3. Fisher, G. 2009, 'Cut the Chaos to Grow Your Business', *Entrepreneur*, 25 October.

4. Hamel, G. 2012, *What Matters Now*, Jossey-Bass, San Francisco, pp. 193–205.

5. Ibid.

6. Ibid.

7. Hamel, G. 2016, 'Want to Bust Bureaucracy? Get Angry', *Management Exchange*, 20 December.

8. Ibid.

9. Silverman, R. 2012, 'Who's the Boss? There Isn't One', *The Wall Street Journal*, 19 June.

10. Kortleven, C. 2016, *Less is Beautiful*, p. 119.

11. Hamel, G. 2012, *What Matters Now*, Jossey-Bass, San Francisco, p. 126.

12. Dyer, J., Gregersen, H. & Christensen, C. 2011, *The Innovator's DNA*, Harvard Business School, p. 169.

13. Anthony, S. 2017, *The Little Black Book of Innovation*, Harvard Business School Publishing, p. 75.

14. Ibid.

15. Gray, J. 2017, 'ANZ Blows Up Bureaucracy as Shayne Elliott Takes the Bank Agile', *The Australian* Financial *Review*, 1 May.

16. Noonan, P. 2011, 'A Caveman Won't Beat a Salesman', *The Wall Street Journal*, 18 November.

17. Dyer, J., Gregersen, H. & Christensen, C. 2011, *The Innovator's DNA*, Harvard Business School, pp. 32–7.

18. Collister, P. 2017, *How to Use Innovation and Creativity in the Workplace*, Pan Macmillan, London, p. 166.

19. Canton, J. 2015, *Future Smart*, Da Capo Press, Philadelphia, p. 50.

20. Hamel, G. 2012, *What Matters Now*, Jossey-Bass, San Francisco, pp. 140–2.

CONCLUSION

1. Musk, E. 2017, 'The Future We're Building—and Boring', *TED Talk*, April.

2. Tibbets, G. 2007, 'Key That Could Have Saved the Titanic', *Telegraph*, 29 August.

APPENDIX B

1. Goodson, S. 2012, 'If You're Not Paying for It, You Become the Product', *Forbes,* 5 March.

2. Schwab, K. 2016, *The Fourth Industrial Revolution,* Penguin, London, p. 104.

3. Whittaker, Z. 2017, 'Accuweather Caught Sending User Location Data, Even When Location Sharing Is Off', *ZDNet,* 22 August.

4. Ross, A. 2016, *Industries of the Future,* Simon & Schuster, New York, p. 177.

5. Shead, S. 2017, 'The UK Data Regulator Has Ruled That Google Deepmind's First Deal with the NHS Was Illegal', *Business Insider,* 3 July.

6. Ford, M. 2015, *Rise of the Robots,* Basic Books, New York, p. 88.

7. 2017, 'The World in 2050', PriceWaterhouseCoopers, February.

8. Ford, M. 2015, *Rise of the Robots,* Basic Books, New York, p. 223.

9. Schwab, K. 2016, *The Fourth Industrial Revolution,* Penguin, London, p. 35.

10. Ford, M. 2015, *Rise of the Robots,* Basic Books, New York, pp. 31, 32.

11. 2017, 'A Future That Works: Automation, Employment, and Productivity', McKinsey Global Institute, January.

12. Aeppel, T. 2015, 'What Clever Robots Mean for Jobs', *The Wall Street Journal,* 24 February.

13. Schwab, K. 2016, *The Fourth Industrial Revolution,* Penguin, London, pp. 38, 39.

14. Egan, M. 2015, 'Robots Threaten These 8 Jobs', *CNN Money,* 14 May.

15. Ford, M. 2015, *Rise of the Robots,* Basic Books, New York, p. 124.

16. Walsh, K. 2017, 'Robots Are Coming to Courts—but They Won't Replace Judges', *The Australian Financial Review,* 30 March.

17. Schwab, K. 2016, *The Fourth Industrial Revolution,* Penguin, London, p. 41.

18. Brynjolfsson, E. & McAfee, A. 2014, *The Second Machine Age,* Norton, New York, p. 139.

19. McAfee, A. & Brynjolfsson, E. 2017, 'Machines Might Actually Be Better Than Humans at Creativity', *TED Ideas,* 4 August.

20. Brynjolfsson, E. & McAfee, A. 2017, 'The Business of Artificial Intelligence', *Harvard Business Review,* July.

21. Ross, A. 2016, *Industries of the Future,* Simon & Schuster, New York, p. 246.

22. Kasanoff, B. 2017, 'Intuition Is the Highest Form of Intelligence', *Forbes,* 21 February.

23. Ibid.

24. Brynjolfsson, E. & McAfee, A. 2014, *The Second Machine Age*, Norton, New York, p. 202.

25. Ibid., p. 193.

26. Ibid., pp. 193, 194.

27. Hamel, G. 2002, *Leading the Revolution*, Penguin, New York, p. 135.

28. Brynjolfsson, E. & McAfee, A. 2014, *The Second Machine Age*, Norton, New York, p. 147.

29. Schwab, K. 2016, *The Fourth Industrial Revolution*, Penguin, London, p. 10.

30. Monga, V. 2015, 'The New Bookkeeper Is a Robot', *The Wall Street Journal*, 5 May.

31. Ford, M. 2015, *Rise of the Robots*, Basic Books, New York, p. 107.

32. 2017, 'Break Through the Hype—Uncover the Reality of A.I.', *Oracle + Bronto*, July.

33. Brynjolfsson, E. & McAfee, A. 2014, *The Second Machine Age*, Norton, New York, p. 99.

34. 2017, 'The Automation Advantage', *AlphaBeta*, August.

35. Kasriel, S. 2017, '6 Ways to Make Sure A.I. Creates Jobs for All and Not the Few', *World Economic Forum*, 14 August.

36. Kellser, A. 2016, 'The Robots Are Coming, Welcome Them', *The Wall Street Journal*, 22 August.

37. Schwab, K. 2016, *The Fourth Industrial Revolution*, Penguin, London, p. 36.

38. Canton, J. 2015, *Future Smart*, Da Capo Press, Philadelphia, pp. 214, 215.

39. 2013, 'It's (Almost) All About Me', *Deloitte Australia*, July.

40. Santens, S. 2015, 'Self-Driving Trucks Are Going to Hit Us Like a Human-Driven Truck', *Medium*, 17 May.

41. Brynjolfsson, E. & McAfee, A. 2014, *The Second Machine Age*, Norton, New York, p. 121.

42. 2017, 'The Automation Advantage', *AlphaBeta*, August.

43. Rothkopf, D. 2017, *The Great Questions of Tomorrow*, Simon & Schuster, New York, p. 61.

44. Brynjolfsson, E. & McAfee, A. 2014, *The Second Machine Age*, Norton, New York, p. 11.

45. Ross, A. 2016, *Industries of the Future*, Simon & Schuster, New York, p. 6.

46. Angus, C. 2015, 'Future Workforce Trends in NSW', *NSW Parliamentary Research Service*, December.

47. West, D. 2015, 'What Happens if Robots Take the Jobs?', *Brookings Centre for Technology Innovation*, October.

48. Ford, M. 2015, *Rise of the Robots*, Basic Books, New York, p. 193.

49. Ibid., p. 197.

50. LoCascio, R. 2017. 'We Need a New Deal to Address the Economic Risks of Automation', *TechCrunch*, 31 March.

51. Brynjolfsson, E. & McAfee, A. 2014, *The Second Machine Age*, Norton, New York, pp. 246, 247.

52. Ibid., pp. 232–4.

53. Ford, M. 2015, *Rise of the Robots*, Basic Books, New York, pp. 257–259.

54. Brynjolfsson, E. & McAfee, A. 2014, *The Second Machine Age*, Norton, New York, pp. 232–4.

INDEX